THE HISTORY OF WATER IN THE LAND ONCE CALLED PALESTINE

THE HISTORY OF WATER IN THE LAND ONCE CALLED PALESTINE

Scarcity, Conflict and Loss in Middle East Water Resources

Christopher Ward
Sandra Ruckstuhl
Isabelle Learmont

BLOOMSBURY ACADEMIC

LONDON • NEW YORK • OXFORD • NEW DELHI • SYDNEY

BLOOMSBURY ACADEMIC
Bloomsbury Publishing Plc
50 Bedford Square, London, WC1B 3DP, UK
1385 Broadway, New York, NY 10018, USA
29 Earlsfort Terrace, Dublin 2, Ireland

BLOOMSBURY, BLOOMSBURY ACADEMIC and the Diana logo
are trademarks of Bloomsbury Publishing Plc

First published in Great Britain 2022
This paperback edition published by Bloomsbury Academic in 2023

Cover image: Jaffa orange culture, boys with baskets of oranges,
1900, Palestine. (© Artokoloro /Alamy Stock Photo)

A catalogue record for this book is available from the British Library.

Library of Congress Cataloging In-Publication Data
Names: Ward, Christopher (Christopher Stuart), author. |
Ruckstuhl, Sandra, author. | Learmont, Isabelle, author.
Title: The history of water in the land once called Palestine: scarcity,
conflict and loss in Middle East water resources / Christopher Ward,
Sandra Ruckstuhl, Isabelle Learmont.
Description: London; New York: I.B. Tauris, 2021. |
Includes bibliographical references and index.
Identifiers: LCCN 2021025813 (print) | LCCN 2021025814 (ebook) |
ISBN 9781788314213 (hardback) ISBN 9780755618057 (epub) |
ISBN 9780755618064 (pdf) | ISBN 9780755618071 (ebook other)
Subjects: LCSH: Water resources development–Palestine–History. |
Water resources development–Israel–History. | Water-supply–Palestine–History. |
Water-supply–Israel–History. | Water security–Palestine–History. | Water security–Israel–History.
Classification: LCC HD1698.I75 W37 2021 (print) |
LCC HD1698.I75 (ebook) | DDC 333.91/15095694–dc23
LC record available at https://lccn .loc .gov /2021025813
LC ebook record available at https://lccn .loc .gov /2021025814

ISBN: HB: 978-1-7883-1421-3
PB: 978-0-7556-3720-1
ePDF: 978-0-7556-1806-4
eBook: 978-0-7556-1805-7

Typeset by Deanta Global Publishing Services, Chennai, India

To find out more about our authors and books visit
www.bloomsbury.com and sign up for our newsletters.

For Wolf Alexander Ward Enoch and River Emanuel Ward Enoch, and
for Robert William Ruckstuhl and Mary Louise Ruckstuhl

CONTENTS

ACKNOWLEDGEMENTS

The authors are entirely responsible for the content of this book, but we must mark our great appreciation of the many friends, colleagues and interlocutors who have helped us to understand the challenges or have provided invaluable information.

The very many people in the Palestinian Territories and in Israel who helped us are too numerous to mention by name, but we would like to extend our thanks to every one of them. We also acknowledge the generous cooperation of many Palestinian communities, including in Jenin, Falamyeh, Jayyous, Yatta, Aqraba and Farkha, and in Gaza City and Khan Younis.

Several experts have unstintingly supported us in various aspects of this endeavour, including Dr Mark Zeitoun, now professor at the University of East Anglia; the late and greatly missed Professor Tony Allan, the doyen of Middle East water studies at King's and SOAS, University of London; and Dr Shimon Tal, former Water Commissioner of Israel. We also thank Professor Eugene Rogan of St Antony's College, University of Oxford; Professor Michael Cernea; and Dr Marc Valéri and his colleagues and students at the Institute of Arab and Islamic Studies of the University of Exeter. We recognize too the work of Professor Ilan Pappé and of Dr Seth Siegel, both of whom have illuminated the scene, albeit from different viewpoints. Our earlier inspirations were our late teachers Albert Hourani; Professor Roger Owen; Professor Freddie Beeston; Dr Robert Mabro; Professor Donald Russell; A. N. Sherwin-White; and Dr Dennis Sandole. We also pay tribute to the late and greatly regretted William St Clair, historian and humanist, whose friendship, wisdom and humour have carried us forward in this as in so many other endeavours.

Colleagues from the World Bank have been an inspiration and a support over the years, and on the subject of this book, in particular, we learned much from Salah Darghouth, Sabine Beddies, Pier Francesco Mantovani and Adnan Ghosheh. We acknowledge a great debt to the work of Jeffrey Sosland. We also recognize the excellent village study of Julia Templin, *Zababdeh: A Palestinian Water History*. Above all, we recognize the unstinting and excellent work of Gidon Bromberg, Nada Majdalani and Yana Abu Taleb, the directors of EcoPeace Middle East and of the former directors, who have done more than any other individuals or organization to further a just, equitable and sustainable peace in the region. Thanks too to the noble enterprise of Wikipedia, a wonderful source and source of sources. We acknowledge the sterling work of our editors, our insightful and dedicated commissioning editor David Stonestreet at I.B. Tauris, and at Bloomsbury, Tomasz Hoskins and Nayiri Kendir, and of Sophie Campbell and the excellent Bloomsbury production team. Finally, we thank Catriona Ward and Antonia Ward for their invaluable help with research and fact-checking.

Needless to say, none of these people who so generously helped us in any way endorses the content of this book, which is our responsibility alone.

PREFACE

This book, together with its companion volume *Water Security for Palestinians and Israelis*, tells the water story of the two peoples who live in the land defined by the borders of Mandate Palestine.

In this first book, *The History of Water in the Land Once Called Palestine*, we look at the water resource and trace the history of its development since Ottoman times up to 2020, a history characterized by a divergence between the two peoples in respect of water and its environment as strong as their divergence in other spheres.

The companion book, *Water Security for Palestinians and Israelis*, carries on the theme to first examine in detail the current security situations of Israelis and Palestinians in respect of water and the environment. We assess the remarkable water security the Israelis have achieved and the corresponding water insecurity and environmental vulnerability of the Palestinians. *Water Security for Palestinians and Israelis* then sets out the practical, economic, legal and ethical rationale for a revised cooperation on water security and the environment between the two peoples.

Christopher Ward, *University of Exeter*
Dr Sandra Ruckstuhl, *International Water Management Institute, Colombo*
Dr Isabelle Learmont, *Hennock, Devon*

Chapter 1

INTRODUCTION

THE DIVERGENCE OF TWO PEOPLES

The story of water in the land that was once called Palestine is the story of two peoples who, a hundred years ago, set out from the same common point, from the same natural endowment, the same technology, the same level of economic development, the same level of water services – and who faced the same risks of drought and flood and insecurity.

It is the story of how the paths of these two peoples began to separate, first to run side by side, and then to diverge, and of how decisions and events in the larger arena started to sunder the two peoples, setting them apart and at odds with one another. Ideas, decisions and events changed the relations of power between these peoples in a profound way so that a state of enmity between them seemed to become rooted and to have an air of permanence.

A book about the history of water in the land first delineated as Palestine under the British Mandate is relevant for several reasons. One reason is memory, identity. The record of what has happened, even if it has no power to change the new reality in the future, is of value to a people – self-knowledge, a realistic sense of identity defined by knowledge of what is lost and of what remains. But another reason, forward looking and more optimistic, is that knowledge and acceptance of loss can drive thoughts of what might nonetheless be different. Amongst all the 'facts on the ground', where is the lever that might move change? In water there may just be such a lever. One new fact on the ground is the coming of desalination. A new possibility has arisen – that if we can now *make* water, then water need no longer be a reason for struggle. It may, instead, be part of a solution to struggle.

And an environmental window is opening, too. The Israelis have developed their natural resources to their limits. Nowadays they recognize the heavy toll taken on the environment. In their prosperity, they have the power to begin to act to correct these harms. And with this awareness and readiness for action comes the reality that their environment is shared with neighbours, and above all, with the Palestinians who live alongside them in the same land. This creates the possibility – and the need – for cooperation and for joint action. Along with this growing concern for the environment comes the menace of climate change, certainly bringing hotter, drier, more erratic weather and shrinking the water resource.

Israelis and Palestinians are in this together, facing the same challenges. There is reasonable impulse that they should work to tackle the challenges together.

And that is the justification of both this book and its companion. If we can understand the long history of gain and loss, we can understand what may drive the parties towards a new understanding and a new compact. Israel now makes water from the sea. This relaxes the old zero-sum game. Already this has helped to bring better agreement between Jordan and Israel. The plundered and stressed environment and the reality of adverse climatic change create a logic of cooperative response.

So this first book is the story of loss, about how Palestinians come to be so dispossessed of water. And for Israelis it is the history of the step-by-step and successful consolidation of a water inventory and of the resulting water security of a nation.

The companion book *Water Security for Palestinians and Israelis* is, then, about hope. How can Israelis consolidate their hard-won water security – and how can Palestinians achieve the same? What are the conditions in which the water security of both peoples can be obtained in a framework of fairness and justice?

Trying to see it from the others' point of view

In these two books we try our best to avoid dwelling on the vast and complex questions of geopolitics which dog debate on Israeli/Palestinian questions and which polarize opinion to the point where it seems that everybody is shouting and nobody is listening. We try to keep to the water question and to discuss that question in the neutral terms of 'water security'. But we also try to understand what water means to either people beyond the simple functions of water security – beyond plain security of water resources, beyond the simple provision of top-notch water and sanitation services, and beyond the ability to manage the risks and protect the environment.

On the Israeli side, it is necessary to understand the deep, the essential connection between water and the Zionist vision. Ben Gurion, a man far-sighted and politically adept, saw from the outset that a continuous space of land and water was essential to the establishment of the Jewish state. He saw, too, what became policy from the establishment of the state, that water should be held and managed by the state for the common good. In his diary for July 1937, the founding father writes:

> we achieve, for the first time in our history, a real Jewish state – an agricultural body of one or more million people, continuous, heavily populated, at one with the land which is completely its own. We achieve the possibility of a giant national settlement on a large area that is all in the hands of the state . . . the difficulties and defeats that preoccupied us until now . . . . [will vanish] . . . . [we will have] an organized economy, rational and pre-determined exploitation of the land and water.[1]

In Israel's story of conquest and redemption, land and the water that fructifies the land have an almost mystical status, beyond the mere platform on which to place a people and a state and to develop an economy. The land and its water are the embodiment of nationhood, both a collective asset and an imaginative symbol of the Jewish people coming home. It was the subordination of the individual to the collective memory of what it meant to be Jewish that drove the early virtues of Zionist pioneering and self-sacrifice, and the same virtues that supported the collective ownership of land and water and the institutions that managed them – the land agency, the water authority. As Israel has evolved into a highly successful modern state, water security has been wonderfully achieved by technology, infrastructure and effort – but to understand the extraordinary emotions and political commitment to that security, we need always to recall these old drivers and basic motives.

Trying to see it from the Palestinian point of view gives a very different perspective. Palestinians see the story of water as a story of dispossession and loss as important as the loss of land, as something so central to a way of life, to a people, that it is not just a negotiable economic service but a central part of a whole struggle – for restitution, for justification, for identity even.

The Palestinians feel they are a people in constant recession, that their loss was not once and for all in 1948. It is understood as constant and still continuing, liberties reduced to a circumscribed home rule in fragments of their old homeland, administered more to the benefit of others than their own by a disempowered and often mistrusted home rule. In this view, identity and history are denied. To Palestinians, everything speaks oppression, disempowerment and loss of hope.

It seems to Palestinians like *less for more.* As with the Sibylline books, the portion that is being offered – of land, of water, of rights, of self-respect – is ever dwindling while the price rises, the price of accepting a humiliating settlement that values at nothing three generations of sacrifice and suffering.[2]

The Palestinians see how the pieces of land left to them in 1948 have largely gone. They consider that the very water that rains on them from the skies and seeps into a rock matrix beneath their feet has been appropriated. The Jordan that once flowed past their lands is now a dirty drain, the water sucked out by others upstream of the West Bank. And today, Palestinians may not even approach the river. Settlement agriculture, military posts and the iron architecture of Area C stand in their way. Even the sea, the vast resources and common culture of the *mare nostrum*, the Mediterranean, is barred to them.

> The teen wrote that if she could have that alternative life, she would move to Acre, 'live by the sea and go swimming. I have only been once – even if the water is only 30 kilometres from my house.'
>
> Ahed Tamimi quoted in *Haaretz*, 7 October 2018

All else set aside, nobody would deny that the Palestinian Arab inhabitants of the land – the Mandate land – are entitled to a fair share of the water resources of that land and to the right to develop those resources as they see fit for the benefit of the people and their economy.

In order to explore what a just and equitable finally agreed resolution on water might look like, we start this volume with a historical narrative, which opens in the twilight of the Ottoman era and traces the development and use of water resources through the Mandate and Independence periods, and through the Occupation up to Oslo and after.

Chapter 2

LAND AND WATER

In this chapter we describe the three main geographical and hydro-geographical regions of the territory covered by Mandate Palestine – the coastal plain with its underlying Coastal Aquifer and the springs and wadis that bring water from the hills; the highlands, underlain by three aquifers recharged by the considerable rains that fall on the higher elevations; and the Jordan Valley and its fabled river that carries water past five present-day riparians from the mountains of Lebanon down to the Dead Sea, the lowest point on earth.

The land is dry and the water that is needed to fructify it is limited and relatively scarce. The population of the territory has multiplied rapidly – fifteen times as many people live there today as at the start of the Mandate after the First World War – and the water needs of a modern economy have led to full development, even to overdevelopment, of the resource. In the charged context of the region, both land and water have inevitably become a locus of competition and contention.

The land before the Mandate[1]

The natural endowment of the land – its structure, geology, topography, physical geography, the climate and hydrology – has changed little in the hundred years since the end of Ottoman rule. Hills are hills, plains are plains, watercourses are watercourses. There are a few changes at the margin caused by the hand of man to the structure of some features – particularly to the vegetation and to the stock and flow of water – and these changes affect both the hydrology and the ecology. Most of the extensive wetlands have now been drained, many springs and wells have dried up, seasonal storm water flows are less in the streambeds, and the natural 'seas' of Galilee and the Dead Sea have shrunk. By contrast, tree cover has increased. But for the rest, beneath the cities and the roads and the irrigation schemes, the natural endowment is by and large unchanged.

So what was this land like a hundred years ago, at the end of Ottoman rule? From north to south, old Palestine runs 'from Dan to Beersheba' and from the Mediterranean to the Jordan. The length is 201 kilometres (130 miles). The width is 145 kilometres (90 miles) in the south, from the Dead Sea to Gaza, narrowing to less than 40 miles in the north, from the Sea of Galilee to Akka. With the Mandate,

Palestine extended another 190 kilometres (120 miles) south from Beersheba, to the Red Sea. In all, the area which Mandate Palestine took over was about 28,000 square kilometres (11,000 square miles). Like so many territories, Mandate Palestine was often said to be 'the size of Wales'.[2]

Geology defines the land into three natural territories: the coastal plain from the River Litani in the north to Gaza and beyond in the south; the hill country; and the deep Jordan Valley between the Sea of Galilee and the Dead Sea. The greatest cause of these geological variations is the massive series of fault lines in the earth's crust that stretches from the Rift Valley in East Africa to the Beqaa Valley in Lebanon.[3] Secondary fracture lines, some running north and south parallel to the fault, and some running from east to west, have produced a great variety of soils and of climate.

The coastal plain

The coastal plain, of varying width, stretches between the central hills and the sea. The plain was made fertile over millennia by soil washed down from the hills in the heavy winter rains. Like Caesar's Gaul, the plain can be divided into three parts: the Philistine plain, the plain of Sharon and the plains north of Carmel.

The Philistine plain The Philistine plain is the largest of the three. Here the climate is always temperate, with an average temperature of 18°C (65°F). The southern, drier part receives some winter rains from October to April, enough for pasture to grow. Its use in Ottoman times was to graze livestock. Around the level of Gaza there was annual cropping of cereals, as the vivid memoirs of the childhood of Salman Abu Sitta well attest.[4] North of Gaza, the whole area, can be cultivated, and by late Ottoman times wells had been dug almost everywhere and there was intensive cultivation, largely of citrus fruit, irrigated orchards and fields of grain. All of this coast is sandy and in the past a widening belt of sand dunes formed over the years south of Jaffa and today's Tel Aviv, between the sea and the plain.

The plain of Sharon At around the level of Jaffa/Tel Aviv, a spur of low hills approaches the coast and narrows a little. Here begins the plain of Sharon, the central section of the coastal plain, extending to Mount Carmel (Jabal al Karmil) in the north. This part of the plain is about 15 kilometres wide (9 miles) and about 90 kilometres (56 miles) from north to south. In ancient times it was covered with an oak forest. In late Ottoman times, the estuaries of the rivers were blocked by silt and parts of the plain became wetlands where the risk of malaria was present. Most of the plain is, however, well watered and drained. In the early twentieth century it was planted with palm trees and orange groves, and fields of corn and melons were laid out between the scattered sandstone ridges where the villages had grown up.

On the eastern fringe of the plain lie low foothills through which run wadis cut into the soft chalky limestone, forming passes that give access into the hills.[5] At the end of the Ottoman period, these mild western slopes were covered with vineyards and cornfields. In winter, the wadis that cut through the low hills carried spate torrents from the highlands across the plain, impeding traffic and transport both from the highlands to the coast and up and down the coast itself. To the north, about three miles north of old Caesarea, is the Wadi al Zarqa'/Taninim. In those days it broke to the sea through wild marshes.

The plains north of Carmel The northernmost section of the coastal plain begins above Mount Carmel, whose foothills reach within 200 metres of the sea. Along the coast here to the north of Haifa lies the plain of Acre, nearly five miles in breadth. The plain ends in the north where the Galilean hills run out in precipitous cliffs into the sea on what is now the Lebanon border. To the southeast of Haifa lies the broad plain of Marj ibn Amir/Esdraelon, below the city of Nazareth. This plain, formed by subsidence along lines of faults, is 26 kilometres (16 miles) across at its widest but narrows to the northwest. Covered with rich basaltic soils washed down from the Galilean hills, the plain is very fertile. The plain drains northwest to the coast between Haifa and Acre which, in late Ottoman times, was an unhealthy swamp. Esdraelon was important in history not only for its fertility but also for the great highway it opened from the Mediterranean through the vale of Jezreel to the Jordan and to the lands beyond the Jordan.

The highlands

The rugged limestone hills that form the highlands continue the line of the Lebanon range, bounded in the north by the deep gorge of the Litani river. These bare hills vary considerably in height but rise to over 1,000 metres in places. The highlands too can be divided into three parts, the southern highlands, the northern highlands and Galilee.

The southern highlands The southern highlands run from Beersheba in the south to the area of present-day Ramallah. North to south the distance is 90 kilometres (55 miles). The widest part is at the southern end, 40 kilometres (25 miles) across. Here the hills rise gradually from the coastal plain to Hebron at over 900 metres (3,000 feet) above sea level. From Hebron to the east, the hills slope sharply down to Ain Jidi/Engedi on the shore of the Dead Sea, dropping 1,200 metres (4,000 feet) in 25 kilometres (15 miles).

Further to the north, at Bethlehem and Jerusalem, elevations are a little lower, about 800 metres (2,500 feet). Jerusalem is surrounded on three sides by valleys. In late Ottoman times, there were many villages here, built around springs sited on the wooded hillsides. North of Jerusalem lies a rocky, broken tableland at an elevation of 600–900 metres (2,000–3,000 feet).

Much of the 3,500 square kilometres (1,350 square miles) of the southern highlands is a rocky wilderness of limestone, with some cultivable land around al Bireh and Hebron. Half the land is desert, with the eastern side of the hills virtually all wilderness leading down to the Dead Sea. A description in late Ottoman times told of 'five to eight hours of desolate waterless waste between the gates of Hebron, Bethlehem and Jerusalem and the Dead Sea. In the shallow soil, vegetation [dies] in the summer months, growing again in the autumn rains and giving pasture to Bedouin goats and hardy mountain sheep.'[6]

But even on these eastern slopes, where there was water, cultivation flourished. In the mid-nineteenth century, the American explorer Edward Robinson found the whole area around Ain Jidi 'covered with gardens, mainly growing cucumbers', all belonging to the Rashidi tribe.[7]

The northern highlands The northern highlands begin beyond modern Ramallah. These hills are broached by wadis from both east and west and are more accessible on all sides than those to the south. Going from south to north, the terrain becomes progressively more open and fertile; the cultivated areas become larger, and the wadis to east and west are less precipitous, leading down to fertile plains even on the eastern side. In the north, the town of Jenin lies on the boundary between the northern highlands and the plain of Marj ibn Amir/Esdraelon. North-east of Jenin is Jabal Faqqua/Mount Gilboa and beyond that is the narrow, steep valley of Jezreel, descending to the Jordan. To the northwest, a long spur runs all the way to Mount Carmel on the coast.

Galilee The northernmost segment of the highlands lies beyond the vale of Jezreel and the plain of Marj ibn Amir/Esdraelon. Here Nazareth 'nestles in a cup-shaped hollow, surrounded by hills'.[8] Back in the day, the main road north to Syria passed through Nazareth's winding streets. From here to the north, interspersed with fertile plains, rise the scattered hills of southern Galilee which run on the east down to Lake Tiberias (the Sea of Galilee). Northern Galilee is more rugged and wild. It forms the foothills of the main Lebanon chain and rises to over 1,200 metres (4,000 feet) at Jebel Jermuk, west of Safed. It is a high tableland broken by many valleys but with a mild climate, and is well watered. In late Ottoman times, it was wooded, with numerous villages. The Litani river forms a natural northern frontier.

The Jordan Valley

The Jordan River lies in a structural depression, part of the East African Rift System, and has the lowest elevation of any river in the world. The river has its ultimate source in the many springs at the foot of Mount Hermon, which rises to 2,800 metres (9,100 feet) at the southern end of the Anti-Lebanon range. Three rivers flow into these upper reaches – the Banias in the Golan, the Hasbani in Lebanon, and what is now the Dan. In the Upper Galilee, the river runs through the Huleh valley where lay, in late Ottoman times, a shallow lake and wetland which had become malarial.[9] At the southern end of this short valley, the river has cut a gorge through a basaltic barrier. The river then tumbles over the rocky river bed into the beginning of the Upper Jordan Valley and later enters, through what was in late Ottoman times a marshy delta, Lake Tiberias or the Sea of Galilee, then 210 metres (682 feet) below the level of the Mediterranean. This lake is 21 kilometres long by 13 across (13 miles by 8).

Descriptions of Tiberias from the early twentieth century tell of 'firm banks and sandy shores [which] have prevented the growth of reeds and the clear pure waters take their colour from the changing lights on the surrounding hills'.[10] The warm, pleasant climate made the lake a popular winter resort in Roman times, when there was also a prosperous fishing industry in which four of the twelve Apostles of Christ played their part. However, storms can be abrupt as furious winds rush down from the Golan and from the hills of Galilee. The fertile land around the shore, fed by many springs, can support rich subtropical vegetation and a hundred years ago 'warm healing springs still flow[ed] near the ruins of ancient Tiberias, once a famous Roman spa'.[11]

Below Tiberias, the river is set in the wide Rift Valley, bounded on each side by steep hills towering 600 metres (2,000 feet) above it. Before all the development of the twentieth century, the river rushed out at high speed from the southern end of the lake, 'cutting its way into the valley like a mill stream', first westward and then turning south along the foot of the hills. In those days the river was clean, a 'clear rapid stream as it leaves the lake . . . about 95 feet wide [30 metres], varying in depth from 3 to 10 feet [1-3 metres]'.[12] However, about 5 miles south of Tiberias, the Yarmouk flowed in from the east, making the water muddier and accelerating the flow. At the time, there was an older river bed that stretched both sides of the Jordan below the junction with the Yarmouk, generally about 100 metres (300 feet) wide but in some places extending to more than a kilometre. This old channel was filled with 'coarse vegetation and dense tangled thorn bushes' and flooded each year when the winter spate and the spring snowmelt arrived.

The valley is about 105 kilometres (65 miles) long from Galilee to the Dead Sea and varies in width from 5 to over 20 kilometres (3–14 miles). In late Ottoman times, the river itself wound and twisted along its length for a distance of nearly 320 kilometres (200 miles) 'like a huge serpent' – see Figure 2.1. There is a considerable drop in the course of the river below Galilee, about 180 metres (590 feet) or some 2 metres per kilometre (9 feet per mile). In descriptions from the late Ottoman period, 'the swiftly flowing stream eats into the whitish grey marl banks and, depositing the mud on the other side, makes the zigzag course ever more tortuous'.[13]

The lower section of the valley widens to a plain where already in the pre-Mandate period there was irrigated agriculture. These were rich lands and many ancient mounds bear witness to a thriving and prosperous population from as early as the fourth millennium BC. Below Jericho, where the valley opens out to its greatest width of 23 kilometres (14 miles), the river runs into the Dead Sea, whose surface then was some 400 metres (1,300 feet) below the level of the Mediterranean. Its bed is as deep again, forming the deepest cleft found in the earth's surface. The streams that feed the Dead Sea are unusually saline; they flow through nitrous soil and are fed by sulphurous springs. Other chemicals rise up from hot springs in the seabed. Along the shore are deposits of sulphur and petroleum. The surrounding strata are rich in bituminous matter. The sea has no outlet except by evaporation, making the water four times as salty as the Atlantic.

A century ago, the sea measured 85 kilometres long by 16 across (53 miles by 10), divided into two sections by a long peninsula of gravel, marl and bitumen, jutting out from the eastern side and rising to 18 metres (60 feet). South of this, the water was shallower, not more than 4 metres (14 feet) deep and running off

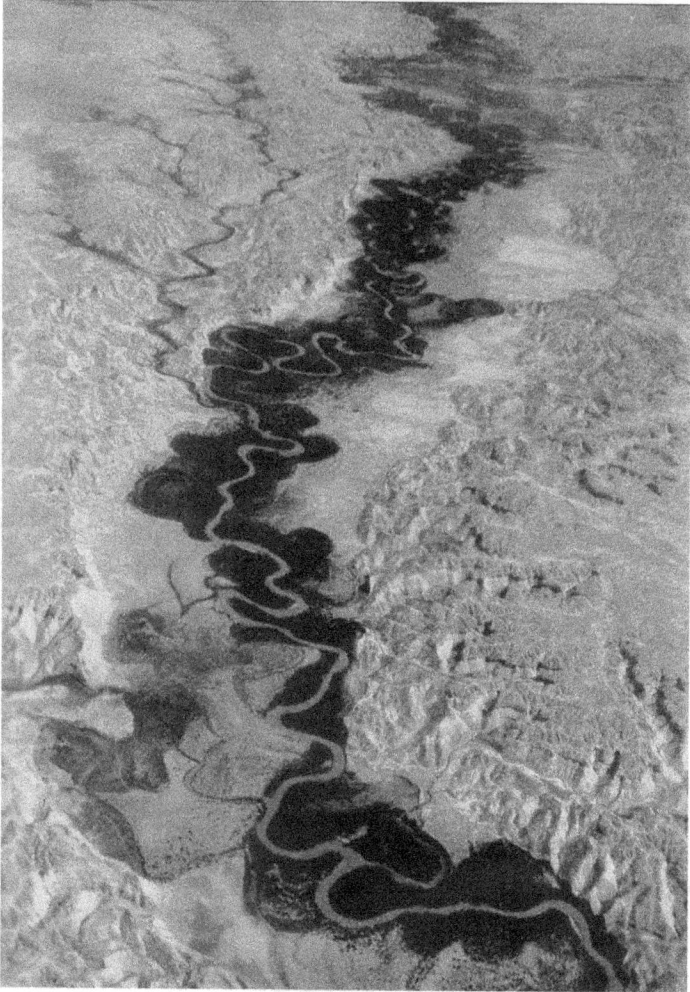

Figure 2.1 The Jordan River. https://upload.wikimedia.org/wikipedia/commons/3/35/The
_Jordan_River_loops%2C_aerial_view_1938.jpg

into marshes. Today the sea has shrunk considerably and comprises essentially
only the main, northern basin, which is about 50 kilometres long by 15 kilometres
wide (30 miles by 10).

The water resources of the land

Water in a dry land

In dry Palestine, access to water has been vital to the growth of human settlements
and to the development of their economies. As in much of the Middle East,

rainfall in most parts of historic Palestine has always been quite limited. Water is a scarce resource and often the scarcest factor of production. Water has thus always been a big constraint, and access to water resources – and control over them – has underlain the viability of human settlements and the agricultural economy.

The innumerable nineteenth-century travellers who published their books on the Holy Land continually reflect on the scarcity of water and on the limits that lack of water must place on the growth of the population and on the economy needed to support them. When the 1939 British White Paper concluded that Palestine could hold a maximum of 2 million people, much of the reasoning was based on the lack of water.[14]

The irony is that today the former Mandate Palestine accommodates a population fifteen times larger than that of a century ago. Today there more than 13 million people living within the borders of this land, well over 8 million in Israel, and nearly 5 million in the Palestinian territories. It is changes in the availability and management of water, as well as shifts away from policies that prioritize food self-sufficiency, that have made this vastly greater carrying capacity possible. How the frontier of water scarcity has been pushed back is an important part of our story – as is the difference in the relative status of the two peoples who occupy the land.[15]

Water-respecting cultures

The first thing to be said is that Palestine is a relatively dry land and since time immemorial its inhabitants have respected and husbanded the scanty resources. All the peoples who have occupied this land have used great ingenuity to get the utmost from the water they have – for drinking, for ablutions, for cleaning, for growing food, for watering stock, for growing trees.

Water is woven into the fabric of myth, history and culture of the peoples who have lived here. The ancient Canaanites and Israelites made sophisticated use of water. In the history of more recent conquerors – the Seleucids, the Romans, the Byzantines, the Arabs – all cared for water and developed great waterworks to supply their cities. And all the while in the countryside, the eternal farmer dug and hewed; irrigated from springs and wells; and clothed the hillsides with terraces to capture the water that ran down the slopes. The villagers worked together to harvest the rain into tanks and to dig shallow wells that would provide their households with water for food and water for life.

Water has seeped deep into the culture of the land. The Bible is full of water – of Moses striking the rock, of St John the Baptist baptizing in the River Jordan, of Christ at the well with the Samaritan girl, the troubled and healing Pool of Siloam. There are 600 mentions of water in the Old Testament. Later, the Muslim conquerors brought with them the liveliest awareness of water and a water-saving culture from their experience in the dry desert margins. The Qur'an has many references to water and the need to safeguard it and use it wisely. Muslim practice and the institutions and architecture that support it give a notable place to water.

Climate and precipitation

The coastal plain has a Mediterranean climate with long, hot, rainless summers and relatively short, cool, rainy winters. Winter temperatures can be in single digits or the low teens, summer temperatures reach 30°C or more. The summer climate is very humid and heat waves are frequent. Rainfall is unevenly distributed, significantly lower in the south. In the desert below Beersheba, rainfall averages barely 30 millimetres annually, whereas in the north of the plain around Carmel, average annual rainfall exceeds 900 millimetres.

In the highlands, the climate is mild apart from the hot sandy desert wind from the east. On the lower western slopes around the modern towns of Tulkarem and Qalqilya, where the elevation is some 200 metres above sea level, the rainfall is about 500 millimetres annually. Where the mountain ridge then rises up to some 1,000 metres above sea level, the elevation of Hebron, Jerusalem and Bethlehem, the precipitation is higher, averaging about 700 millimetres annually. Beyond the mountains, where the land falls away sharply towards the Jordan Valley and the Dead Sea, the climate is hot and dry with precipitation no more than 100 millimetres a year.

The rainy season is the six months of winter, with 70 per cent of annual rainfall occurring in just four months, from November to February. Summers are hot and dry with high rates of evaporation. In winter, precipitation often takes the form of snow at the higher elevations of the central highlands, including Jerusalem. Rainfall patterns have always been unpredictable and variability appears to have become more pronounced, with more frequent and larger variations from the long-term average – from 25 per cent of annual long-term averages in dry years to 160 per cent in wet years.[16] A prolonged drought spell in the second part of the 1980s raised the possibility of secular shifts in climatic patterns. Since 1993, it is estimated that the annual rainfall trend has decreased by 9 per cent, and high and low extremes in rainfall have become more frequent.

A changing climate

In a speech in 2014, Benjamin Netanyahu claimed that Israel's rainfall was only half of what it had been when the state was founded in 1948.[17] Although this is exaggerated, it is certain that, as with other lands of the Levant bordering the Mediterranean Sea, climate in the territory that was Mandate Palestine is changing and the pace of change is likely to pick up. Overall, there is a rising level of aridity caused by a generally drier climate, with less rain, particularly in winter, and increased temperatures in both winter and summer. There is already increasing unpredictability about the weather and this is likely to worsen, with delayed winter rains, increased rain intensity and a shortened rainy season. The outlook is for a further decline in annual rainfall and a resulting 25 per cent drop in natural water resources by the end of the twenty first century against 1961–90 averages.[18] Greater variations in temperature between seasons and increased frequency and severity of extreme climate events are expected, with the incidence of heat waves likely to continue to increase. By 2100, mean temperatures are forecast to increase by 1.6–1.8°C and precipitation to reduce by 4–8 per cent, with an overall rise in evapotranspiration of 10 per cent.

Anticipated impacts are reduced soil moisture and lower streamflow and aquifer recharge, more frequent droughts and greater spatial and temporal climatic uncertainty. The availability of natural water will decrease, and demand for water, particularly in agriculture for both permanent and just-in-time irrigation and for watering stock, will rise. Higher temperatures in the hills and mountains may lengthen the summer growing season and boost yields where irrigation water is available, but lower and more erratic rainfall and lower stores of water will reduce the availability of natural water for both agriculture and domestic uses. The Mediterranean coastline will be exposed to sea-level rise which at the extreme could be up to nearly one metre (with a range between 12 and 88 centimetres), causing flooding of settlements and agricultural lands and risking accelerated saline intrusion into the aquifers.[19]

Water sources

The natural water sources in the coastal plain are the rainfall, which provides significant soil moisture in the north but dwindles towards the south; the Coastal Aquifer; and the short rivers between the hills and the sea, which were in the past fed largely by springs in the foothills as well as by winter spate flows from the highland wadis.

The average total amount of rainwater falling on the highlands each year has been estimated at between 2,000 and 3,000 million cubic metres, two to three billion tons of water. Most of the rain falls on the higher elevations, on the mountain ridges. Roughly three-quarters of the rainfall evaporates, the remaining water runs off into streamflow, enters the soil profile as soil moisture, or infiltrates into the ground where the soft limestone absorbs it, recharging the groundwater aquifers or reappearing as springs that charge rivers and streams, most of them ephemeral. As the western slopes of the mountain range are gentler than the eastern slopes and receive considerably more rain, the western aquifers have a much higher recharge rate than the eastern aquifers which drain towards the Jordan Valley.[20]

Apart from a handful of streams where there is some modest baseflow, the only perennial river is the Jordan. Elsewhere there are seasonal flows where surface water run-off produced by heavy rains appears in ephemeral form in the valleys and wadis. Historically, there were about 300 springs arising from groundwater flows. Only about 120 of these springs flowed throughout the year, while the remaining ones carried water only during the rainy season, in the winter months and into the early spring. The total annual discharge of all these springs was estimated to reach about 100 million cubic metres a year. However, only half of this amount was fresh water. The other half – largely from the springs on the eastern escarpment and in the Jordan Valley and along the shores of the Dead Sea – has a high salt content. Today development has altered the hydrology and reduced both the number of these springs and their flow.

The water resources of the land can be divided into three parts which roughly follow the three natural territories we looked at earlier: the Mountain Aquifers, the Coastal Aquifer and the Jordan River system. In discussing each of these resources, we describe the resource as it was at the start of the story, in the late Ottoman period. Although the developments of modern times and the problems that have arisen over the division and use of the resource are the subject of later chapters and of our companion volume, here we also touch on how each resource presents today.

The Mountain Aquifers

The Mountain Aquifers are composed of three distinct formations, each draining in its own direction – see Figure 2.2. All three derive virtually all of their recharge from rainfall and snowmelt in the highlands.[21] The largest of the three aquifers, the Western Aquifer, has a flow that follows the surface topography, from the highlands

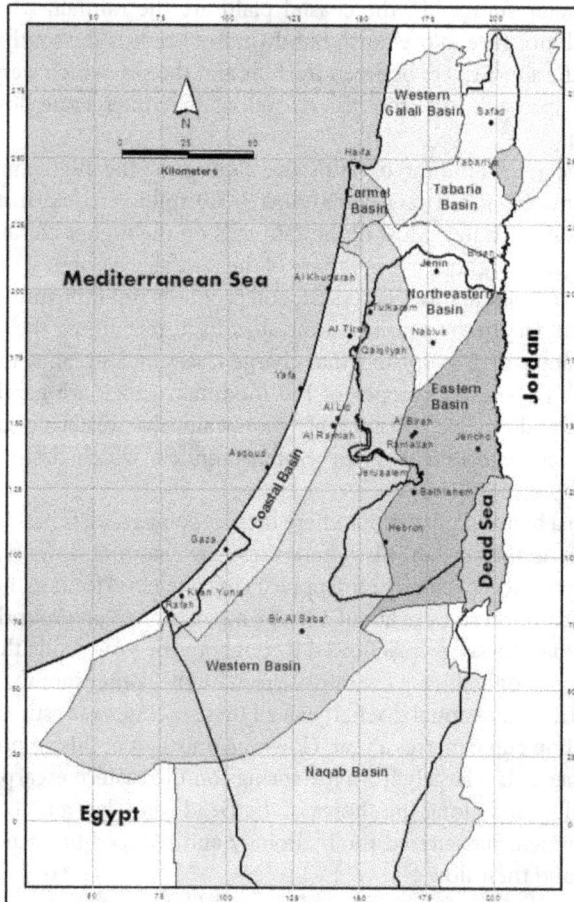

Figure 2.2 Shared and Non-Shared Aquifers. *Source*: PWA/SUSMAQ.

towards the coast. The smaller Northeastern or Northern Aquifer flows northwards from the northern highlands towards the plain of Marj ibn Amir/Esdraelon. The third aquifer – the Eastern – flows down the escarpment and discharges towards the Jordan Valley and the Dead Sea. All three aquifers share the same predominant geology, largely karstic limestone formations, and are hydrologically characterized by generally rapid flow, although flow rates can be very variable – see *Managing the Mountain Aquifers* in what follows. Depth to water declines from upstream to downstream. In the Western Aquifer, depths to water may be as much as 700–800 metres in the upper parts of the hills and along the ridges, but depths descend to 150–200 metres in the foothills, and to as little as 60 metres in the plains.[22]

The table *Estimated Recharge and Estimated Potential* shows a range of estimates of recharge, together with the planning assumption of 'estimated potential' that was adopted in the 1993 Oslo negotiations (see Chapter 7) and the long-term average yields recorded by the Hydrological Service of Israel.

Table 2.1 Estimated Recharge and Estimated Potential of the Mountain Aquifers (million m³/year)

Aquifer	Estimated recharge range	'Estimated potential'	HSI observed yield 1988–2005
Western	335–450	362	405.3
Northeastern	130–200	145	138.6
Eastern	155–237	172	165.3
Total	**620–887**	**679**	**709.2**

Sources: Recharge range from Tal and Abed-Rabbo: 24.
'Estimated potential' from Article 40.
HSI observed yield from HSI Development of Utilization and Status of Water Resources: 211, 296.

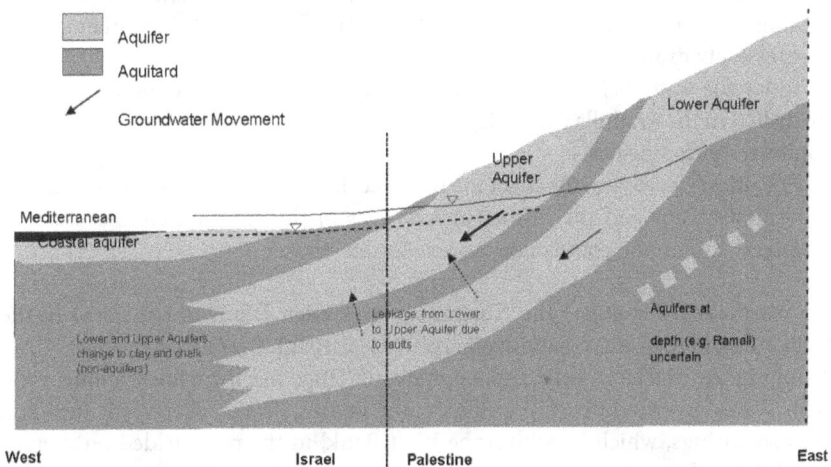

Figure 2.3 Schematic cross-section of the Western Aquifer. *Source*: PWA/SUSMAQ.

The Western Aquifer The Western Aquifer is the largest of the three aquifer formations beneath the highlands. It is, in fact, two aquifers, an upper and a lower – see Figure 2.3.

Both aquifers are predominantly composed of karstic limestone formations very capable of absorbing water within the structure of the rock. The rock matrix has high hydraulic transmissivities – that is, the rain that falls on the highlands seeps down to the aquifer quite speedily and then is transmitted towards the foot of the mountains. However, karstic limestone may also store reserves of water in fissures and cavities and some of this water may flow out only very slowly.

The upper aquifer, which can be up to 400 metres thick, comprises dolomites and chalk in addition to limestone. The lower aquifer is made up of dolomites in addition to the limestone and can be more than 300 metres thick. Groundwater in this layer flows largely through joints and fissures. The karstified layers at the top of the aquifer make for particularly rapid groundwater flow.

Recharge of the two aquifers takes place in areas of the higher elevations where the two layers outcrop. Further west, as elevations decline, the aquifers are overlain by rocks that are impermeable or of low permeability. As a result, little recharge can take place and the aquifers are also protected from contamination. Hence the quality of the water is first rate, with chloride concentrations of less than 100 mg per litre. There is probably some seepage from the upper to the lower aquifer.

Further west towards the Mediterranean, the lithology becomes richer in clay and chalk which stem the flow of groundwater. Historically this led the aquifers to discharge much of their water in major springs in the foothills, principally the Nahr al Auja (now called the Yarkon by the Israelis) near Jaffa and Tel Aviv and, to the south of Haifa, the Wadi al Zarqa', now called the Taninim by the Israelis. The average outflow from the springs was considerable by local standards, about 330 million cubic metres annually or 370 tons of water per second. Historically, much of this discharge ran into wetlands and malarial swamps along the coast. Beginning in the Ottoman period, these wetlands were progressively drained.

Today the water is largely extracted from the very numerous boreholes which are drilled in the foothills where depth to water is low and where artesian pressure minimizes pumping costs.

How these developments affect the resource, its division amongst users – Israeli and Palestinian – and the history and politics of this division are discussed in Chapter 7, and in the companion volume to this book.

The Northeastern Aquifer The Northeastern Aquifer drains to the north of the highlands where its main natural emergence is through the Gilboa and Beit Shean springs in the Marj ibn Amir/Esdraelon plain.[23] Together the natural annual yield of these springs would be 110 million cubic metres. The smaller Wadi Far'a and Bardala Springs, which lie within the West Bank, in the past yielded on average 25 million cubic metres, although yields appear to have declined in recent years.

Since the Mandate period, the water of this aquifer has been used largely for agriculture.[24]

The Eastern Aquifer The Eastern Aquifer is, in fact, composed of a series of small aquifers which discharge to numerous springs on the steep eastern escarpment of the highlands as it descends to the Jordan Valley and the Dead Sea. The principal amongst these springs are the ancient named springs of Auja (with a yield of 10 million cubic metres); Samiya (5 million cubic metres); Feshka (40 million cubic metres, but warm and saline); Wadi Qilt (5 million cubic metres); Jericho (13 million cubic metres); and Ein Gedi (3 million cubic metres). There are many smaller springs and, towards the lower slopes of the escarpment as it dips below sea level, there are some very salty springs.[25]

Managing the Mountain Aquifers Several factors complicate the management of the Mountain Aquifers. The first of these factors is that more than 80 per cent of the recharge occurs in the upland areas, but most of the natural outflow is in the foothills and the plain. It is in the lower elevations that the water can be most economically abstracted. This zone lies principally in a narrow band on either side of the Green Line, between Israeli territory and the Palestinian West Bank. As we shall see (Chapter 7), this divergence between hydrogeology and political jurisdiction has led to enormous contention.

The second factor is that the natural groundwater regime is complex and hard to model and manage. This complexity is a result of both climatic patterns and hydrogeology. Rainfall across the highlands is quite variable both across different areas and within and between years so that infiltration also is consequently variable. Geologically, the strata of the mountains dictate considerable depths to water across large parts of the West Bank and also, in places, long-time scales between recharge and discharge. With much of the formation karstic, the aquifers have a character of dual porosity, with flows both through fissures and through the rock matrix which are hard to model. Spring flows, for example, may have both a fast-flow fissure component and a slow matrix component. Some of the water resident in the aquifer and being tapped by deep wells today may be thousands of years old, and contemporary recharge may be very different. Thus quantifying the resource and estimating 'natural flows' – a prerequisite for rational allocation – is difficult.[26]

A third factor is that development and patterns of use of the aquifers were established simply by the law of capture, and have been established without consultation. There is always potential for conflict in the development of an aquifer – between wells and springs, between wells upstream and wells downstream, between deep wells and shallow wells. In the case of the Mountain Aquifers, water allocation has been almost entirely determined by Israel, both through action to drain off the water in the foothills and, following the 1967 Occupation, through regulation of drilling and water use within the West Bank, and by development of water resources within the West Bank for the benefit of its own citizens. Inevitably this pattern of development and management has occasioned bitter dispute, as we shall see later in this book and also in the companion volume.

The Coastal Aquifer

The Coastal Aquifer basin extends over the full width and length of the Gaza Strip and along most of the coastal plain of Israel. Its estimated sustainable yield is 375 million cubic metres a year, of which 320 million cubic metres lie beneath Israeli territory and 55 million cubic metres beneath the Gaza Strip.[27] In its early years, Israel overdrew on this resource and, because of the proximity of the sea, this caused saline water to flow into parts of the aquifer. Since the early 2000s, however, Israel has moderated its offtake and today extracts no more than the sustainable yield.

By contrast the Palestinians in Gaza have no other natural water source. They have long heavily overdrawn the aquifer and continue to do so. In 2014 the Palestinians pumped out more than 170 million cubic metres, over three times the sustainable yield.[28] As a result of continuous overdraft over a number of years, the quality of the water in the Gaza portion of the aquifer has been badly affected by seawater saline intrusion and also by pollution from sewage and agricultural chemicals. The water quality is nowadays notoriously poor with nitrate levels exceeding 200 milligrams per litre (the US EPA standard is 10 milligrams) and chloride levels exceeding 400 milligrams per litre (the EPA standard is 250 milligrams).[29]

The Jordan River system[30]

The Jordan River is the largest source of water in the region. The total annual discharge of the Jordan and its principal tributary, the Yarmouk, is more than 1 billion cubic metres – it varies annually between 1,240 and 1,350 million cubic metres. The combined river can deliver on average 1,500 tons of water every second, a massive resource in so arid an environment.

The river rises on the slopes of Mount Hermon, on the border between Syria and Lebanon, and flows southward through northern Israel to the Sea of Galilee (Lake Tiberias). Tiberias forms excellent natural storage – it can hold a whole year's average run-off, some two and a half billion cubic metres of water. This capacity allows the lake to be used as a natural reservoir, holding water over from the flood season to the dry, hot summer months. However, lake levels need careful management to preserve water quality. Reducing the lake level by just one metre will give an extra 160 million cubic metres of water, invaluable in times of drought, but with this gain comes risk because at lower levels in the lake lie saline waters. If too much water is taken off and lake levels drop below a 'red line', the saline water at the bottom can rise up and ruin the entire resource irreversibly.

Below Tiberias, the Jordan is joined by the Yarmouk and by two lesser tributaries. Today, the Yarmouk marks part of the frontier between Syria and Jordan, and between Israel and Jordan. In earlier times, inflow from the Yarmouk once nearly doubled the Jordan's flow, but upstream damming and diversion have reduced flows.

The Jordan is world-famous, revered by Christians, Jews and Muslims alike. It was in its waters that Jesus was baptized. Almost ever since, the river has remained a religious destination and a site for baptisms.

Today the Jordan is an international river, shared by four riparian countries, although not by the fifth riparian, the Palestinians. Israel is the largest user of water from the basin, with an annual withdrawal of between 580 and 640 million cubic metres, and the sole user of water from Lake Tiberias apart from 50 million cubic metres allocated to Jordan under the 1994 Israel/Jordan Peace Treaty. In total, Jordan uses about 290 million cubic metres, diverting water from the Yarmouk and the lower Zarqa tributary to the King Abdullah Canal for irrigation of crops in the Jordan Valley and for municipal and industrial use. Syria uses 450 million cubic metres of surface and groundwater resources in the Yarmouk basin, mainly for agricultural purposes. Annual abstractions in the Hasbani sub-basin in Lebanon are estimated at 9–10 million cubic metres, mainly used for domestic water supply.[31]

*　*　*

This chapter has discussed the land and water of the territory first delineated as Palestine by the League of Nations Mandate. These resources are scanty by international standards. The present-day population of the land, around 13 million, would make population density over 450 people per square kilometre and would rank the territory the sixth most populous in the world. In water scarcity also, the land is world-beating. Where the global average of water available each year per capita exceeds 6,000 cubic metres (6,000 tons), the present population of the land have access to only a small fraction of that, little more than 200 cubic metres per head, perhaps three or four per cent of the worldwide average. It is not surprising that this scanty natural endowment has led to bitter contention and to struggle. More encouraging is that it has also led to levels of ingenuity and innovation in the use of both land and water, which are world-beating.

The story of the rest of this book is thus of how the Palestinian Arabs, who at the end of the Ottoman era and the start of the Mandate had title or access to the vast majority of the water resources of the territory, ended up with an ever-diminishing share, so that by today, a century later, each Palestinian has access to about 39 cubic metres of natural water each year, while each Israeli has access to three times that, about 114 cubic metres.[32] The story is one of asymmetrical water development, of the emergence of apparently intractable dispute over water, of the attempts to find resolution, and of ways cleverly devised to eke out the exiguous natural endowment. It is also the story of an environment stretched to the limit and of, as yet, only partial and unilateral attempts to conserve and restore a bruised ecology and an overexploited natural resource base.

Contention over the Jordan River has been intense – Chapter 5 tells the story. Groundwater, the main source of water available to Palestinians in both the West Bank and the Gaza Strip, has been equally disputed. The Oslo Accords of 1994 contained interim provisions that allocated shares of the groundwater between

Israelis and Palestinians and provided for management of the resource. These provisions have long been bitterly contested by the Palestinians and have resulted in growing inequity between the parties. These disputes on groundwater are discussed in detail in Chapter 7 of this book.

The companion volume takes up the story, describing the contemporary situation and the issues the parties face today. In this second book, we also trace out a hopeful path for the future. We discuss the scope and incentives for a rebalancing of water resource allocation and for genuinely cooperative and sustainable management of the resource and of its environmental setting. We assess how cooperation between Israelis and Palestinians on water resources could be reset and water security achieved for both peoples in a solution that would bring benefits to both parties.

Chapter 3

MODERNIZATION AND WATER IN THE TWILIGHT OF THE OTTOMAN ERA, 1850–1918

The modernization of the economy and society

In the mid-nineteenth century, the lands and people that later made up Mandate Palestine were part of the Ottoman Empire, beneath a yoke which was firm but relatively easy. The economy and society were overwhelmingly traditional. Local politics was stable and hierarchical. But in the three-quarters of a century from the mid-Victorian era to the end of the First World War, the territory stirred from its secular slumber. From 1850 external influences began to bring change. The Ottomans set about a modernization which altered the old balance in Palestine's rural economy. Foreign investment, trade and immigration grew and the first Zionists began to arrive, inspired by the radical vision of a Jewish homeland in Palestine.

The conditions for the emergence of a modern economy and society began to form: political stability, an educated middle class, the growth of the population and of cities. Infrastructure began to connect Palestine to the world. Capital investment and the development of modern patterns of production and commerce marked the early stages of a market economy. Laws and institutions supported banking and markets and the growth of transactions in real property.

As we shall see, change also came to the land and to the water resources essential to life and to agriculture. New ways of managing water and land were adopted that drove economic growth and increased employment and prosperity. Ottoman reforms created a market in land, and the wealthy of the Levant put together sizeable estates. Investors developed irrigated groves of citrus and built up a profitable export trade in the prized Jaffa orange. And two waves of Jewish immigrants, inspired by the new vision of Zionism, fled troubles in Eastern Europe to settle in Palestine.

By the turn of the twentieth century, these vectors of change grew stronger. A new Palestinian middle-class was forming. Arab political consciousness expanded, and opposition to the Zionist enterprise grew. The First World War strengthened Britain's prospects of control in the Fertile Crescent and sharpened its interest in the idea of a sympathetic European colony in Palestine on Egypt's flank, protecting the route to India.

By 1918, the conditions were right for the emergence of Palestine as an early modern state. The dissolution of the old Ottoman Empire provided the opportunity. But world politics produced two constraints to this. One was the imperial design of Great Britain. The other was the determination of European Jews to set up a homeland in the territory now called Palestine.

*　*　*

With this background we turn to the water economy of late Ottoman Palestine. We look first at the agricultural economy, the user of more than nine-tenths of Palestine's water, where rural people continued their age-old daily toil to wrest a living from the soil and to eke out the scant water resources of this dry land. We then look at how water was managed, at changes in its development and use, and at the development of water and sanitation services to communities.

Agriculture and water, 1850–1918[1]

The condition of Palestine in the nineteenth century

It is hard to have a clear picture of the Palestinian countryside in the late nineteenth century, because almost all the witnesses who wrote about it seem to have had an axe to grind or to have seen but little of the country and that through a foreigner's lens. Some travellers described a run-down land and a run-down impoverished people with scant farming capacity. Many saw only Jaffa where they disembarked and the narrow stony valley that led from the coast up to Jerusalem, which even today is a dreary enough passage. Most famous is Mark Twain's dour report from his visit in 1867:

> [a] desolate country whose soil is rich enough, but is given over wholly to weeds
> – a silent mournful expanse . . . . Desolation is here that not even imagination
> can grace with the pomp of life and action . . . . We never saw a human being on
> the whole route . . . there was hardly a tree or a shrub anywhere. Even the olive
> and the cactus, those fast friends of the worthless soil, had almost deserted the
> country.[2]

The coastal zone was found to be particularly desolate. Disdainful travellers described tracts of sandy soil of low fertility and swampy stretches that precluded agriculture and harboured the malarial mosquito. A 1913 account describes the coastal plain:

> The road leading from Gaza to the north was only a summer track suitable for
> transport by camels and carts . . . no orange groves, orchards or vineyards were
> to be seen until one reached [the Jewish village of] Yabna [Yavne] . . . . Houses
> were all of mud. No windows were anywhere to be seen . . . . The ploughs used
> were of wood . . . . The yields were very poor . . . . The sanitary conditions in

the village were horrible. Schools did not exist . . . . The western part, towards the sea, was almost a desert . . . . The villages in this area were few and thinly populated. Many ruins of villages were scattered over the area, as owing to the prevalence of malaria, many villages were deserted by their inhabitants.[3]

A meta-study of nineteenth-century Palestine by the Israeli geographer Arie L. Avnieri is a little more balanced in depicting this deplorable scene.[4] He accepts the fertility of the soil and the industry of the inhabitants, but again there is the litany of desolate and deserted lands. Along the marshy areas of the coastal plain and in the valleys of the Hula and Kinorot, and of the Nahr el-Mokatta,[5] the problem was malaria. Other areas were said to be prey to Bedouin exactions – the valleys of Baysan (Beit Shean) and Marj Ibn Amir (Jezreel), and the coastal area stretching along the Bay of Acre, from Acre to Haifa.[6] Mount Carmel is a wasteland 'development ruined by foreign and local wars . . . the western slope malaria-ridden . . . seventeen villages abandoned *before Jewish settlers arrived in 1882* (our emphasis).'[7] Where villages did exist, they were 'miserable and half in ruins, the villagers downtrodden and browbeaten by money-thirsty absentee landlords'.[8]

Much of this doleful geography is political polemic. The title of Avnieri's book reveals an underlying purpose: *The Claim of Dispossession*. The lands were empty, abandoned, the population wretched, disease-ridden, prey to plunder until the redeeming Zionists arrived. Ilan Pappé in his *History of Modern Palestine* provides quite a different picture, almost a Theocritean idyll of the hill villages, the whitewashed houses with their blue symbols to ward off the evil eye clustered amidst fruit trees and bougainvillea along a hillside or lying scattered around a village square and mosque, the little forum of rural life.

In fact, there is considerable evidence of productive agriculture throughout this period. The most remarkable, as we shall see in what follows, is the development of citrus cultivation, but even in the dry south of the coastal plain there could be a buoyant agriculture when the rains were ample. In the 1880s, Edward Hull, who led the Palestine Exploration Fund survey of the geology of Palestine, describes how 'the extent of the ground [near Beersheba] cultivated, as well as on the way to Gaza, is immense and the crops of wheat, barley and maize vastly exceed the requirements of the population'. W. M. Thomson, the American missionary who spent twenty-five years in the Levant, arrived in the Gaza area in the spring of 1859 and exclaimed 'Wheat, wheat, an ocean of wheat'.[9]

The traditional agricultural economy

In the second half of the nineteenth century, Palestinian society was largely rural and the economy predominantly agricultural. Farming was the mainstay of the economy, providing a limited but relatively stable livelihood. Around 15 per cent of the rural population were not farmers themselves but nonetheless depended on agriculture – traders, wholesalers, transporters.[10]

The traditional agricultural economy was for the most part subsistence, but excess rural produce would be marketed in town. Until the rise of citrus cultivation, the main cash crops were cotton on the coastal plain and olives on the terraced slopes. In the valley bottoms and on terraces in the highlands and on the coastal plain, cereals – wheat and barley – were grown, and some sesame, too. In the mountains, the most valuable and appreciated crop was the olive, which provided not only home-produced olives for the dinner table but also the oil that could be used for cooking and fuel or could be made into soap.[11]

Social relations were organized around the clan, patriarchal but with an egalitarian approach to property and production. Land was typically owned collectively but farmed individually, with plots rotating amongst farmers, a system known as *musha'*. The Bedouin moved on the fringes of the cultivated area, guardians of the long-distance trade routes. As always in the delicate balance between the settled and the nomad, there were frequent frictions and exactions.[12]

Most agriculture in the Palestinian highlands was rain fed. The heavy clay soils of much of the mountain area were well suited to the traditional cereal crops generally sown in early winter, in November, just before the onset of the rainy season. These winter crops would be harvested in mid-summer, in June. Double cropping – two crops in one year on the same piece of land – was common. Hard durum wheat or sesame might be planted as the summer crop on fields where there was still enough moisture in the soil profile or where some supplementary irrigation was available. These crops would be harvested in autumn, before the land was prepared for the next winter cereal crops. Some farmers might practise a biennial cereals–legume rotation, with a cereal crop followed the next year by a crop like chickpeas that requires little water and which restores nitrogen to the soil.[13]

If the rains were good, moisture stored in the soil profile also allowed vegetable crops to be produced without any supplementary irrigation. A decade ago, the researcher Julia Templin recorded traditional agricultural practices in the highland village of Zababdeh which have remained largely unchanged since a century before. One farmer named Alad said that on his twelve dunums[14] '[we] plant all the vegetables in the land . . . for the winter in the winter, and for the summer in the summer . . . . And the soil will be wet, from the winter water, so it will be enough for the vegetables in the summer'. Another informant, Naziha, recalled the crops her family planted, including 'tomatoes, potatoes, peas, chickpeas . . . . In March [we] plant watermelon and tomatoes, potatoes, and in the summer, other products . . . and the next year [we] plant wheat . . . . Because[we] plant the land twice.'[15]

Seeds of change

In the late Ottoman period, change began to affect the agricultural economy. Two factors started this process. First, and most obviously, was the growth of the population, particularly the growth in the towns that came with the settled political conditions and the emergence of a more market-oriented economy. This demographic factor, combined with the rise in income attendant on economic growth, led to the emergence of a much larger market for food. Subsistence crops began to give way to cash crops. For certain products, particularly citrus, export markets were also opening up, as we shall see later.

A second factor was that in order to promote modernization and increase tax revenues, the Ottoman land law reform of 1858 changed the basis of land tenure, with far-reaching effects. In the past, land had been leased from the state in return for services to the sultan. Under the reforms, anybody could own land provided they paid the taxes. Real property had to be registered in the state land registry, the *tapu*. In 1865, the Ottomans conducted a land survey in Palestine under the new law. Land in private hands was registered as *mulk*, freehold property. The owners had to pay for the title deed and were liable to tax at 4 per mill of the capital value and 4 per cent of the annual crop. Those farming land that remained in government hands (*mir*) paid the annual *'ushr*, 12.5 per cent of the sale value of the crop. By bribing officials, many investors managed to get land registered as *mulk*. In this way they paid the lower taxes and had a saleable asset.

A land market emerged, and land became the object of speculation. Notables began to register in their own names the lands of peasants and Bedouin who were unwilling to pay for the title deed or who simply did not grasp the significance of the changes in land tenure that were brought about by the new law. The old practices and rights of collective usufruct under *musha*[16] proved incompatible with the new rights. By law, many small peasant farmers in the villages no longer had rights over the land they had farmed for generations.[17]

These beginnings of modernization and a more commercial economy brought benefits, but also costs and risks. Private property rights and the creation of a market in land encouraged investment, particularly in high-value tree crops, notably in the Jaffa orange. The growth of urban and export markets led to a cash crop economy that increased incentives for consolidating land holdings and for planting high-value crops.

However, the new tax burdens began to create high levels of indebtedness. There came also for the first time the possibility of land being sold outside the community. Small landowners began to sell their land to big landowners and to rich urban families. Land ownership by absentee landlords was on the increase. The Ottoman civil servant Musa al-Husayni, for example, was able to purchase 400 hectares (1,000 acres) of fertile irrigated land around Jericho in 1872. It was said at the time that this constituted some two-thirds of the total cultivated land in the area. All this reduced the scope for family farming in areas where land transfer and consolidation were taking place. With the beginning of land sales came the first emergence of landless agricultural labourers.[18]

The rise of a new commercial irrigated agriculture: the Jaffa orange[19]

In areas with water sources, Palestinian farmers had practised irrigation since ancient times. Where there were springs, farmers used small earth canals to convey the water to irrigate their crops – fruit and vegetables and, in the hot Jordan Valley, date palms and bananas. In the highlands, some crops were historically irrigated from cisterns that captured rainwater, although quantities were small and this method could be used only to supplement rainfall.

It was the development from the mid-nineteenth century of the Jaffa orange in the coastal plain that brought commercial irrigated agriculture to Palestine on a large scale and revolutionized the agricultural economy, both water use and farming. Citrus had long been grown in the Jaffa area.[20] The germ of its rapid expansion lay in the variety of orange that local farmers had developed over the years. Originally produced by Palestinian farmers around Jaffa from the native (*baladi*) orange in the mid-nineteenth century, the Jaffa orange (also known as the *shamouti* orange) is large and juicy, thick-skinned so it keeps well and, above all, it has few or no seeds.

This *shamouti* orange emerged by a process that combined varietal selection with chance. It is said that the farmers who developed it gradually selected cultivars where the seeds were clustered near the top of the orange until, with selection over the years, a cultivar was produced with virtually no seeds at all. The Jaffa orange is, along with the navel and bitter orange, one of three main varieties of the fruit grown in the Mediterranean region. It ripens early and ships well. As Palestine opened to the world, the Jaffa orange quickly became an international favourite. Queen Victoria is known to have relished it.

The Jaffa region did not spring up as the centre of this new production by chance. The soils were suitable for citrus cultivation. A shallow depth to water in the Coastal Aquifer made irrigated agriculture possible even with traditional water-lifting techniques. The irrigated gardens which ringed Jaffa town were often mentioned by travellers in the first half of the nineteenth century. Historically the crops irrigated here were many and various – lemons, oranges, pomegranates, figs, peaches, apricots, almonds, grapes, vegetables, watermelons, sugar cane, tobacco. With the economic changes in the mid-nineteenth century, the port town of Jaffa provided not only an outlet for produce to the local and regional market but also a gateway to exports by steamship within the region and beyond, and in particular to the growing European market for fresh produce.

The first cash crop to take off in this new era of opportunity was, in fact, not the orange but the mulberry tree, for silk production. Silk had become a driver of the Lebanese economy and from the middle of the nineteenth century it took off in Palestine as well. This, however, proved short-lived. Competition from other lower-cost producers and, above all, from artificial silk was strong and by 1880 the mulberry tree and silk production had all but disappeared from the Palestinian landscape.

But as the mulberry declined, citrus – and especially the Jaffa orange – took first place amongst the cash crops of Palestine. By 1880, there were 3,000 citrus groves, and by the end of that decade there were more than 9,000. The area planted was more than 36,000 dunums, or nearly 4,000 hectares.[21] An account of around 1880 gives a snapshot of these groves:

> . . . reservoirs [are] used to irrigate them. The water in these reservoirs is deep. Horses and mules are harnessed to a wheel which raises the water and causes it

to overflow into a pool at garden level, and then into ditches which water all the trees.

It has been some thirty years since gardens have begun to be planted, and they have multiplied to such an extent that there are now close to five hundred large ones around the city. All are profitable to their owners, for the land is fertile and can produce all manner of fruit.[22]

And so from tiny beginnings – just 1,400 cases exported in 1845 – the trade took off.[23] In 1880, 200,000 cases were exported from Jaffa – 30 million oranges. In 1910, 950,000 cases were sent out – over 125 million oranges. For the first time, fresh citrus fruit, tasty and rich in Vitamin C, became available throughout Europe, and the Palestinian citrus industry prospered. Fruits carrying the Jaffa orange label were first marketed by Sarona, a German Templar colony established in 1871.

Until the 1880s, cultivation followed the old ways. A grove would be established from a nursery where lemon seeds would be planted. When seedlings had grown into saplings, usually in two to three years, the *shamouti* orange was grafted on to the lemon tree root stock. The young trees were planted out quite densely – 250–300 trees per dunum, up to 3,000 trees per hectare. While the trees were maturing, vegetables would be planted between the rows. The farmer who grew the vegetables would tend the young trees for free.

Irrigation was essential for much of the year. A well would be dug by hand and a waterwheel with wooden buckets built above it. Donkeys would power the wheel, drawing on a pulley. As the buckets rose one by one until they were at the top of the wheel, they tipped water into a tank or pool with a head of height above the orange grove. From the tank, small stone-lined canals ran through the grove to water the trees. The tank would be filled by day and the grove irrigated by night to keep down losses to evaporation in the warm, dry climate. Typically, about 5,000–6,000 cubic metres – or 5,000–6,000 tons – of water were required in a year for each hectare of orange grove. This volume of water was expensive – labour and wear and tear were big costs, but the biggest cost was usually the donkey and its feed. The cost of water amounted to about a quarter of the sale value of the crop.[24]

As the young trees grew, there would be considerable cash expenses – for labour, for fertilizer, for the donkeys – or for water if it were purchased. Although the production techniques were not advanced and farm bookkeeping was largely absent, the high level of investment and the rapid growth of exports showed how profitable orange production was. As is still common today in the Arab world, the owners of the grove would usually sell the crop on the trees as it approached maturity. The intermediary or the merchant who bought it would take care of guarding the trees until the oranges were ready, and then would arrange for picking, crating, transporting and shipping. Most exports went to Britain and Europe via the great entrepot of Liverpool.

Until the end of the century, almost all the groves were in Arab hands. Only a few Jews and a handful of German immigrants took up the business at the time. An account of 1880 shows early but small-scale Jewish interest:

Some of these gardens belong to our Jewish brethren, and one was purchased by the righteous Sir Moses Montefiore, may God bless and keep him.[25]

But towards 1900, foreign interest grew. With this came the European experts, supercilious, finger-wagging, contemptuous of the simple traditional production techniques which were well adapted to the environment. Despite the success of the orange business and its profitability, the experts expressed both pity and ridicule over the errors in planting, irrigation and pest control. However, a recent (2005) study advanced the idea that the traditional methods were 'ultimately more cost-efficient' than the 'modern' enterprises that developed later.[26]

The German Templars and a handful of American settlers began to innovate. Despite high tariffs, the Templars brought in irrigation piping and mechanical water pumps, and used organic fertilizer. The traditional waterwheel began to be replaced by kerosene-powered motor pumps. These early pumps were typically 3–4 horsepower and could yield 20–40 cubic metres an hour, ten times the yield of the traditional donkey-powered waterwheel. By 1906 there were 200 of these motor pumps installed around Jaffa.[27] Steel waterwheels also came in, and wider, more even spacing of the trees was practised. Of course, these new methods demanded higher levels of capital, with investment in a grove irrigated by motor power up to three times that in a traditional grove.[28] As the yield of wells increased, so did the size of groves they could irrigate. The new capital-intensive groves were often 50 dunums (5 hectares), twice the size of traditional ones.

Jaffa grew prosperous on the orange trade. Local notables, Arab merchants, churches and settlers from the United States and Germany, and incoming Jews – all snapped up land. Land prices rose. Land that in the 1880s cost 30–50 francs per dunum (the equivalent of about US$1,500–2,500 per hectare in today's money) was being sold after the turn of the century for 300–600 francs per dunum (US$15,000 or more in today's money). If the land was already planted to citrus, the price could be up to 2,500 francs per dunum, equivalent to an astronomical US$125,000 a hectare today.[29]

The economic success of the Jaffa orange business was remarkable. Already in 1885, Jaffa oranges accounted for 20 per cent of all exports from Palestine and by 1913 this had grown to 40 per cent. Most of the value added stayed locally, with the majority of the groves and virtually all the trade in Jaffa oranges in the hands of local residents. Much employment was created, ranging from those who dug the wells, all through the planting, production and harvesting processes, to those who built the crates and wrapped the oranges.[30] The overwhelming preponderance of this value added was in Palestinian Arab hands, although settler interest strengthened from around the turn of the century. By 1905, there were 30,000 dunums (3,000 hectares) under citrus with a few hundred dunums in Jewish hands.[31]

Early settler agriculture

Meanwhile, elsewhere in Palestine, settler agriculture was growing fast. The early Zionists began to arrive at just the moment that a land market was emerging, and this enabled them to make their first purchases. Zionist thinking was grounded in acquiring and developing land and water in Palestine using modern agricultural techniques. Already in 1870, a visionary Frenchman, Charles Netter, founded *Mikveh Israel*, the first Jewish agricultural school, with the aim of training up a cadre of young agronomists and farmers who would then establish villages and settlements throughout the land. This school was near Jaffa, established on a tract of land leased from the Ottoman sultan. Netter became the first headmaster and introduced new methods of agricultural training. Baron Edmond de Rothschild contributed to the running costs. The school published manuals on agriculture, and staff served as agricultural advisers to settlements. Later the school also served for a time as an agricultural research centre.[32]

The earliest settlements of the first *aliya* (1881–1903) had to struggle to survive. To take one example, Zikhron Ya'akov was founded in December 1882 when 100 Jewish pioneers from Romania, members of the Hibbat Zion movement, purchased land in Zammarin. The families all came from the same town, Moineşti, in Moldavia. These very early Zionists were led and inspired by a scholar, Moses Gaster. Despite their enthusiasm, the endeavour proved too hard for many. The unyielding rocky soil and the scourge of malaria caused many to quit within the first twelve months.

However, the next year, in 1883, Baron de Rothschild was persuaded to become the patron of the settlement, which was named Ya'akov after the Baron's father. Rothschild paid for town planning, and housing lots were assigned to each farm family along the main road.[33] Each lot included a house facing the street, a long interior courtyard and a rear building for storing agricultural implements. The French-inspired architecture included tiled roofs and painted wooden windows. Rothschild also drew up an agricultural plan. Much of this plan failed but one project did prosper – grape production and a winery. Carmel Winery was the first in the country, and it survives to this day.[34] Each farmer was given a salary and placed under the direction of Elijah Shaid, the Baron's clerk.

There were some benefits for the local population from this early phase of settlement. For example, at Zikhron Ya'akov both Jewish and Arab workers were initially employed as labourers, each earning (in 1894) a wage of six piastres.[35] However, Jewish workers also received free housing and a supplement of four piastres from a charity fund. When Rothschild withdrew his financial support from plantations in Palestine in 1900, the subsidy was discontinued and Jewish workers were quickly replaced by Arab ones who would accept the reduced conditions.

The situation of agriculture on the eve of the Mandate

By the end of the Ottoman period, we see two agricultures side by side in Palestine. In the highlands and in parts of the coastal plain, traditional agriculture continued much as it had for centuries. Alongside it there was a modern, commercial, export-oriented farm sector springing up, predominantly in Palestinian hands but with the new Jewish settlements fast catching up. We see consolidation of farmland in fewer hands and the decline of the old collective ownership and farming systems, with the first emergence of the landless labourer and the drift to towns. We see the adoption of modern techniques of irrigation and crop husbandry, but also the first signs of separate development of agriculture between the Jewish and Arab communities, with a fast-rising and modernizing Jewish sector and a two-track Arab sector – modern production, particularly of the Jaffa orange, and traditional production in the highlands and the rainfed lands of the coastal plain.

Water and water management

We have seen the main and most valuable use of water – in agriculture – and also the improvements in water management in agriculture, particularly in irrigated citrus production. But what of the water resource and its management – water rights, water resource development, water services to communities?

Water rights

Traditional water rights in Palestine were a combination of local custom and Muslim common law. The *sharia'* approach is that water is *mubah, res nullius,* the property of no one person or entity, but a free good jointly owned by all. Yet the *sharia'* recognizes that although there may be no private property in either groundwater or surface water, private use rights may be acquired. As everywhere in the traditional Islamic world, a landowner in Palestine could hold the exclusive right to use water – a well, a stream or a spring – developed within that individual's property, subject to 'the right of thirst', the right that allows everybody to quench their thirst at a water source. In Palestine private rights to springs or wells developed on owned land could thus be held and could be transferred with the land.

Rights to springs and streams could also be shared, either with riparians according to their land holdings or amongst a community as a common drinking source. Rules for shares and for maintenance were hammered out over the generations. Water sales did occur, but were frowned on, particularly when the water was for drinking. As late as the 1930s, the people in Zababdeh were so incensed at a local family who began a business bringing drinking water for sale from the mountains on camelback that they attacked the camels and killed them.[36]

In their modernizing reforms of the 1870s, the Ottomans attempted to codify water rights in the *mejelle*, the new civil code based on the Code Napoleon. In principle, the *mejelle* vested property in water in the state as a public good. All existing and future uses had to be registered and were subject to licensing and regulation. Commissions were to survey and recognize existing water rights.

However, the *mejelle* formulation added little to traditional practice. The new code essentially recognized that the use of water within a property was the right of the landowner. In any case, the proposed commissions and registration process appear not to have been implemented in Palestine. No central water administration was set up. Landowners continued to control the water on their land and communities controlled communal sources, with rights protected and disputes resolved according to Islamic law and local custom.[37]

Water development

Although there were no major public works in water resources development in this period, the Ottoman administration did begin the long effort to drain the marshes. This was intended to reduce the incidence of 'Jerusalem fever', the malaria that ravaged the land, and to reclaim the drained land for cultivation.[38]

In the countryside, water development and storage remained largely traditional. In many villages there were communal cisterns, typically fed by springs or by rainwater harvested from slopes. Across the Palestinian highlands there were countless examples of these rock-hewn chambers, usually lined with a thick layer of plaster. They were not too deep – up to 5 metres (20 feet) at the most – so that water could easily be drawn out, or a man could slip in and carry out periodic maintenance and cleaning every three or four years. The cistern was filled by channels cut in the slopes above to capture and convey the run-off from the hillsides. The water first passed through a small settling basin where dirt and sediment were deposited or filtered out. The cleaned water then entered the cistern through an opening deliberately made narrow to keep the water clean.

The technology persevered well into the twentieth century, basically unchanged since biblical times. The water collected from the slopes was generally quite clean and was used mainly for drinking, and for domestic tasks. The women and girls would trek to the cistern and collect the water in heavy clay jars. By contrast, any water collected within the village itself was usually dirty and used only for livestock. In some areas, cisterns were also used to irrigate crops, but this was very expensive. Masterman in 1900 records 'about fifty cisterns' to supply supplementary irrigation water to a vineyard of just two acres.[39]

One fairly elaborate example was Ein Battir pool in Battir village northwest of Bethlehem.[40] The dimensions of the pool were 10 metres square, with a depth of 4 metres. The pool was fed from springs, and the water was used for both domestic and agricultural purposes. The supply from the springs ran along lined channels or pipes to reduce losses and maintain quality. A traditional system of water management divided up the water and resolved any conflict:

> The elder of the clan used to distribute the rationed water according to a certain quota. The share of the beneficiary was determined in accordance with the irrigated land area. At the middle of the pool's floor, there was a point which represented the level of the water. A graded scale rod was placed at this point, and each grade was equivalent to a particular share. The water shares of the beneficiaries were distributed throughout the week. One day, for example, was allotted to one benefiting clan. One of the clan members was assigned on that day to divide water among his clansmen. One and a half shares were allotted for each 20–30-m^2 plot of irrigated land. The landowner could either directly use the water or store it up in supplementary pools for use on waterless days. This system is still operative in many Palestinian villages.[41]

Urban water supply

Until the latter half of the nineteenth century, investment and management of urban water supply was largely a local and individual affair. The coastal cities all drew their water from wells sunk into the shallow aquifer. A few towns, notably Jerusalem, had aquaducts bringing water by gravity from nearby springs to public fountains and to mosques. Some mosques and churches would invest in their own water supply system, often water drawn by hand from wells. Households would invest in individual cisterns to capture rooftop and other run-off and this served to provide the bulk of domestic water. Water was also provided from shared and communal sources. Sanitation was typically a hand-dug cesspit.

In every town there was a private trade in the small quantities of clean safe water needed for drinking. Typically the local administration would regulate distribution within the city by licensed carriers who delivered drinking water to houses and shops for a fee set by the Wali, who also determined working hours. Most towns also had public drinking fountains (*sabil*) which supplied free drinking water in line with the 'right of thirst'.[42] In some towns, ponds that collected both rainwater and spring water were used to carry water over from the winter rains to the dry summers. These ponds were supervised by officials who were entrusted with their maintenance and protection from pollution.

With the rapid increase in the urban population from mid-century, the Ottoman government and local municipalities and other agencies began to plan for urban services. The city councils got new life under the Young Turks and this led to the start of development of modern municipal services of water supply and sanitation. However, there was considerable doubt about consumer willingness to pay for piped water services. An 1893 proposal to convey water by pipe from the Nahr al Auja river (which Israelis later called the Yarkon) and distribute it through a piped network within Jaffa – the Franghia-Navon Scheme – was dismissed as too expensive and not financially viable because residents would not be willing to pay the tariffs.[43] The new settlements began to develop their own systems. In 1879, a piped water system was installed in the German Templar colony of Sarona. A piped water system was also installed in Ahuzat Bayit, the new Zionist quarter of Jaffa, established in 1909, which was later to become Tel Aviv.[44]

Water supply of Jerusalem[45]

The most ambitious challenge was the water supply of Jerusalem, and this can be taken as an example of developments in the late Ottoman period. The site of the city, on top of a dry mountain amidst barren hills, is well suited for defence but not for water supply. In fact, throughout history, securing a water supply has been a persistent concern, 'a source of collective anxiety and permanent conflicts'.[46]

The nearby Gihon spring supplied the city at its beginnings but as the spring was seasonal and flowed only intermittently a few times each day, early residents constructed the Pool of Siloam to store the water.[47] From the time of the Canaanites in the eighteenth century BC onwards, rock-cut tunnels conveyed the water to within the city to ensure the water supply in times of siege, and webs of underground pipelines were developed by subsequent rulers to distribute the water.

In the middle of the nineteenth century, piped networks were local and limited. The main sources of supply were the private cisterns designed to collect and store rainwater. Almost every private home had its cistern that collected water from the rooftops and from the streets and gardens, and the Ottoman building code required the construction of a cistern for every new building.[48] In 1850, estimates were that consumption from these cisterns was about 300 cubic metres a day, which would have provided about 30 litres of domestic water per person for the then population of 10,000 inhabitants. The engineer E. Pierotti, in his exploration of Jerusalem published in 1864, counted 992 private cisterns in the city. By the end of the Ottoman era in 1918, there were over 7,000, which would match the sevenfold increase in the population of the city over the half century since 1864.[49] But there were health problems related to these cisterns. The Ottoman Director of Public Works for Palestine, the excellent and tireless engineer Franghia Bey,[50] wrote: 'the dirtiness of the water from the cisterns is particularly high at the end of the summer when the water levels are low, and this results in serious health risks, including malaria.'

Most households used their cistern water for all domestic purposes except drinking and then purchased small quantities of clean potable water – 1.5–2 litres per person per day – from the carriers at the water market at the Mugrabim Gate. The carriers sourced this water from local springs, mainly the Gihon spring and Bir Ayub in the Kidron valley. A number of public fountains – the *sabil* – also provided water, including for Islamic ritual ablutions. The most notable were the six public fountains built by Suleiman the Magnificent in 1536 along the pilgrimage route to the Haram al Sharif.

Solomon's Pools, located several miles from Jerusalem, near Al-Khader village to the southwest of Bethlehem, were the major public water supply. These ancient pools had a capacity of over 150,000 cubic metres and an aqueduct conveyed the water to Jerusalem from a slight altitude above the town (768 metres) to basins located under the Haram al Sharif, the lowest point of the city, at 736 metres. Because the difference in altitude was so slight, flows were sluggish. The municipal authorities were constantly repairing the system. An 1894 report (by Franghia Bey) records that the pools 'were restored by Izet Pasha, the Governor of Jerusalem . . . the aqueduct underwent its last repair in 1888 which apparently was not very efficient since the aqueduct currently doesn't work'. Repairs were carried out by a corvée of forced labour[51] but the system was nonetheless often out of commission. Part of the problem was that Jerusalem water carriers sabotaged it to protect their businesses. The residents of Bethlehem, who contested Jerusalem's right to the water, also sought to cut the supply.

Problems intensified as the population continued to grow. The Jewish population of the city rose from 4,000 in 1850 to almost 40,000 by the end of the century, and the Christian and Moslem population doubled over the same period, from 4,000 to 10,000, respectively. The total population went from 10,000 inhabitants in

1850 to 70,000 in 1910, which increased basic water requirements from 300 cubic metres per day to more than 2,000. In a report of the 1880s, Franghia Bey wrote:

> The suffering of the inhabitants of Jerusalem, the main cause of which is the lack of water, has made public opinion rank water supply highest among all the issues which involve the Holy City for more than ten years. As the days go by, the need becomes more pressing, more urgent.

The Ottoman administration was active in seeking solutions to the challenge.[52] Engineer Franghia Bey discusses the consumption figures: '35 to 40 litres of very pure spring water per day, in addition to the water captured in the cisterns is amply sufficient to place the city within the ranks of happy towns.' In 1908 the Ottoman authorities published Franghia's report which proposed the diversion of the sources of the Arub and the modernization of the aqueduct in order to bring 2,000 cubic metres of water per day by gravity to the city.

The following year the German engineer Max Magnus, the director of the Carl Franck Institute of Bremen, published an alternative proposal: to divert the spring at Ein Fara, located 13 kilometres north of Jerusalem. As the spring was 500 metres lower in altitude than Jerusalem, Magnus proposed to lift the water by electric pumps. The cost was estimated at 4 million francs (about $20 million today), double what the Franghia Plan would have cost, and operating costs to run the pumps would also have been very high. In any case, the financial viability of either scheme was doubtful. Although the theoretical need was great, residents were likely to be reluctant to pay money for a fully potable supply when they could meet most of their needs from their cisterns.

The Zionists were also planning for Jerusalem water supply. At the start of 1910, the Zionist Executive Committee sent a Dutch engineer called Meyer to Jerusalem to study the question. When his report was published later that year, the Zionists favoured the scheme Meyer proposed, arguing that a good water supply system would encourage middle-class Jewish immigration and would be profitable if combined with the award of other contracts, such as electricity supply or tramways. A report by Jacob H. Kann, a member of the Interior Committee of the Zionist Organization and a director of the Jewish Colonial Trust Bank, proposed that the water supply scheme be financed by the banks and that it could be profitable or at least viable financially because it would help to jump-start the local economy.

Progress was halting. The municipality did tender works under the Franghia Plan in 1910, but then cancelled the tender. In 1914, the Jerusalem press was criticizing the city council for its failure to maintain the existing water and sanitation system.[53] Finally, on 27 January 1914, a concession agreement was signed with a Greek Ottoman citizen from Istanbul, Euripides Mavrommatis, for the 'building and operation of the supply of drinking water to the city of Jerusalem' together with concessions related to an electric tramway system and the supply of electric light and power. The concession allowed Mavrommatis to propose how the drinking water supply was to be accomplished, although he was expected to adopt either Franghia's Arub springs scheme or the Ein Fara scheme of Max

Magnus. The contract explicitly forbade a monopoly of water supply, providing that both household cisterns and the drinking water market would continue in use. The contract also required the construction and maintenance of twenty public fountains. An agreement for similar concessions for the city of Jaffa was concluded in 1916. However, the war interrupted the implementation of these concessions and at the start of the Mandate the British awarded a concession to Pinhas Rutenberg (see Chapter 4), which effectively cancelled out the previous arrangements. Protracted international legal battles followed, but Mavrommatis never implemented the works.

Sanitation

The typical means of disposing of the small quantities of wastewater and sewage generated under traditional water and sanitation practices was the cesspit system, in which the wastewater simply drains away into the earth and is, it is hoped, filtered and cleaned by the soil before it reaches groundwater. However, this system was far from safe and the population suffered annual episodes of cholera, with a particularly bad outbreak in Haifa in 1910.[54]

To manage the risks, the founders of Ahurat Bayit, the future Tel Aviv, set out by-laws on how cess pits should be constructed, maintained and cleaned. They set up a sanitation committee headed by the municipal physician to supervise sanitary conditions, including checking the pits. Liquids were absorbed into the sandy soil; the solid residues cleaned out by Arab or Yemeni Jewish labourers.[55] But already, only two years after the founding of the city, in the autumn of 1913, the committee wrote to the Tel Aviv Executive Committee recommending a sewerage system. It would, however, be more than a decade before this could be realized.

*　*　*

We see in the closing decades of the long Ottoman rule over Palestine a certain energy, driven by the modernization of institutions and by the rapid growth of the economy and the population. As a result, new patterns emerged of market-oriented irrigated agriculture and of urbanization and the start of modern water and sanitation services. These changes affected most of the population to some degree, but mostly the emerging Palestinian middle-class and the settler community. In fact, the Palestinian Arab economy in this period was thriving from the growth of water use in high-value agriculture. Future patterns of separate development and differential access to opportunity were not yet firmly traced. How these patterns grew more pronounced is discussed in the following chapters, culminating in the strongly contrasted situations in respect of water today, which are the subject of our companion volume.

Chapter 4

WATER IN THE ERA OF THE BRITISH MANDATE, 1918–48

Nationalism and development in the Mandate era

The Mandate, surely one of the least glorious episodes in the long history of the Empire . . . productive of . . . more criticism than any other part of that vast enterprise.

A. J. Sherman, Mandate Days: 11

The contradictions of the Mandate

In 1920, the San Remo Conference awarded the Mandate for Palestine to Britain. The British aim was largely to secure imperial interests, and above all to safeguard the route through the Suez Canal to India by protecting Egypt's flank. Despite strong Arab opposition, the final terms of the Mandate confirmed the promise of a Jewish homeland. With its provision for specifically Jewish institutions and rights, the Mandate was weighted towards fostering what was essentially the development of a Jewish state within a state and according a favourable treatment to the Jewish economy that aided its separate development. This was an innovation in international law and practice, an internationally sanctioned framework of institutionalized discrimination in favour of one group of inhabitants of a territory over another group. The arrangement, to a large extent, elided the Palestinian Arabs, who were the overwhelming majority of the population, ignored their concerns and was silent about their rights in the new state

Although many of the British officials on the ground were at best lukewarm towards the idea of Jewish settlement, the Mandate authorities set about their task of helping Jewish immigration, land acquisition and economic development. The Zionists mobilized their community behind the project of creating institutions that would prefigure a Zionist state. The Jewish Agency emerged as an effective political and executive body, and the Yishuv began to build considerable economic autonomy.

In counterbalance, the reality that for the first time in millennia Palestine was administered as a single unit contributed to Arab political thinking. A Palestinian Arab nationalism began to form. Already in 1919, the first Palestine Arab Congress had convened. During the 1920s, popular Arab opposition to Zionist settlement increased and Arab leaders attempted to bring some order to Arab national aspirations and to the rejection of Zionism. The British struggled to imagine a political settlement that could bring the two communities together but by 1930, it was clear to the Mandate authorities that common political institutions were not possible. Both communities grew hostile to collaboration, and ideas of bi-nationalism attracted only very limited support. Palestinian aspirations were spurred by the sight of other Arab territories achieving increasing degrees of independence and hopes rose briefly when the 1930 Shaw Commission called for limiting Jewish immigration.

In the 1930s, the ghost of a political settlement – a two-nation state under a benign British rule – was quickly dispelled by increased Jewish settlement in flight from an increasingly savage Europe and by the growing anger of the Palestinian Arabs at what they saw as the loss of their land and livelihoods. By 1936, political options seemed exhausted and an Arab revolt broke out. Despite a garrison that already in 1936 numbered 20,000 men, the British simply lost control of much of the country. Armed Arab bands roamed the hills, their bravery much admired by the British. Martial law was imposed and the revolt was eventually put down with considerable savagery. From Government House atop the incongruously named Hill of Evil Counsel, the high commissioner, Sir Arthur Wauchope, looked down and wrote to Humphrey Bowman, the director of education:

> I was up early this morning and could have wept as I saw the walls of Jerusalem turn golden under the cloudless sky and thought of – what you and I think of every sorrowful day.[1]

At this time, thinking began to turn to the possibility of partition. However, soon war came and all the horrors for the Jewish people. Zionism gathered strength from immigration and new settlements, and from the military experience gained by the more than 27,000 Palestinian Jews who served with the British forces. By contrast, divided loyalties weakened Palestinian leadership and resolve, and when the time of crisis arrived, the Arabs were ill-prepared.

Uneven and increasingly separate development

Despite the troubled politics, the years of the Mandate saw the continuation of the modernization of Palestine. Towns, manufacture and trade grew rapidly. Marshlands were drained and brought under cultivation. Water was mobilized for a prosperous irrigated agriculture. The peasant economy in the highlands grew in fits and starts. Water resources were developed for hydropower and for modern water supply and sanitation. Amenity and health improved in consequence.

There was, nonetheless, an underlying inequality which grew out of both structural and specific origins. The Mandate accorded privileges to Jewish institutions and the British therefore gave, amidst loud Arab protests, a broad concession over all the running waters of Palestine to a Jewish enterprise. And the Yishuv mobilized private capital, experience and pioneering energy to develop irrigated agriculture and the modern water supply and sanitation services that Europeans expected.

The Mandate authorities and Palestinian Arab institutions moved to do the same for Palestinian Arabs but could never achieve the same level of investment and services. As a result, the water sector developed a lopsided character. By the 1930s, even the question of sewage systems was an issue between Jews and Arabs that could only be resolved by separation.

The triumph of Zionism

After just three decades of the turbulent Mandate, the Yishuv emerged as the only gainers. The British had expended huge administrative and military effort before being bundled ignominiously out of the country. Instead of a complaisant new state on the flank of Egypt, they had a fiercely independent new country together with a humanitarian and ethical catastrophe and a hostile and bewildered Arab world. Even the imperial goal, the protection of the Jewel in the Crown, had gone when India gained its independence in 1947.

The Arab Palestinians had wasted thirty years in largely peaceful outcry at what was taking place. Their enraged outbursts of violence had been met not with concessions but with fierce repression. Their economy had, for sure, grown, but as a shadowy appanage of the dynamic and well-resourced Jewish economy. And their politics were in disarray, even their identity was in question. As the British fled, most Palestinian Arabs ended up as refugees, dispossessed and homeless.

Only the Zionists achieved their goal, and that beyond their imagining. They soared to nationhood in a way and in a space of time that even the early visionaries could not have anticipated. These sturdy, resolute immigrants bound together the disparate elements and created a firm homeland for the wretched Jewry of Europe.

*   *   *

With this background we now look in detail at the questions of water. First, we discuss the economic setting and then look at water resources development. We continue with a review of agriculture and water under the Mandate, and end the chapter with the spread of water and sanitation services.

The economy during the Mandate

Economic prospects for Palestine at the start of the Mandate

When Allenby arrived in Palestine in 1917, he found a country battered by war, especially along the coastal plain. The population of 800,000 – 650,000 Muslims, 80,000 Christians, 60,000 Jews – had shrunk by 50,000 through the ravages of conflict – through military actions, famine and disease.[2] Nonetheless, the structure of the economy that had developed over the previous half century remained and a post-war revival could build on this base. Commerce and the export trade held promise for further growth and the Arab population had shown a capacity to adapt to the evolving political and economic circumstances. A rich source of future growth lay in the prospective influx of Jewish manpower, know-how and capital, although how this would affect the economy as a whole was as vexed a question as its effect on politics and on society. But in any case, the British Mandate was to bring a legal and administrative framework that provided a stable base for economic growth, provided that political and security conditions allowed it.[3]

The economy, concessions and the Yishuv

Generally, economic policy was laissez faire and public spending on infrastructure and services was limited. Outlays were largely for administration, defence and security. During the 1920s and 1930s, only 12 per cent of the government budget went towards public works, health and education. The generally low level of public spending on infrastructure and services affected mainly the Arabs as the Jewish Agency made up for it by spending nearly half (40 per cent) of their own recurrent budget, generated largely from foreign donations, on education and welfare.[4] The government did invest in roads and railways but expected them to pay their way.[5] One exception was port facilities. Up to the 1930s, Palestine lacked a deep water seaport. Heavy equipment and goods – steam engines for the railways, for example, or factory or construction plant – had to be landed at Port Said in Egypt, taken by train to El Kantara, trans-shipped across the Suez Canal, and then re-embarked on the railway and freighted up to Palestine. In 1933 a deep water seaport was constructed at Haifa.

Utilities such as water supply and electricity were seen primarily as a domain for private investment. Concessions were granted to stimulate development and to raise revenues, including the Rutenberg Concession on water and electricity (on which see what follows). Rights to exploit the mineral resources of the Dead Sea were granted to the Jewish-owned Palestine Potash Company.[6] In awarding these concessions to Jewish entrepreneurs, the British were influenced by the preferential provisions in the Mandate that 'the Administration may arrange with the Jewish agency to construct or operate . . . any public works, services and utilities, and to develop any of the natural resources of the country' [Article 11].

This legal stipulation could serve to effectively exclude 'the thousands of Arab businessmen, many of them returning from [overseas], who sought to profit from imperial development schemes'. Essentially the old Arab merchant classes now found themselves squeezed out of their former role as the operators of public works concessions and government development projects. And yet many of these businessman were as capable and had as much access to capital as any of the Jewish immigrants.[7] It is likely that this preference for Jewish investment and entrepreneurship was also driven by a *non dit* that today would be called racist, a belief that European Jews were better suited to play the role of Palestine's entrepreneurs, 'acting as the catalyst for a new era of development and industrialization' in the region.[8]

Growth of the Yishuv economy and the separate development of the two economies

Overall, Palestine enjoyed high but uneven rates of economic growth during much of the Mandate. This growth occurred mainly in the Jewish economy where annual GDP per capita increased from around £P 20 in 1923–4 to perhaps as much as £P 50 in 1935. Arab manufacturing and trading enterprises also grew, largely concentrated on the coast, along with the large expanses of Arab citrus groves.[9] However, the Arab economy could not match the rapid growth of the Jewish sector – in 1935, Arab per capita GDP was estimated at only one-third of that of the Yishuv, at about £P 17. By 1936, despite the much larger Arab population, the Jewish and Arab economies were roughly the same size. In that year, one estimate was that the Yishuv produced three times more goods and services – £P 9.5 million – than the Arab sector, and exported overseas three times what they sold to the Arab sector – £P 3 million against £P 1 million.[10]

There was some interdependence between the Arab and Jewish economies. Despite the Zionists' promotion of 'Hebrew labour', by 1935 there were 12,000 Arabs working for Jewish enterprises. However, Zionist policy essentially favoured separate development and, inevitably and perforce, this became Arab practice too. With few exceptions such as the citrus export trade, cooperation and collaboration dwindled rather than grew and by the 1930s the two economies were becoming increasingly separated.[11]

The wartime boom[12]

By contrast with the Great War, the Second World War proved quite a boom time economically for Palestine. During the 1920s and 1930s, considerable new infrastructure had been built, notably rail networks and asphalt roads. This served Palestine well when the Second World War brought increased economic opportunity in serving the large military presence in the country.[13] The war in North Africa threatened Egypt and the Suez Canal. As a result, Palestine became a huge army base and source of goods and services. Most sectors of the economy grew fast. Jewish industry thrived, producing a wide range of industrial goods, spares, electrical appliances, etc. Scientists at the Hebrew University supported innovation for Jewish factory owners. Arab industry expanded, too, and by the end of the war was producing half of Palestine's output of cigarettes and a fifth of the country's total production of woven cloth and footwear. The main economic casualty of the war, which badly affected the Arab economy, was the principal export, citrus, where markets were virtually closed for the duration of the war.

Water resources regulation and development

Mandate water policy and legislation

Water management by the British under the Mandate was done with a light touch, but there were changes in water governance and administration that prefigured later more centralized approaches. For most local water uses, the British did little to alter the traditional system of decentralized water management with individual use rights essentially tied to the land and with community-based practices of managing resources held in common. The Mandate authorities did, however, introduce the legal basis for more centralized control through an Order in Council of 1922, as amended in 1940, that declared that '[All] waters . . . in Palestine shall be vested . . . in the Government of Palestine'.[14] In principle, the orders severed all private rights and invested power in a Water Commissioner to enact ordinances concerning the beneficial and economic use of all water sources, including groundwater. The Mandate authorities argued that this provision was in line with the Ottoman *mejelle* (see Chapter 3). However, this broad right of the Mandate authorities to essentially nationalize all water resources was never applied, largely because members of the Yishuv raised objections.[15] It was, nonetheless, the 1922 Order which empowered the Mandate authorities to grant a concession the following year (see later) giving the Palestine Electric Company exclusive rights to develop 'all the running water in western Palestine'.

In the later years of the Mandate, the authorities promulgated two further instruments regulating water, a 1937 ordinance on public water supplies and a 1942 ordinance on surface water drainage. The 1937 ordinance *Safeguarding of Public Water Supplies Ordinance*[16] dealt with the licensing of water resources development, particularly the digging of wells and the construction of canals to transport water. There were provisions for registering existing water rights at the Water Department and for protecting these rights. Once registered, water rights were restricted to the owner of the land or whoever actually farmed the land and could not be diverted elsewhere for any purpose. Licenses were issued by the District Commissioner.

The 1942 ordinance *Drainage (Surface Water) Ordinance*[17] provided for drainage and land reclamation in the public interest. Drainage areas were declared by the government under the management of the Water Department. The main purposes were to drain the malarial swamps and to reclaim the drained lands for agriculture. Fees for land betterment were to be recovered from beneficiaries.

Zionists and water resources

In 2003, the Israeli economist Ariel Dinar wrote:

> The issue of water . . . is an issue intertwined in asymmetries and power relationships, history and ideological beliefs. Not only did the early Zionists view water ideologically but they were also able to demonstrate their power over the Arab inhabitants through several schemes. The issue of water security and scarcity also played a large role in how the Zionists viewed water and the necessity to control it and reluctance to share it. There is a kind of psychological scarcity, a scarcity of resource in the eye of the beholder.[18]

Trottier, writing in 1999, said:

The real founders of the new-old country were the hydraulic engineers.[19]

The early preoccupations of the Zionists with water to support Jewish immigration and to green a dry land are well known. Herzl wrote a novel in which water engineers are heroes and in which much of northern Palestine 'all the way from Acco to Carmel' was 'what seemed to be one great park'.[20] Ben Gurion[21] never stopped thinking and planning for the water that would be needed to make the homeland, and later the state, a viable entity. Shimon Peres recounted how 'Ben Gurion talked about water *all the time*'.[22]

With the prospect of the realization of a Jewish homeland after the Balfour Declaration, the Zionist leaders began planning as early as 1919 how to develop the water resources of Palestine. In that year, the Zionists sent a powerful delegation to Versailles, where the shape of the future British Mandate was being discussed. In correspondence with the British prime minister David Lloyd George in 1919, Zionist leader Chaim Weizmann argued that 'the whole economic future of Palestine is dependent on its water supply for irrigation and electric power'. Weizmann was clear: Palestine must have access to all the run-off from Mount Hermon and to the entire Jordan resource from the headwaters down, and to the Litani for '25 miles above the bend'.[23]

With these objectives, the Zionist delegation to Versailles tried to persuade the British and French governments to extend the borders of the proposed Palestine mandated territory to include the headwaters of the Jordan.[24] They also proposed that the Litani river should be diverted into the Jordan basin. The Litani rises in the Beqaa Valley between the Lebanon and Anti-Lebanon mountains and flows south parallel to the Syrian border for most of its 100-mile length. There is, however, a point where it turns abruptly west to plunge towards the sea. This 'bend' is only three or four miles from the Jordan basin. The Zionists proposed to divert what they argued was wasted water – and the river delivers almost a billion cubic metres of water annually (920 million cubic metres), more than the Jordan above the Yarmouk – and put it to use in the valley of the Jordan.[25]

A short tunnel was proposed that would divert the bulk of the Litani flow into the Hasbani, the first tributary of the Jordan. Because the Jordan lies at a much lower altitude, deep in the first beginnings of the Great Rift Valley, the diversion would be a nearly costless gravity flow and could also generate hydropower.[26] The hitch was that the Litani lay entirely in the proposed new territory of Lebanon, which fell, under the Sykes–Picot Agreement of 1916, to the French, and the sources of the Hasbani also rose in territory reserved for French administration when the Mandate jurisdictions were determined. So the idea of diversion was laid aside.[27] The focus shifted to the internal resources of Palestine and to the Jordan River itself.

Zionist development of land and water

The early Zionist development of land and water was built around remarkable ideals of group colonization perfectly adapted to the purposes and constraints of the

Zionist conception. The main idea was to fill the land with people and productive, extensive enterprise. This essentially meant farming and the development of a viable agricultural economy that would create both incomes and self-sufficiency in basic food to maintain a growing population that would spread progressively across the face of Palestine. This approach would take advantage of the main asset Zionists possessed when capital and infrastructure were scarce and standards of living were low – the energy and toil of needy immigrants. And it would also sow the seed for a national consciousness by the practice of living and working together on the new land.

There is no doubt that there was an almost mystical element to this attachment to the land and water, and to the agricultural activity and way of life that the natural resources supported – 'a source of spiritual renewal' for the new migrants, matched by a sense of redemption of the land from the desolate state they perceived it to be in.[28] Money coming from abroad enabled the Jewish Agency to expand its purchases and development of land – three quarters of its investment budget went towards this goal. From 1919, Zionist officials toured the country, purchasing land largely from the absentee landlords who owned more than 20 per cent of the private land in Palestine – big landowners like the Damascus-based Abdul Rahman Pasha who owned 200,000 dunums (20,000 hectares). The Zionists also took over uncultivated lands – wastes and marshes. A key criterion was access to water and the possibility of irrigated farming which was essential to grow cash crops and generate sufficient revenue to keep the farms viable.[29]

Jewish settlements and cooperative farms sprang up on the land acquired, particularly concentrated along the coast and in the upper part of the Jordan Valley watershed, around Lake Huleh and the Sea of Galilee and in the Jezreel Valley. Typically these settlements were fenced and guarded. In these areas there were some natural springs. In former swamps, like the area around Lake Huleh, water that had previously inundated the land could now be canalized or pumped out. There was also local rainfall. To supplement these sources, many of these farms relied on the pumping of shallow groundwater by the new technology of the day: the kerosene or diesel engine and the shallow lift pump. Quantities that could be pumped were, however, small by comparison to the yield of later pump and tube well technology.[30] A particular success was in the western Jezreel Valley, south of Nazareth, where in 1935 wells were drilled and the water pumped through a network of pipes to farms all through the valley.[31]

The Rutenberg Concession

It was right at the beginning of the Mandate that a decisive event occurred that in principle put considerable control of Palestine's water resources into the hands of the Yishuv. This was the Rutenberg Concession which granted to a Zionist entrepreneur the exclusive right to 'utilize all the running water in western Palestine for seventy years'. This remarkable concession illustrates the determined approach of the Zionists to water resources development, as well as the privileges accorded to the Yishuv under the Mandate. It also illustrates the economic exclusion of the Arab population from key resources and businesses– and the strong Arab opposition from the outset to the discriminatory privileges accorded to the Yishuv.

The beneficiary of this concession, Pinhas Rutenberg, was an old Russian socialist with a murky past in the early stages of the Russian Revolution in 1905–6. After fleeing his native Russia, he developed skills as a hydraulic engineer and became a fervent Zionist, helping to found the American Jewish Congress. Already before the end of the First World War he had drafted a detailed plan for developing irrigation and thirteen hydropower projects in Palestine. He took these plans to Paris in 1919 during the negotiation of the Treaty of Versailles and won financial support from the French Rothschilds for the schemes.[32]

The Jewish Agency, which was set up under the Mandate to help Jewish immigration to Palestine, took up the idea vigorously, and in 1921 Rutenberg obtained a concession from the British for 'waterpower and irrigation installations' in Palestine. This first concession was quite limited, to generate hydroelectricity from the Nahr al Auja (later called the Yarkon by the Israelis) to supply towns on the coast, principally Jaffa and the new Jewish town of Tel Aviv. Operating under the name of the Jaffa Electric Company, Rutenberg in 1923 built a grid that gradually covered Jaffa, Tel Aviv, neighbouring (mainly Jewish) settlements and the British military installations in Sarafend. However, Rutenberg never honoured the original commitment to build a hydroelectric power station on the Nahr al Auja. The electricity was supplied, instead, by generators driven by diesel engines.

In 1923, Rutenberg founded the Palestine Electric Company (PEC). To mobilize the full support of the Mandatory power behind his projects, Rutenberg consulted directly with the then Colonial Secretary Winston Churchill. He also invited influential British figures onto the board, including the politician Herbert Samuel, who was the first British high commissioner in Palestine, Lord Reading and Hugo Hirst, chairman of the British General Electric Company.[33] Rutenberg mobilized finance from world Jewry – American Jews contributed $1 million to finance the project.[34]

With the company established and with such powerful backing, Rutenberg was able in to obtain a second concession in 1926. It was this concession that granted the PEC the exclusive right to utilize all the running water in western Palestine for seventy years. The grant of such sweeping rights over water led to fierce Arab protests against what they considered, as Rouyer puts it, 'a virtual monopoly over much of the Jordan river basin'.[35] Essentially, any other potential user of Jordan water would have to seek the permission of the PEC. There is no record that this permission was ever granted. The Arabs also considered that the Yishuv would probably gain better access to electricity, with consequent economic advantage.

Under this broad concession, the PEC developed a large hydropower installation at the confluence of the Jordan and the Yarmouk. The site was chosen for the strong water flow and the possibility of regulating the flow-through storage in Tiberias during the winter rainy season and release of the water reserves in the summer.

Construction began in 1927 and continued for five years, providing employment for 3,000 workers. The site, known in Arabic as Baqoura, was renamed Naharayim, Hebrew for 'Two Rivers'.[36] The plant began production in 1932 and until 1948 produced much of the electricity consumed in Palestine.[37]

Lowdermilk's influential book on water and Zionism

A decade later, Walter Clay Lowdermilk entered this dynamic arena. It is worth looking at this scientist and religious visionary in some detail because of Lowdermilk's later influence and the extent to which his ideas actually came to pass in the state of Israel. He perfectly captured the contemporary meme that good stewards shall inherit the earth, and he was in no doubt that it was the Jewish farmers and not their neglectful Arab neighbours who were the heirs to Palestine. For Lowdermilk, the 'answer lay in the soil'. A land and water man through and through, he had been a 1911 Rhodes Scholar at Oxford and had extensive overseas experience in Europe and China, as well as serving as assistant chief of the Soil Conservation Service in the US Department of Agriculture. His views were a remarkable joining of the science of soil conservation and an almost mystical devotion to the notion of mankind's stewardship of the earth. On his visit to Palestine in 1939, he was so impressed by the soil conservation techniques he saw in certain Jewish villages that he was inspired to draft The Eleventh Commandment, which he broadcast over the radio from Jerusalem in June of that year.

> Thou shalt inherit the holy earth as a faithful steward conserving its resources and productivity from generation to generation. Thou shalt safeguard thy fields from soil erosion, thy living waters from drying up, thy forests from desolation, and protect thy hills from overgrazing by the herds, that thy descendants may have abundance forever.

Lowdermilk was by contrast appalled by what he saw as the Arab neglect of the good earth and the abandonment of old practices like terrace agriculture, and there was a warning for these poor stewards.

> If any shall fail in this stewardship of the land, thy fruitful fields shall become sterile stony ground or wasting gullies, and thy descendants shall decrease and live in poverty or perish from off the face of the earth.

Lowdermilk became a hero with Zionists[38] and an evangelist for their ideas. Although a Christian, he was a committed supporter of Zionism and Jewish settlement in Palestine. He spent many months in the country and wrote an advocacy piece *Palestine, Land of Promise* (1944). The ideas for water development which he outlined in this influential book became known as the Lowdermilk Plan. The book was extensively used by Zionists and their supporters, particularly in the United States. Copies were given to every member of Congress and, according to Siegel, FDR's copy was open on his desk on the day he died.[39]

In his book, Lowdermilk proposed several large infrastructure projects. The most ambitious was the idea of inter-basin transfer from the Jordan to the Negev. This massive project was to begin with the diversion of the Litani into the Jordan as the Zionists had proposed at Versailles. The idea was then to pump the water out of Lake Tiberias, sunk deep in the Rift Valley, and lift it through pipes up to the coastal plain. The water would then be transported the length of the land to irrigate the Negev desert in the far south.[40] Water would be available, too, to 'reforest a land last heavily wooded two thousand years earlier during the last Jewish Commonwealth in the Second Temple era.'[41]

Lowdermilk also came up with an outline of a 'Med-Dead' project. This idea, which was to have a long afterlife, was that water could be taken from the Mediterranean around the level of Gaza and transported by gravity to the Dead Sea, which lies some 400 metres below sea level. The difference in elevation would allow the production of hydroelectricity that would not only supply power to Palestine but would also serve to desalinate water for drinking and irrigation.

Like many of the Victorian evangelicals and imperial thinkers who preceded him, Lowdermilk saw Jewish settlement as positive for both Arabs and Jews. He considered that the prosperity of the Arab population was on the rise along with that of the Zionists, pointing out, for example, that Arab mortality rates were falling. Attributing these perceived results to Zionist settlement, he saw beneficial effects even beyond the border of Palestine: 'Jewish settlement will lift the entire Near East from its present desolate condition to a dignified place in a free world.' The thought is consistent with notions of the time about the effects of colonialism throughout the world. The settler develops the country and all rise together, even if not equally. The contrast with what actually happened a few years later could not be more stark.[42]

The Palestinian point of view

There is no doubt that the Palestinian Arabs were against Jewish immigration and settlement. The means at their disposal to oppose it were, however, frail. Jewish settlement, a Jewish homeland, Jewish political institutions and Jewish economic preferences and privileges were written into the Mandate that was the basic law of the country, and this was supported by the legal and administrative system.

Nonetheless, the Palestinian Arabs were not silent on these issues. From the outset their organized opposition protested against Zionist land purchases, against the Rutenberg Concession and their exclusion both from the concession itself and from the waters of their own land, and against the drainage projects which opened uplands to be assigned to the Zionist colonists. Jamal Husseini, general secretary of the Executive Committee of the Palestinian Arab Congress, bombarded the Mandate authorities with memoranda protesting the privileges accorded to the Zionists in the Mandate and opposing specific infrastructure development projects. The fifth Congress, held in Nablus in August 1922, called for a boycott of the Rutenberg electricity supply. All to no avail, however.

Early plans for Jordan Valley irrigation

Although by global standards, the volume of water in the Jordan basin is small – about 1,300 million cubic metres annually (see Chapter 2) – the resource is a precious one in this very arid region.[43] It is not surprising that from the beginnings of modern Palestine, many engineers put their minds to developing schemes to harness these waters for irrigation, hydropower and potable water supply.

One challenge that most plans tried to address is that of storage. The main natural flows in the Jordan basin occur in the rainy wintertime when irrigation is least needed. For the winter floodwaters of the Upper Jordan and its tributaries, this is not so much a problem as they flow into the natural reservoir of Lake Tiberias where they can be stored and released when needed for irrigation downstream during the hot dry summer. However, the main Jordan tributary, the Yarmouk, which provides almost half of the water in the basin, has no such natural storage. Planners therefore devised schemes for diverting the Yarmouk to the nearby Lake Tiberias so that its winter flood flows could be stored there.

Already in the late Ottoman period, plans had been hatched. In 1913 the Ottoman director of Public Works for Palestine, the energetic engineer Franghia Bey whom we met in Chapter 3, had proposed a plan to transfer Yarmouk water to Lake Tiberias, both to generate electricity and to store up to 100 million cubic metres of Yarmouk water in the lake.

These plans for storage were matched with schemes for developing irrigation in the Jordan Valley. As early as 1901, Abraham Bourcart had developed outline proposals[44] and during the Mandate, several further plans were devised. In 1919, even before the official start of British authority, a Norwegian group headed by Moltke-Hansen proposed irrigation in the Jordan Valley and an early version of Lowdermilk's Med-Dead scheme to transfer water to the Dead Sea and thus produce hydroelectricity.[45] Then in 1922, Euripides Mavrommatis, whom we have already met in Chapter 3, came up with a revision to the Franghia Plan that would not only have transferred Yarmouk river flows to Lake Tiberias for hydropower generation and storage but would also have diverted water to irrigate the East and West Banks to the south of Tiberias. In 1928 another engineer, Henrique, proposed additions to the Mavrommatis scheme of transferring Yarmouk flows to Tiberias by adding the irrigation of the Yarmouk Triangle, the land that lies to the south of Tiberias in the angle of the two rivers.

The 1938 Woodhead Commission and the Ionides Plan

None of these ideas received any official support until the Arab Revolt of 1936–9 led to serious thought about the future of Palestine. In 1938 a commission of enquiry was set up under Sir John Woodhead to assess the feasibility of dividing Palestine into three parts: an Arab state, a Jewish state and a British enclave for Jerusalem and Bethlehem.[46] The Arab state would join parts of Palestine with Transjordan in a single state. Then, the economic question was posed: What would be the economic and fiscal viability of this Arab state? One answer was sought in irrigated agriculture, using the ample waters of the Jordan River and profiting from the fact that most of the Jordan Valley would lie within the boundaries of the proposed Arab state. To provide a more detailed answer, the Mandatory authority in Transjordan commissioned a study from Michael G. Ionides – *The Report on Water Resources of the Transjordan and their Development*. The 1938 Ionides plan found that there was ample scope for development of the Jordan Valley between Lake Tiberias and the Dead Sea[47] and recommended irrigating the East Bank from both the main Jordan River and from the Yarmouk tributary. As peak flows were in winter and irrigation need was highest in summer, the report took up the idea of storing the winter flood waters of both the Jordan and the Yarmouk in Lake Tiberias. Feeder canals from the south end of Tiberias could then supply the eastern side of the lower Jordan Valley – known as the East Ghor[48] – with irrigation water in both summer and winter. Up to 75,000 acres (30,000 hectares) could be thus irrigated.

The Ionides plan came to nothing as the British subsequently rejected partition as impractical, but the proposals – storage in Lake Tiberias and large-scale irrigation of the East Ghor – were taken up in subsequent plans and have been partly realized today (see Chapters 5 and 6).[49] The leaders of the Yishuv vigorously opposed the Ionides plan and, instead, proposed out-of-basin transfer. In their view the water resources available within the borders of Mandate Palestine were not enough to sustain the big new population of Jewish immigrants that they hoped to build up. Water was needed not only for the drinking and domestic needs of the anticipated flood of immigrants from Europe but also for the agricultural economy of the cooperative settlements, the *kibbutzim*, that were beginning to dot the land in an N-shaped swathe. Their proposal was, instead, that taken up by Lowdermilk, to transfer Jordan water out of its natural basin and to pump it up to the coastal plain.

Ironically, when Lowdermilk had first looked at the Jordan Valley, he had rejected out-of-basin transfer on the principle that water belonged in its own basin. The cost and engineering challenge of pumping water up from 210 metres (682 feet) below sea level to 100 metres (330 feet) above sea level and then transporting it the length of the Palestine coast, as the Yishuv dreamed of doing, looked prohibitive. Yet, the transfer and pumping scheme was the one that Lowdermilk was persuaded to adopt – and within a specifically Zionist perspective. He ultimately concluded that transporting water from the Jordan basin to the Negev was feasible although costly and that it could support the settlement in Palestine of four million immigrants, which was a pearl beyond price for the Zionists.

The Arabs opposed any out-of-basin transfer. Insofar as there was a decided Palestinian Arab point of view about this, it was to see out-of-basin transfer as Jewish appropriation of the water of Palestine. The Lowdermilk idea was perceived to be both uneconomic and highly tilted towards the Yishuv's interests to the detriment of the interests of the Arab population. The Mandatory authority maintained a more neutral view: that the water resources of Palestine should be developed on an economic basis for the benefit of the population. Given the potential for irrigation by low-cost gravity flow in the Jordan Valley, this meant that policy would favour in-basin use for both irrigation and hydropower as the most economic option. However, during the Mandate there was no public development of irrigation in the Valley.

Rural Palestine, agriculture and water under the Mandate

> Very barren hill lands, no sanitation, no electricity, no roads. Peasants . . .
> walked, went on donkeys . . . the very rich people had a horse, and camels
> for transport . . . they were using wooden nail ploughs that only ploughed a
> few inches. It was very Biblical and beautiful to watch the winnowing of the
> corn, throwing it up with shovels and letting the wind blow away the chaff.
>
> Edwin Samuel, District Officer in Ramallah (and son
> of the High Commissioner)[50]

Rural society and its economy were changing only slowly. In 1918, the Arab
population remained largely rural, living in some thousand villages still mainly in
the hills, built on the terraced hillsides and in the mountain valleys.[51]

Almost all agriculture – more than 90 per cent – was rainfed or drew on
springs and streams. As we saw in Chapter 3, some modern irrigation was used
to grow citrus or fresh fruit and vegetables for the market.[52] Subsistence crops still
predominated but the commercialization of farming was on the rise. In traditional
farming, cereals, sesame and sorghum remained the main field crops. At the start
of the Mandate, winter wheat was by far the predominant crop. However, over
the life of the Mandate, barley production increased progressively and by 1945
had outstripped wheat production. Barley tolerates dry conditions better and was
essential as livestock feed.

Production of cash crops, particularly olives, citrus and vegetables, shot up.
Olive production rose by five or six times – see the table *Estimated Production
1920–45* – between 1920 and 1945. Vegetable production went up by a multiple of
ten times or more, supplying the growing towns. Irrigation was developing mostly
in the coastal plain for citrus, fruit and vegetables. This reflected the growing
commercialization of farming as the population grew and urban and export
markets developed. By 1935, two-thirds of Palestinian agricultural production
was being sold outside of the Palestinian Arab economy, largely to the Jewish
population but also for export.[53]

The Mandate government paid some attention to traditional agriculture, taking,
at least initially, a rural development approach and investing in rural infrastructure.
The main motive seems to have been to prevent a wholesale move to towns. An
important policy was the development of education in rural areas. Elementary

Table 4.1 Estimated Production 1920–45 (annual averages in thousands of metric tonnes)

	1920–4	1925–9	1930–4	1935–9	1940–2	1945
Wheat	84.7	90.5	69.1	88.3	110.3	58.4
Barley	38.9	49.5	45.6	70.5	95.3	74.9
Olives	n.a.	12.9	11.1	36.4	40.6	79.5
Vegetables	n.a.	16.1	22.0	99.4	194.1	244.8

Source: Owen 1988: 21.

schools were to be opened in every village, financed on a matching grant basis. In the first year of British rule, 1919, fifty-two schools opened in Palestinian villages. Later on, in 1931, the inspired director of education, Humphry Bowman, opened the Kedourie College for Agriculture in Tulkarem, specifically reserved for Arab students – the Yishuv was already well-served by specifically Jewish agricultural institutions.[54]

However, none of this really equipped the peasant economy to compete with the modernizing, go-ahead agriculture systems of the Zionists. By 1930 it was clear that income disparities were increasing. Arab rural poverty was on the rise and rural landlessness became an increasing problem. Village families that neither owned land nor held a tenancy either sought work as labourers or moved to towns. Already by 1931 this rural proletariat represented one-third of the peasant population.[55] Initially, a measure of stability and the increase in market opportunities stimulated a general pattern of growth but this was reversed in the early 1930s. A succession of bad harvests and a fall in prices affected production, while an increase in taxes particularly hit the producers of low-value cereals. The government had to step in to remit taxes and to provide loans for purchase of inputs. Thereafter, as can be seen from the previous table , growth in output picked up again.

Growth was primarily concentrated in the larger and more commercial farms. Farmers who could invest in cash crop production generally prospered, particularly in the citrus industry. In addition, Jewish farming was promoted by a considerable level of external funding. By contrast, the Arab small farm sector in the hills struggled and indebtedness grew. The 1930 Johnson–Crosbie survey of over 25,000 Palestinian Arab families found small farm sizes, too small to sustain a family. Amongst the bottom quarter of the agricultural population, the average household debt was £P 27 against an annual income in the range of £P 25-30. One issue was the tax burden which Palestinian Arabs claimed fell unfairly on poorer rural households. Attempts to overhaul the tax system to introduce an income tax that would be assessed mainly on higher-earning city dwellers were opposed by the Jewish Agency. Only in 1941, and due to the exigencies of war, was income tax finally introduced in Palestine.[56]

Attempts by the Mandate authorities to develop Arab agriculture were patchy and half-hearted. One main focus of the 1930 Shaw Report was to propose a more active development policy in Palestine, particularly to increase agricultural productivity. The British experts on agriculture who contributed to the report were deeply shocked by their government's neglect of rural areas. They claimed that development policy had hitherto fostered only Zionist and imperial interests, and made landowners richer while impoverishing the peasants. Lewis French, the newly appointed Director of Development, insisted on the need for investment in rural Palestine and a massive budget of £7 million was proposed for investment in rural areas. As a result, there were some initiatives. Credit cooperatives were, for example, set up. However, they never proved very effective as links to the banking system provided credit only to larger commercial farmers. Edwin Samuel describes:

Most of the people were heavily in debt, you couldn't get bank loans because the title deeds were defective . . . . The Government began issuing agricultural loans and one of my jobs was to dish out the money and try and recover them later.[57]

A pilot agricultural development project was set up at Tel al-Suq near Beisan. However, projects like this were few and far between and had scant impact on overall rural poverty or productivity. One problem was that the Labour/Liberal coalition government that came to power in Britain in 1931 preferred a free-market approach of encouraging immigration of Jewish capitalists who would, it was hoped, invest in an economic structure that would ultimately benefit Palestine's rural poor. However, by this time the Yishuv were set on a path of separate development and only the growth of urban markets had much impact on Palestinian agriculture.[58]

Citrus

The most successful crop in Palestine remained citrus by far. We saw in the previous chapter how Palestinian Arabs had invested in citrus and developed a profitable export trade. Citrus was ideally suited to the climate and soils of the coastal plain where it grew well with the rainfall and supplementary irrigation. Under the Mandate, the Yishuv also invested heavily in citrus. The land planted to oranges, lemons and grapefruit rose rapidly, up from 30,000 dunums (3,000 hectares) in 1905 to nearly 300,000 dunums (30,000 hectares) in 1937.

This was a sector where there was more or less parity in investment and ownership and in productivity and profits between Arabs and Jews. Arab groves were typically smaller, production methods were less advanced and they enjoyed weaker access to credit and marketing support, but these drawbacks were largely compensated by lower labour costs. The citrus industry is also one of the few examples of economic cooperation between the two communities. This was mainly due to the energetic Palestinian chairman of the Arab Citrus Industry, Shuqri Taji al-Faruqi.[59] Yet, even here there was a parallel track of development when the Jewish Agency set up the Citrus ResearchLaboratory in Rehoboth in 1931 as part of its Agricultural Experimental Station. The director, Dr Kasteliansky, commented: 'The Station is really our pathfinder, our only guide in the desert.' There was no indication of Arab participation in this research, which could certainly have been of benefit to both Arab and Jewish growers.[60]

Through the 1930s and up to the Second World War, citrus was Palestine's main export. In fact, the 1930s were boom years. Citrus exports rose from 2.4 million cases in 1930/1 to a peak of 13 million cases in 1938–9 – representing a massive 1.5 billion oranges. In that year, Jaffa oranges commanded almost one-quarter (23 per cent) of the world orange market.[61] Domestic demand was by this time consuming almost all Palestinian production of other agricultural and manufactured products. As a result, citrus was far and away Palestine's leading export business, accounting for over 70 per cent of export value in 1935–9: £P 3.31 million annual average out of total export proceeds of £P 4.76 million.[62] However, the industry was very hard hit by the war which brought an abrupt halt to exports. Citrus exports almost disappeared and production languished. Nonetheless, growers maintained their groves and production quickly recovered after the war towards pre-war levels in the two years before the events of 1948, events which essentially finished off Arab citrus production for good.[63]

Water supply and sanitation during the Mandate

Modern water supply

The Mandate authorities promoted safe water supply and aimed to bring piped water to all major towns. As a result, a number of municipalities developed piped water supply systems. In Nablus, for example, the local authority established a water network in 1932, supplied from four nearby wells: Deir Sharaf, Far'a, al Badan and Audala.[64]

In the fast-developing coastal towns of Jaffa, Tel Aviv and Haifa, modern systems of water supply developed on a large scale. Water was available in generous quantities through piped networks in Tel Aviv. By 1934, consumption in the hot climate of that city was 230 litres per person daily, considerably more than most European cities. By 1947, consumption in Tel Aviv had reached 350 litres daily for each person, amongst the highest in the world, compared to just 114 litres in London. Highland cities fared less well –Jerusalem remained water-constrained, with consumption per head in 1934 just 45 litres a day.[65] The chronic water problems of Jerusalem were alleviated only when water from the strong perennial springs of the Nahr al Auja[66] was pumped up to supply the city – see Figure 4.1.

The water supply of both Jaffa and Tel Aviv was from wells. However, by the 1930s, the extraction of groundwater and the drop in the water table were leading to intrusion of seawater and salinization of the Coastal Aquifer (see Chapter 2). In 1936, the Colonial Office despatched the engineer Howard Humphreys who considered that the Nahr al Auja which was already supplying Jerusalem would also provide the most reliable and high-quality resource for Jaffa and Tel Aviv. However, the cost of developing this source and piping it to the towns was considered too high and the municipalities preferred to dig deeper wells in the Coastal Aquifer. As a result, by the end of the Mandate, Tel Aviv was being served by a total of twenty-seven wells linked into a grid with a central control system. Regulations required safe distances between wells and cess pits. Chlorination was gradually introduced.

Although Jaffa and Tel Aviv were adjacent communities and it would have been efficient to have invested in a single supply, Jaffa had its own separate system. This was because the British had early on recognized the Yishuv's desire for separate development by granting the infant Tel Aviv municipality status in 1921. Ironically, this move had been resisted by the old Sephardic neighbourhoods of Jaffa that were to be incorporated into the new town. They saw no good reason to

Figure 4.1 Piping water from the Nahr al Auja to Jerusalem towards the end of the Mandate. Laying water pipe to Jerusalem, c. 1946 Werner Braun - kkl-jnf photo archive via the PikiWiki - Israel free image collection project https://en.wikipedia.org/wiki/Water_supply_and_sanitation_in_Israel#/media/File:PikiWiki_Israel_14794_water_to_Jerusalem .jpg.

be separated from their old urban culture and multi-faith ties. The mayor of Tel Aviv, Meir Dizengoff, described this Sephardic resistance as a 'collision between a European way of life and a passive oriental one'. As a result of the sundering of the two settlements, water supply in Jaffa remained a private affair. The Mandate authorities asked Humphreys to develop plans for a reticulated system for Jaffa but this was set aside in the wake of the disturbances of 1936–9.[67]

Sanitation

As water supply increased in towns, it led to increased problems of disposal of wastewater, both grey water and sewage. As we saw in Chapter 3, the almost universal system in towns was the cess pit, and as water supply increased, cess pits began to overflow and sanitary conditions became a hazard to health. As a result, despite the newness of Tel Aviv and the high hopes of the pioneers, the town was often described as rather squalid.[68] Already in 1924, the Tel Aviv municipal engineer, Uriel Avigdor, had proposed a reticulated sewerage system for the town but this was dismissed as too expensive. The situation continued to deteriorate and the municipality turned to the Mandate authorities for support in contracting a loan to finance construction.

In 1926, the Crown Agents despatched two consulting engineers, the brothers John and David Watson, to prepare sewerage plans for Jerusalem, Haifa, Jaffa and Tel Aviv. The engineers recommended a joint system for Tel Aviv and Jaffa that would discharge into the Mediterranean through a common outfall at the Bassa swamps. The logic of joint development of the infrastructure seems, at this stage, to have been persuasive enough to get the two municipalities to form a joint committee. The main Salameh sewer was constructed in the early 1930s, and districts of both municipalities were connected to it. However, this joint project was not achieved without some tensions typical of the relations between the Yishuv and the Palestinian Arabs at the time. Karlinsky notes:

in accordance with common perceptions and attitudes of the period, Tel Aviv's municipal engineer, Yaíakov Shiffman (Ben Sira) . . . belittled the Jaffa municipality's technological and administrative ability to carry out complex technological projects. In 1938, Israel Rokach, the Mayor of Tel Aviv, portrayed the Jewish neighbourhoods within Jaffa city limits as captives in an urban space of cultural, economic and social degeneration.[69]

Residents in unconnected areas continued to use cess pits. In 1935, many households in Jaffa's old city were draining their wastewater directly to the sea through masonry conduits. By this time, relations between the two municipalities had deteriorated along community lines. Engineer Shiffman of the Tel Aviv municipality explained to the Watson brothers whom the Crown Agents had again sent out:

based on the records of the existing cooperation, and since this cooperation is undesirable for us *in both its political and its technical-financial aspect*, the Municipality wishes to reserve the right to decide on the extent of said cooperation and, in any event, it should be minimized as much as possible.[70]

This time the Watsons' report recommended two separate systems with two separate collectors. This separation reflected not only the separatist policies of the Yishuv and the antagonistic relations between the two communities but also the open revolt of the Arabs in the period between 1936 and 1939 and the views of the Peel Commission which, in July 1937, recommended a scheme of partition of Palestine as the solution. In the Watsons' plan, there would be a complete separation of Jewish and Arab sewage which effectively reflected larger ideas and realities of separation.[71] In the event, the cost of the Watson scheme was held to be prohibitive. The estimate for Tel Aviv was over £P 600,000, more than twice the annual municipal budget. For Jaffa, the bill was £P 284,000 against a 1936–7 municipal budget of £P 56,000. As a result, the scheme was only partly implemented and the Salameh sewer main and the Bassa outfall continued to be in use.

By 1939, sewerage household connections were still limited, with only just over one-quarter (28 per cent) of Tel Aviv's 8,000 houses having sewerage connections. Other houses in Jaffa and Tel Aviv were still connected to smaller conduits into the Mediterranean, with six lines in total discharging sewage to the sea. During the war, Tel Aviv municipality continued to connect houses and by 1946 two-fifths (39 per cent) of households were hooked up. In addition, new hygiene practices greatly improved health. Palestine had been prone to many public health problems, largely water-related or due to the absence of hygiene amongst both communities.[72] The British medical services introduced new health and hygiene services, regulations and practices. Ultimately this helped make Palestine one of the healthiest societies in the Eastern Mediterranean.[73]

Water supply in the villages

The water collected from springs and cisterns continued to provide nearly the entire domestic water supply for rural Palestine. Cisterns dug during the British Mandate era were often dug by the same back-breaking manual labour that had been used in ancient times. Later, elderly Palestinians looked back to these times and gave a good account of the conditions. A man in Zababdeh, Abu Jilal, described hewing a cistern in the limestone rock using a pulley system to remove large stones:

> They were digging this [cistern] . . . they were making a wood-like circle, making the rope going around it while they are pulling the soil, or the rocks from inside the [cistern], to take them out . . . . They [took] three months to dig [it], the whole summer to finish.[74]

The digging was often a communal effort, involving the whole family or even multiple families working together to dig cisterns big enough to store water for their families all summer long. Two or three related families usually shared a cistern built on their lands. Women had to walk to the particular cistern owned by their families, often uphill several kilometres from their homes. A Zababdeh woman, Rosa, remarked that three trips to the cistern every day were needed to provide for her family of six. The cistern was over a kilometre from her home. She would go with the other women, each balancing a large clay jar on her head. Water was drawn from the cistern in buckets and poured into the jars. After the effort, water was a precious commodity, to be handled carefully and used in moderation. One villager, Abu Jilal, commented to Julia Templin:

> I never washed [my] face with clean water until [I] reached twenty years old . . . . [We] don't want to waste the clean water [for washing], so [I] was using the dirty water for the animals . . . that's what [I] was using to wash [my] face.

Sometimes, in the hot rainless summers, the cistern would be dry and villagers would have to go far afield to fetch water. In 2008, an eighty-one-year-old Zababdeh woman named Fairuz recalled a summer around 1940 when she was thirteen or fourteen years old and she went with some other girls to collect water from a cistern. When the bucket came out of the cistern empty, the girls tied a rope around Fairuz's body and lowered her into the dark shaft. She reached the bottom only to discover that it was indeed dry. The girls then checked twelve more cisterns nearby, with the same result. Because it did not rain for another one or two months, the girls then had to tramp 10 miles or so to Jenin in search of its plentiful springs:

> [We] would go, like, groups of people, and [we] took donkeys with [us]. And [we] were holding [the jars on our] heads and hands [in order to bring water back here], just for drinking. And that lasts for two days. And [we] have to go the next day to search again.[75]

*   *   *

The period of the Mandate, just three decades, marked a time of decisive change in Palestine. For most, but not all, of the population, modernization of the economy brought higher standards of living. Towns continued to grow and industry thrived. Water was mobilized for hydropower, and piped water and sanitation services came to the larger towns. Commercial irrigated agriculture prospered, and the production of both oranges and olives brought prosperity to many. Traditional rural households saw less change and some lost access to the land altogether.

The most decisive feature of this period in Palestine's history was the change in the character of the population. For the Yishuv, the growth of the Jewish population and the development of largely separate institutions and of an increasingly separate economy came to resemble a state within a state, almost a state in waiting. For the Palestinian Arabs, the political functioning of Palestine lent a growing sense of identity and national consciousness which only expanded with the increasingly abrasive relations between the communities.[76] The widening political, economic and social gap between the two peoples inhabiting the land is reflected in an emerging disparity and apartness in access to water and water services.

In the Mandate period, the Palestinian Arabs lost a measure of control over their water resources. The 'development of the running waters of Western Palestine', and notably the entire waters of the Jordan River, became the monopoly of a Yishuv enterprise. The Palestinian Arabs were effectively excluded from these resources. As land came into Zionist hands, the surface and groundwater resources attached to the land were developed by the acquirers. Wetlands were drained. A lopsided development of water resources and services began that prefigured the wholesale losses that the Palestinian Arabs were to experience after 1948.

As we shall see in the following chapters, this unevenness and separation in respect of water was strengthened and consolidated in the decades after the independence of Israel. With hindsight, the economic, demographic and institutional transformation in the Mandate period was less an interlude than a prelude to the struggles and shocks of 1948 and of all that followed. This was as true for water as for the other resources and activities of the territory first defined as Palestine under the short-lived and uneasy Mandate of the British.

Chapter 5

BUILDING ISRAEL'S WATER SECURITY, 1948–67

After a couple of minutes of shock, of lips parted as though in thirst and eyes wide open, our faraway street on the edge of northern Jerusalem roared all at once . . . a cataclysmic shout that could shift rocks . . . then roars of joy . . . and everyone was singing.

Amos Oz, recalling when news came that the UN had voted to adopt Resolution 181 on the creation of a Jewish state in Palestine[1]

The year 1948 was the decisive moment in which Israel was born. Endorsed by the two great powers and with the guilty sympathy of much of the Western world, the new nation sprang into being on a scale and possessed of powers which few Zionists had dared to dream of. The story of the next two decades is of Israelis' intense and intelligent endeavour to build a state and an economy. This turned out to be a supremely successful enterprise and one in which the creation of institutions and infrastructure for water played a determining part.

Israelis worked hard, fought hard and invested hard and achieved 'water independence', essentially complete security of water resources. This came about through a combination of two master strokes. One was a visionary project to unify all water resources in a national grid. The other was the appropriation of regional water resources, notably the incorporation into the unified system of the bulk of the resources of the Mountain Aquifers and of the Jordan River.

By 1967, Israel had created the world's most integrated water system and had extended its reach to the shared waters of the Jordan basin and the Mountain Aquifers that lay beneath the West Bank. Towns were progressively served with good water and sanitation services. A prosperous and innovative agriculture played a big role in Israel's economy and in employment.

All this came at a high cost, and it was largely the Palestinian Arabs who paid, dispossessed of most of their land and water, of their livelihoods and belongings, and even of their identity and memory. The former owners of the land and water of all of Palestine were crammed into shrunken territories or exiled to other countries. Many lived in tents or, later, in concrete huts. They struggled for survival, as refugees do. Many found success in one way or another, and in one country or another. Those in the West Bank and in Jordan fared somewhat better than other Palestinians in the years to 1967. But for the most part the Palestinian story is the story of loss. The Western powers made attempts to help them but to little effect.

In the early days there remained some optimism that a resolution could be reached. The politics at the time were more fluid and less locked into confrontation and conflict than they later became. For a time there was a belief that somehow reconciling conflicting proposals and promoting the cooperative or at least non-conflictual development of water could not only help the Palestinians but also contribute to peacemaking. However, most of the attempts to provide water and to settle the refugees in the Jordan Valley came to nothing. The window of opportunity began to close and with hindsight the optimism appears naïve. The tough stance of Israel over every issue, the rise of Arab nationalism and the growing militarization on all sides began to make compromises less likely, while the strengthening US–Soviet competition in the region hardened positions. Hopes for collaborative approaches to water resources progressively faded. In particular, Israel's single-minded pursuit of transfer of Jordan water did much to feed the growing tensions. And when confrontation on water began to put Israelis and Arabs on the path towards war, it was likely to be once again the Palestinians who would be the losers.

The end of the Mandate and the creation of the state of Israel

Failing to reach agreement on a political settlement, the British surrendered their responsibilities in Palestine to the UN. Early on in the deliberations, the two great powers – the United States and the USSR – decided on partition but when the UN presented a partition recommendation in November 1947, the country immediately descended into violence. Exhausted and disgusted, the mandarins and military of the vaunted British Empire abandoned their trust to a bloody struggle. In May 1948, the state of Israel was declared and Arab countries sent invasion forces. Months later, by August 1948, Israel had achieved a decisive victory and an armistice was concluded. The fighting ended and the way was clear to consolidate gains and build the new nation state.

Taking over the land and the water

This new state possessed considerably more land than the UN had originally allotted to it. As Palestinian Arabs fled or were expelled from these lands, the population of the new country became predominantly Jewish. The administration then came in to inventory and take over Arab land and property. Anti-repatriation laws prevented any Arab from 'returning' to the new state or from reclaiming land or property. The new government either destroyed or took over Palestinian property thus 'vacated'. From August 1948, bulldozers flattened former Palestinian villages. About 370 of Palestine's 1,000 or so villages were simply wiped out.

A particular case was the century-old Jaffa orange industry which, as we have seen in previous chapters, had been an important part of the Palestinian Arab economy. According to the 1947 UN Partition Plan, the city of Jaffa was to be part of a future Arab state. At first Jewish and Arab orange growers signed an agreement that, in case of hostilities, the groves should not be harmed and that harvest and exports should go ahead. However in April and May 1948, the Haganah militia started conducting random attacks and bombardments on Jaffa and most of the inhabitants fled the city by boat. By the middle of May, fewer than 5,000 of the 70,000 Palestinian Arabs who had lived in Jaffa, remained. The new state of Israel then confiscated Arab orange groves as 'abandoned assets'.[2]

There began, too, a process of erasing old names and replacing them with new or even older ones. Between 1949 and 1951, Ben Gurion oversaw a huge project to 'give Hebrew names to all the places, valleys, springs and roads' in the country. Everything was renamed by a specialist committee. The part of Arab Palestine that had fallen to Israel began to disappear from the map and from memory through a deliberate policy of erasure.

Israel continued this process of Judaization by encouraging mass immigration. Many of the incomers were installed in houses that had belonged to Arabs. In the countryside, settlers were installed on the emptied Arab lands, often close to the new border to strengthen claims and establish defensive bulwarks.[3] With the land went the water without which the land was fruitless. It was not for nothing that the early visionary Zionists had dreamed and planned for water. Inheriting from the British the precedent of nationalization of water, the new government assumed the right to take over all the water resources of their new land, a practice later written into Israeli water law.[4]

Israeli plans for water

From the outset, the Zionists had always conceived vast water plans. We have seen already in Chapter 4 the intense interest and top priority that the Zionists consistently accorded to water resources. Water was the resource that made land productive, and water would allow the footprint of the national home to grow to fill as much of former Mandate Palestine as possible. Water was the economic resource that would allow the maximum number of immigrants. It would bring self-sufficiency in basic foods and boost the 'carrying capacity'.[5]

During the 1940s, the Jewish Agency had already carried out many surveys of Palestine's water resources. This culminated at the time of independence in the Hays Plan of 1948, in which the engineer James B. Hays filled in the engineering details of most of the ideas that Lowdermilk had sketched out a decade earlier. Hays proposed eight stages of water development for the new state, beginning with intensive exploitation of the Coastal Aquifer, reclamation of the Huleh wetlands and development of the Yarmouk jointly with Jordan on a fifty-fifty basis. Hays also detailed projects for the 'Med-Dead' hydroelectric scheme (see Chapter 4) as well as for hydroelectric development on the Hasbani.[6]

In 1952, building on the work of Hays, the Water Department of the Ministry of Agriculture produced Israel's first national water plan. This proposed integration of all water resources in a single, comprehensive state-wide system, with massive north–south water transfer to 'reclaim the desert'. The cost of the proposals was stupendous, but the impulse was for development of water and land at almost any cost. The young country saw the benefits of economic development, water security and nation building as far greater than any mere financial cost.[7]

And so began what Mark Zeitoun characterized as a 'hydraulic-driven nation building exercise'. In the period between 1948 and 1967, Israeli extraction of groundwater went up by a multiple of three, increasing from 300 million cubic metres in 1948 to 1,000 million cubic metres in 1966. In addition to the systematic development of the groundwater resources of the Coastal Aquifer, this period saw the rapid and intensive development of well fields all around the new borders between Israel and the West Bank and Gaza. A glance at the hydraulic map will show how this operated. Wells around the West Bank drew the downstream flow of the Western and Northeastern Aquifers (see Chapter 2). The rain fell on the West Bank hills, seeped into groundwater and flowed down a hydraulic gradient towards the new state where it could easily be captured by relatively shallow wells under artesian pressure with little or no pumping.

This intensive development of the Western Aquifer provided a readily available, highly potable, low-cost resource for the growing towns along Israel's coastline. Development of the Northeastern Aquifer fed the towns and settlements of the northern part of the new country and provided reliable year-round supplies for intensive agricultural development. Soon Israeli planners had the idea of connecting all these sources into a national grid. This pattern of development and abstraction was seen by Israel as establishing a right to the water it exploited. Years later, when the West Bank came to develop its water resources on a larger scale, Palestinian Arabs were confronted with a status quo in which the downstream riparian claimed a historic right to the water it had developed years before and which it had been using for a considerable time – on these claims and counterclaims, see Chapter 7.

Development around Gaza followed a similar pattern but a contrary logic. The water source of Gaza is principally the shallow Coastal Aquifer, together with the seasonal flows in the wadis where for a few days a year the water rushes down from the highlands and across the desert to the sea. As Israel developed the northern Negev, both these resources were intercepted. Wells were drilled all around the Gaza border, and the spate flows in the wadis were intercepted. And here it was the upstream riparian, Israel, that later came to claim historic rights.

At the same time (1948–67), Israel completed the draining of the marshes that had begun under the Ottomans and continued under the British Mandate. The main focus was on the lower reaches of the Yarkon/Nahr el Auja and on the wetlands around Huleh Lake – on draining the Huleh marshes and the resulting adverse environmental consequences, see the discussion in the section *Developing the Jordan*.

The Negev

It was not for nothing that the early visionary Zionists had dreamed and planned for water. When the Zionist delegation at Versailles had argued for the inclusion of the headwaters of the Jordan in Mandate Palestine and had set out the case for the diversion of the Litani (see Chapter 4), they had in mind a bold project – that the water should be lifted out of the Jordan basin to the coastal plain and used for domestic and industrial purposes and for irrigating the fields of Palestine – and not just the existing fields but also the arid lands that lay in the deep south, in the Negev desert.[8]

From early in the Zionist dream, the collection and transfer of water from the north to the south of the land had been considered. The basis of the idea was that there was more water in the north and more land in the south. Through the thinking of Lowdermilk and others, the idea became more concrete – to transfer water from the Jordan basin to the vast empty Negev, establishing a huge tract of land for Jewish settlement. Early thinking on the feasibility was inspired by US experience with similarly vast projects of inter-basin transfer and long-distance conveyance, for example by the inter-basin diversion of the Colorado River to the cities of the California coast and to Californian irrigated agriculture. For the Zionists and, after independence, the new state, these projects promised not only water security but also all the allure of pioneering farmers populating this new frontier and reclaiming the desert and making it bloom.

Grafted on to this bold idea was another just as bold – to use a single pipeline to convey bulk water to all points of the entire country, with water feeding in from all sources and out to the points of use, a perfectly controlled and optimized integrated water sourcing and supply system for an entire territory. This visionary concept drew on the experience of the Tennessee Valley Authority (TVA). The TVA also inspired the Israelis with ideas about the laws, regulation and agencies that would be needed to support this unified water system.[9]

The Negev is more than half (55 per cent) of Israel's land area but, with very low rainfall and high temperatures, it is largely a desert with a seasonal 'green bite' of pasture. Only in the north and west is rainfall adequate to allow the rainfed production of cereals – the vast seasonal wheat fields that Abu Sitta recalled from his youth (see Chapter 2). Historically the arid zones to the south and east were an area of shifting nomadic animal husbandry. The Ottomans had largely left the area alone to self-rule by the tribal system, although in the early twentieth century they began to develop Beer Sheba, largely as a military outpost and, during the First World War, as a railway terminus. The British continued this hands-off approach, leaving the Bedouin population of some 50,000–70,000 largely to their own devices.

From the beginning, the Zionists showed interest in colonizing and developing the Negev, and in the turbulent times after the Second World War, Zionist settlers began to move in to stake a claim. Siegel tells the story of the pioneers who clandestinely established eleven new farms in the northern Negev in 1946. They drilled a deep well in one location and, finding water, used every effort to obtain pipes and were able to hook up all eleven farms through a pipe network.[10] That these lands were owned and farmed by Palestinians is elided from the story. Today, the Negev has been intensively developed by Israel but even so is home to only 8 per cent of its population.

Developing the Jordan

We saw in Chapter 2 the extraordinary character of the Jordan Valley and its river, the lowest-lying on earth, and the importance of the river within the limited water resources of the region. For over a century before the establishment of the state of Israel, planners had been intent on converting this rich resource to human and economic use. Chapter 4 sketched out some of the early Ottoman, British and Zionist ambitions and plans for its development. But all planning for the Jordan River was confronted by the same two natural challenges. The first was the reason that had at first made Lowdermilk doubtful about transferring water out of the valley: that because the valley is sunk so far below the lands on either side of it – over 200 metres – by far the most economic use of the water lies within the rather confined spaces of the narrow Rift Valley itself. The second challenge lay, as we saw in Chapter 4, in the seasonal pattern of rainfall in the catchment. There is a hydrological mismatch between the peak flows which occur in winter and the peak demand for irrigation water which comes in the dry summer. Whatever the use of the water, some means to match the flows to demand is needed if most of the winter floods are not to be lost to the Dead Sea. In fact, storage is required. On the main Jordan River, Lake Tiberias provides considerable natural storage. On the Yarmouk tributary, no such natural storage exists. To these natural challenges was added the geopolitical challenge of a transboundary water course. With the break-up of the Ottoman Empire, the basin had already acquired an international character, with four separately governed mandated territories constituting the riparians. After 1948, the basin was shared by four independent sovereign nations – Israel, Jordan, Syria and Lebanon – as well as by the West Bank Palestinians then under Jordanian administration.

Early plans and issues

Right at the start of the twentieth century, in 1901, the first plans for developing the Jordan valley for irrigation had been prepared, and several more followed under both the Ottomans and the British. The latest study of the question – the 1938 study by Michael Ionides – had proposed the use of the Jordan waters for irrigation on the East Bank (Chapter 4). Nothing came of this at the time but after 1948, interest in the Jordan Valley water resource strengthened amongst the new states. The economic potential of the valley for agricultural development was seen as considerable. Large quantities of water ran unused to the sink of the Dead Sea and all this water had, in the view of the planners, to be put to use – no one at the time thought or cared much about the ecological integrity of this extraordinary natural feature.[11] The waters of both the main river and of the Yarmouk could be used to irrigate by gravity the large, flat plains and platforms in the Rift Valley that were naturally commanded by the river. The climate of the low-lying depression was dry and hot, inimical to rainfed agriculture but ideally suited for year-round irrigated cultivation. Up to three cropping seasons a year were possible in this natural greenhouse.

However, planning for the development of the Jordan Valley was not a simple matter of gauging and developing the optimal irrigation scheme. Now that there were four sovereign nation riparians, development of the Jordan system had become an area of contest, a mirror of a larger regional political dissension. All four nations were water-scarce and anxious to develop more water resources. Two of them – Israel and Jordan – were exceptionally water-scarce. They needed more water if they were to develop profitable agriculture, quality water services and a modern economy.

And here came a strong divergence of interest. Jordan saw the potential for use in agriculture within the basin in the East Ghor, the east bank of the river, where there were at least 30,000 irrigable hectares. Jordan in this period also controlled much of the west bank of the river and there was irrigation potential there too. Israel, which was in at least partial possession of the resources of the Upper Jordan, had little land downstream within the Jordan Valley to irrigate. Instead, Israel's burning aim was to divert as much water as it possibly could, lifting it out of the Jordan basin entirely to bring water to households and industry in the narrow coastal strip and to agriculture in the desert south of the new country. The political reflection of these economic plans highlighted the divergent interests of the riparians. The new and very poor state of Jordan hoped to develop the basin's water resources to enlarge its economy and employment. Israel wished to transfer the water to its coastal plain to provide water for the hoped-for influx of new Jewish immigrants and to build its infant economy and state.

In the water sphere, these ideas were not necessarily incompatible. Both in-basin and out-of-basin uses could have been accommodated by agreement and by infrastructure. But the wider complicating factor for planning and development was that the three Arab nations – Jordan, Syria and Lebanon – were states that had bitterly opposed the creation of the state of Israel and would not wish to see the new country prosper on the basis of Jordan water. The Israelis, for their part, had no wish to see a strong and prosperous Jordanian (or Palestinian) farming population installed along much of the length of the Jordan Valley. Thus both development needs and political antagonisms made planning a contentious rather than a cooperative process in which rivalry over water resources and their development reflected the larger regional rivalries. To complicate matters, the international community looked at the river as an untapped resource that could be used as a solution to at least part of the Palestinian refugee problem.[12]

In just a few years, several quite detailed plans for the development of the Jordan Valley were prepared, none of which was implemented because of objections by one side or the other. In 1951, Jordan and UNRWA[13] commissioned the Cambridge firm of Murdoch MacDonald & Partners to prepare an irrigation plan to settle Palestinian refugees on both East and West Banks. The resulting MacDonald Plan built on the Ionides concept of year-round irrigation within the Jordan Valley. The basic approach was that Jordan and Yarmouk waters should stay within the basin, reserved for in-basin use only. Jordan – and the Palestinian refugees it harboured – were to be the main beneficiaries. There was some rationale to this as, having taken over the West Bank, Jordan was now the most important riparian, controlling most of the main river below Tiberias as well as the south bank of the Yarmouk. The report assumed that Israel and Jordan would agree on the in-basin use and on the use of Tiberias as a shared reservoir. However, it quickly became clear that Israel would not agree, partly because it had other plans for the Jordan water and partly because it was simply unwilling to cooperate with an Arab country in this way.[14]

The Bunger plan

Plans now proliferated as the United States stepped in to try to resolve the refugee problem. The next year, 1952, saw the US-sponsored Bunger plan for hydropower and for irrigation from the Yarmouk for Palestinian refugees. This plan came about almost by chance. An American engineer, Mills Bunger, was flying from Amman to Beirut. Bunger was working in Amman for the United States Technical Cooperation Agency, the precursor of USAID. Flying above the Yarmouk river, Bunger had one of those 'airplane moments' when someone in the development business suddenly spots a nation's destiny from a mile high. Gazing from his window, Bunger saw the perfect site for a reservoir. Where the Yarmouk river valley narrowed, at Maqarin, below the tributaries that Bunger could see flowing from the Yarmouk watershed in Syria and Jordan, there was the perfect place to construct a dam, a dam that would impound and regulate half the flow of the river and leave the other half to flow downstream unregulated. It seemed to Mills Bunger the perfect scheme. Hydropower and downstream irrigation would generate huge value – and no riparian would be deprived of access to water. And Israel did not need to be involved as the scheme did not touch on the waters of the main river or of Tiberias.[15]

Back in Amman, Bunger presented his idea – a large storage dam on the Yarmouk that would generate hydropower and irrigate the Jordan Valley for the benefit of Palestinian refugees. With the plight of the refugees a lively concern at the time, Jordan, UNRWA and the United States' *Point 4 Program* jointly commissioned the 1952 'Bunger Plan' with the specific objective of providing for resettlement of as many Palestinian refugees as possible. The Syrian government, interested in the hydropower, was party to the planning, too. The proposal was to 'aim at the maximum development of the Jordan Valley without involving international negotiations that might not be feasible at the moment'. The proposal was also to be capable of being 'easily fitted into any subsequent schemes derived from the use of Lake Tiberias'[16]

The plan proposed irrigation on the west and east banks of the Jordan Valley, sufficient to settle 100,000 refugees based only on water from the River Yarmouk. A large 140-metre-high dam would be constructed upstream at Maqarin, with a storage capacity of 500 million cubic metres. The dam was to capture the winter flood flows of the Yarmouk without the need to store water in Lake Tiberias, which was essentially controlled by the Israelis. Most of the water would be allocated to Jordan, but 65 million cubic metres would be allocated each year to Syria. The dam would also generate hydropower of 281 million kilowatt-hours. A weir downstream on the Yarmouk at Adasiya would divert water into a canal running down the East Bank of the Jordan to irrigate the lands there, and a siphon under the main Jordan River would also transfer Yarmouk water to a canal to irrigate land on the West Bank.

As it was becoming clear that the interests of Israel and its Arab neighbours were hard to reconcile, and as broader political tensions persisted, the Bunger plan was designed to meet Jordanian and Syrian needs and to help the refugees without requiring the cooperation of Israel. It was expected that the dam would not attract opposition from that quarter as it did not apparently affect Israeli water rights and did not require cooperation over storage in Tiberias. Seeing the project as critical to refugee resettlement, the four sponsors – Jordan, Syria, UNRWA and the United States – agreed to go ahead. On 4 June 1953, Jordan and Syria signed a treaty on utilization of the Yarmouk that would allow implementation of the plan. Jordan was to pay most of the costs of the dam as it would be getting most of the water, while Syria would benefit from 75 per cent of the hydropower generated. Jordan and UNRWA endorsed the project, and in July 1953 *Point 4* appropriated the necessary funds.[17]

However, quite unexpectedly this plan too met with Israeli objections. Israel claimed water rights on the Yarmouk, protesting to the United States and the UN that the dam would alter its 'historic Yarmouk allocation' and the flow of water to its Yarmouk Triangle region. Israel based its claim to 'historical Yarmouk rights' in part on the rights of the Palestine Electric Corporation (PEC) which, as we saw in Chapter 4, had obtained from the British Mandatory authorities of Transjordan the 'Rutenberg Concession' and the right to develop hydropower on the Yarmouk. These concession lands lay within the former Transjordan, and hence in the new state of Jordan. When the Jordanian government became aware of the issue in 1953, it promptly cancelled the concession. Nonetheless, the Israeli successor to the PEC wrote to the United States government asserting its rights on the Yarmouk and saying it was 'entitled to full recognition in the implementation of the agreement'.

The Israeli government also claimed water rights as a Yarmouk riparian. The land between Tiberias, the main Jordan River and the Yarmouk – the Yarmouk Triangle – had formed part of Mandate Palestine and in September 1950, Israel had crossed the Jordan River and occupied it, apparently in contravention of the 1949 armistice terms. The land in question was negligible in size (about 2,600 hectares, of which some 830 hectares was cultivable land), but it gave Israel a frontage of some seven kilometres on the north bank of the Yarmouk, on the basis of which Israel now claimed Yarmouk riparian rights. The claim was denied by Jordan. This tiny issue threw a spanner in the works of the entire Bunger plan.[18] Unnerved by the Israeli claims, the United States dropped its support. Mills Bunger continued to push for it and for his pains, he was given a transfer within his Agency to Brazil. As a man of principle he refused to accept this sidelining and he resigned from the service.[19]

The Main Plan

With the issue of the Palestinian refugees still not settled, UNRWA sought to build an 'apolitical' approach. The TVA, a source presumed to be trusted by all sides, was brought in to review all proposals for the Jordan and to propose the 'most efficient method of utilizing the whole of the watershed in the best interests of the area', disregarding political boundaries. The plan was to be developed based on economic principles.

TVA delegated the work to a Boston consulting firm, Charles T. Main. The resulting Main Plan was published in August 1953 – *The Unified Development of the Water Resources of the Jordan Valley Region*. To keep costs down and to maximize benefits, the plan provided for both irrigation and hydropower, keeping all waters within the basin, relying on gravity rather than on pumping, and using natural reservoirs – particularly Tiberias – for floodwater storage rather than investing in costly dam construction. Jordan would store the winter floodwaters of the Yarmouk in Lake Tiberias. A dam would be built at Maqarin but at a much lower cost as it would be only for hydroelectricity. Total hydroelectric output would be 210 million kWh. Canals would bring water by gravity to Huleh and the Galilee hills in the north, and to the East and West Ghor, also by gravity. The total cost of the Main Plan was estimated at $121 million, primarily to be financed by the United States.[20] There was no immediate decision on this plan but, as we shall see, it was to form the starting point of US attempts to reach a definitive agreement on the Jordan.

Israel's original diversion project

Having stymied the various proposals designed to benefit the refugees, Israel at this time conceived its own project on the Jordan within its 1952 national water plan. This was an ambitious project for out-of-basin transfer, building on Lowdermilk's concepts from the 1930s which had been further detailed in the Hays Plan of 1948 (see *Israeli plans for water* earlier). The project was to divert the Jordan at B'Not Yacov Bridge (the Bridge of Jacob's Daughters), just south of Lake Huleh. From there, a 13-kilometre diversion canal would carry the water to the northwest corner of Lake Tiberias. The considerable difference in elevation – a 280-metre drop down to the level of the lake – would allow hydroelectricity to be produced at a hydroelectric power station on the lake and the power produced would be enough to pump the water right up out of the Jordan basin more than 250 metres to the level of the coastal plain and on to the south of Israel. Inevitably this proposal to transfer most of the water of the main Jordan River out of the basin and convey it to the south of Israel met strong opposition from all the other riparians. This Israeli plan was seen by the Arab countries as a hostile act.[21]

Meanwhile, Israel was pressing on with other steps in its water plan. Two of these steps also provoked tensions and opposition as they were seen as contraventions of the 1949 armistice agreements. The first, as we have seen, was the occupation of the Yarmouk Triangle in September 1950. The second occurred the following year when, in March 1951, Israel began to drain the Huleh Lake and the adjacent marshes. This ran into difficulties with the Syrians because much of the lakeshore lay within the 1949 Armistice Demilitarized Zone.[22]

The Johnston Plan

1953 Dulles Mission

With no basis or will for regional cooperation on water, the parties appeared to be racing headlong to confrontation. Alarmed at the risks but also sensing opportunity, President Eisenhower proposed the United States as an impartial arbiter and this proved generally acceptable to the riparians. Although the United States was the principal supporter of Israel and there was strong popular feeling amongst Americans in favour of the new state, the United States at this time did not provide the almost unquestioning support for Israel that later characterized its policies in the region.

This early US stance of fairness was prompted by an appreciation of unrighted wrongs, in particular the plight of the refugees, and by the genuine poverty of the Arab countries. There were also fears of the Arab states leaning towards the Soviets who were increasingly interested in the region and looking to establish a *point d'appui*. Essentially, US policy at this time was to try to achieve Middle East stability in order to protect US oil interests and to keep the USSR out. The State Department interpreted this policy as requiring a resolution of the Palestinian refugee issue together with the more general economic development of the Middle Eastern states, with the Arab states and Israel rising together on a tide of co-prosperity. The approach was to be similar to that successfully pursued under the Marshall Plan in Western Europe or the Truman doctrine for Greece and Turkey, with economic cooperation leading to political cooperation. The United States would back up policy initiatives with development aid under the *Point Four Program*.[23]

The United States was particularly interested in the development of the Jordan Valley because they saw it as an opportunity to achieve both economic prosperity and the settlement of a large number of refugees. In addition, settlement in the Jordan Valley alongside the territory that the refugees had once called home seemed to offer an opportunity to improve the refugees' social and economic status without impairing their rights to repatriation or compensation.

In May 1953, Eisenhower's secretary of state, John Foster Dulles, travelled to the Middle East to see for himself, proclaiming his administration's policy of 'true impartiality' in Arab–Israeli matters. He was appalled at the poverty he found, particularly amongst the refugees. He confirmed that the United States earnestly sought a solution to the refugee problem, and saw water in the Jordan Valley as a key means of resettlement. A memorandum prior to the trip says: 'development of the Jordan Valley water resources provides the most immediate hope for a partial solution to the Palestinian refugee problem.' Dulles himself maintained that 'an effective irrigation system would allow more land to be farmed and provide more refugees with work and hope for the future'. Later the same year a special ambassador, Eric Johnston, was despatched to the region to sort matters out.[24]

However, this approach was to come up against two hard contradictions. The first was that, as we have seen, the Israelis on the one side and the US and the

Arab states on the other had very different plans for the waters of the Jordan basin. The second, more fundamental problem was that neither the Israelis nor the Arab states were prepared to cooperate with each other on either economic or political projects. The reality was that Israel – and the Arab attitude to Israel – represented a political challenge in which compromise and cooperation were not strong options. Yet, because the Jordan was an international river, its equitable development depended precisely and absolutely on agreement and cooperation amongst the main riparians. In the absence of agreement and cooperation, hard power and facts on the ground would determine the division and use of the Jordan waters.

Prior to the Johnston mission

Israel continued its uncompromising stance on water. In fact, Israel had already begun tentative moves to transfer water from Tiberias as early as 1951, when, contrary to the armistice agreements and over the protests of US and UN officials, it began moving military units and bulldozers into the demilitarized zone (DMZ) on the Syrian border. Throughout 1952 and the first half of 1953 there were many armed clashes in the basin. It appears that the Israelis were anticipating that the United States would come out against out-of-basin transfers. In September 1953, perhaps in an attempt to establish 'facts on the ground' that might pre-empt any American plan, Israel secretly began a crash programme to construct the planned diversion project at B'Not Yacov Bridge. As this lay within the DMZ between Lake Huleh and Tiberias, there were immediate protests to the Security Council. Jordan complained that the quantity and quality of water being released was compromised. Syria protested that the works were being undertaken in the DMZ established under its 1949 Armistice Agreement with Israel. The Americans were enraged and on 18 September 1953, President Eisenhower suspended vital economic aid until Israel halted the works and cooperated with the United Nations in the DMZ.[25] By the end of October, Israel agreed to suspend work on the diversion project and US aid was resumed.[26]

Johnston's Mandate

On 7 October 1953, Eric Johnston arrived in the region as personal representative of the president with the rank of ambassador. The Americans believed that an economic and equitable settlement acceptable to all riparians could still be worked out. Although Johnston had no experience whatever of the Middle East or of water, he had two extraordinary advantages – the total trust of the administration, and the skills of a negotiator who had got on well with Stalin and later with Khrushchev. His most significant achievement to date had been as president of the Motion Picture Association of America (MPAA) when he convened the infamous closed-door meeting of motion picture company executives at New York City's Waldorf-Astoria Hotel that led to the Waldorf Statement in 1947 and to the Hollywood blacklist.[27]

The State Department set four main criteria for what Johnston was to come up with: that the plan should make use of all water without waste or extravagance; that all schemes proposed must be economically and technically sound; that the outcome should be equitable with no riparian denied fair use; and that the overall plan should be accepted by all interested countries. The understanding was that Johnston would essentially work out how to implement the Main Plan, which after all had the *imprimatur* of the revered TVA upon it. The United States was clear from the outset that this would require Israel to agree to major departures from its own plans. Dulles spelled out some of the imperatives to the Israelis: that they relinquish claims to exclusive territorial control over Tiberias, agree to a fixed allocation of water and play an active role in refugee resettlement.[28]

Johnston himself was a firm believer that agreement on water could provide a gateway to peace. He considered that agreement on a cooperative plan for development of the Jordan Valley would not only allow the resettlement of many refugees but also help many political problems to disappear. He wrote to Eisenhower that 'if we grasp the key firmly and turn it carefully, it may open the way to eventual rapprochement between the parties to the Palestinian dispute.'[29]

The history of the Johnston mission

When Johnston arrived in the region on 21 October 1953, he was presented with various plans. The Arab League, representing a united front of the three Arab riparians – Syria, Jordan and Lebanon – submitted its proposal based on the Ionides, MacDonald and Bunger plans. The salient points were no out-of-basin transfer, no storage in Tiberias and construction of the Maqarin Dam to store Yarmouk floodwaters.[30] Israel submitted a radical counterproposal, the Cotton Plan, which called not only for out-of-basin transfer but also for diversion of the Litani river, which lay in a completely separate basin within Lebanon beyond the Jordan watershed. As we have seen in Chapter 4, the Zionists had for years looked on the Litani as a potential resource, considering that its actual and possible uses within Lebanon were limited. Now the Israelis brought up the old proposal that had been mooted at Versailles – that if the Litani were diverted through a short tunnel under the mountains it could be joined to the Jordan into which it would flow costlessly by gravity.[31]

Over the course of some eighteen months, Johnston visited the region four times before coming up with his plan. However, it was some 'side discussions' in 1955 between Johnston and the Israelis that resulted in a radical overhaul of Johnston's ideas. Arnon Soffer, the Israeli water expert, writes: 'In the period between Johnston's third and fourth visits to the region, [Johnston] hosted Israeli experts, and *together they made progress on his revised proposals.*'[32]

Siegel explains that Johnston 'originally wanted all Jordan water to stay in the Jordan Valley' – but was persuaded to change his mind.

> He understood that unused water was needlessly flowing to the sea and thereby being wasted. Johnston agreed to significantly increase Israel's share of the water

so that Israel could make productive use of it. In addition, Israel succeeded in persuading Johnston that water should be diverted out of the basin and transported the length of Israel, as far as the Negev.[33]

This diversion was, of course, directly contrary to Arab views and wishes. In fact, it appeared not only to the other riparians but also to neutral observers to breach both economic logic and basic principles of water management. The costs of this transfer, which involved pumping up water from over 200 metres below sea level to Israel's coastal plain, a total lift of more than 250 metres, and then transporting water over a distance of more than 200 kilometres, were phenomenal. The diversion also breached a common understanding of transboundary water management – that riparians (and in-basin users) should have first say in what happens to the water, and that benefits should be shared fairly. But it would represent a huge boost for Israel, not just in terms of developing the country and settling and fructifying the land but also in terms of water security and even nation building.

The Johnston Plan

Amazingly, despite its fame and long influence, it is not completely clear what the Johnston Plan consisted of. It is certainly not a formal agreement between anyone. Often it seems as though every party has its own version. The only fixed rule was that states that subsequently took US aid for water projects had to follow some version of the plan. There is, however, no single 'Johnston Plan', just a series of documents which, taken together, are referred to as the plan.

There are even two written versions. There is an 'Israeli version' contained in a draft Memorandum of Understanding dated 5 July 1955 and completed by details in other exchanges between Israel and the United States. There is also the 'United States version', which includes the same documents as the Israeli version together with a further 'US–Arab Memorandum of Understanding' of 11 October 1955. This 'US–Arab MoU' was approved by the Arab League Technical Committee. There are significant differences between the two versions, particularly differences in the quantities allocated to Israel from the Yarmouk and to Jordan from the Jordan River.[34] The 'United States' version also provides for UN involvement in supervision, but this was stoutly rejected by Israel and is absent from the 'Israeli version'. The essentials of the plan cover storage, allocation and distribution systems.[35]

Storage

The Johnston Plan provided for Jordan to have the lion's share of Yarmouk winter floodwaters to be used for summer irrigation both on the East Bank of the river, within Jordan proper, and on the West Bank, territory then administered by Jordan. For this to work, storage was needed to carry over water from the winter flood flows to the main irrigation season in the hot, dry summer. The plan therefore provided for two mechanisms to store Yarmouk water for irrigation by

Jordan. One was for a somewhat smaller version of the Maqarin Dam that had been proposed by Bunger (see earlier, *The Bunger plan*), on the Upper Yarmouk between Syria and Jordan. The dam was to be built by Jordan with US finance. It would be 126 metres in height and would store 300 million cubic metres of water for downstream irrigation in the Jordan Valley. The dam was also to generate 150 million kilowatt-hours of hydropower – very important as Syria would get no irrigation benefit but would, instead, receive hydropower.

However, this scaled-down Maqarin Dam would be too small to store all the floodwaters. A second storage mechanism was therefore proposed, a short canal at Adasiya from the Yarmouk to Lake Tiberias, which lies at a lower level. This would allow 80 million cubic metres of Yarmouk floodwater to be stored in Tiberias. In total, 300 million cubic metres of Lake Tiberias storage was to be made available to Jordan.[36]

Allocation

The allocations under Johnston were based on fixed quotas for certain riparians from each of the four rivers considered: from the Hasbani, 35 million cubic metres annually for Lebanon; from the Banias, 20 million cubic metres for Syria; from the Jordan, 22 million cubic metres for Syria and 100 million cubic metres for Jordan; and from the Yarmouk, 90 million cubic metres for Syria and 25 million cubic metres for Israel. The residual of the Jordan, estimated at 375 million cubic metres, was to go to Israel; and the residual of the Yarmouk, estimated at 620 million cubic metres, was to go to Jordan. The two tables below show the final allocations proposed by Johnston in his 1955 plan, and the differences between the Johnston Plan and the other plans presented to him.

Distribution systems

Both versions of the plan spell out the distribution infrastructure proposed for Jordan, Lebanon and Syria. For Jordan, this infrastructure included the diversion weir at Adasiya to divert water from the Yarmouk into two canals, an East Ghor canal to irrigate the East Bank lands and a siphon under the main Jordan River and

Table 5.1 Allocations in the Johnston Plan (in millions of m³)

	Hasbani	Banias	Jordan	Yarmouk	Total available
Lebanon	35				35
Syria		20	22	90	132
Jordan			100	Residual of Yarmouk river (estimated at 620)	720
Israel			Residual of Jordan River (estimated at 375)	25	400
Total	35	20	497	735	1,287

The 'Israeli version' has 40 million cubic metres of Yarmouk water for Israel for the Yarmouk Triangle farms.

Table 5.2 Plans Presented to Johnston (allocations in millions of m³)

	Arab League plan (March 1954)	UN plan (Main, 1953)	Israeli plan (Cotton)	First Johnston Plan	Revised Johnston Plan (1955)
Lebanon	35	-	451	-	35
Syria	132	45	30	50	132
Jordan	1,047	774	575	829	720
Total for the three Arab states	*1,214*	*819*	*1,056*	*879*	*887*
Israel	182	394	1,290	426	400
Total	**1,396**	**1,213**	**2,345**	**1,307**	**1,287**

Note: The Cotton Plan includes the waters of the Litani.
Source: Soffer in Isaac & Shuval: 110.

a West Ghor canal to irrigate the lands on the West Bank. There was also to be the short canal from Adasiya to Lake Tiberias for Jordan to convey excess Yarmouk winter floodwaters to be stored in the lake, together with the works needed to accommodate and then release these flood flows from Tiberias in summer. For Lebanon, a storage dam and irrigation works on the Hasbani were foreseen, and for Syria, diversion works on the Jordan and a canal leading from the river to convey Syria's Jordan allocation of 22 million cubic metres to its Boteiha farms. As we have seen, the Maqarin Dam on the Yarmouk was also foreseen, to store 300 million cubic metres of water and to generate hydropower.

Only the Israeli version is specific about Israeli intentions to divert water out of the basin. Both versions state that 'residual water of the Jordan will be available for unconditional use of Israel'. Israel was able to construe this to mean that the plan allowed it to proceed with out-of-basin use. However, only the Israeli version says anything about Israeli infrastructure. Where the United States version is silent on any water project for Israel, the Israeli version states clearly that water will be taken out of the basin at Israel's will and that 'the principal Israeli diversion structure will be located at or near B'Not Jacov Bridge'.[37]

Assessment of the Johnston Plan

The Johnston Plan in whatever form represented some significant shifts away from the original principles of Johnston's mission.[38] While in general terms, the plan would 'make use of all water without waste or extravagance' with 'schemes proposed that are economically and technically sound', it is far from clear that the proposed outcomes were equitable, and the overall plan was certainly not accepted by all riparians. In addition, the specific requirements that Secretary of State Dulles placed on Israel were certainly not going to be fulfilled by the plan. Israel did not relinquish its claim to exclusive territorial control over Tiberias or agree to a fixed allocation of water. Still less did Israel play an active role in refugee resettlement.[39]

The plan corresponded to few of the announced principles and requirements, and all the departures benefited Israel. By adroit political legerdemain, Israel frustrated most of the declared US objectives while achieving all its own objectives – while yet claiming that its plans and projects were in accordance with Johnston. Somehow the plan was no longer about resettlement of refugees but about finding acceptable water-sharing agreements between the states. There was no more insistence on the basic principle of the 'Main Plan' of in-basin use, gravity conveyance and natural reservoirs. The refugee resettlement notion was altogether lost sight of. Water for the West Ghor never materialized. All the unused water in the Jordan was siphoned off to Israel's coast. How did this striking reversal take place?

The first shift was the 'Gardiner formula' that gave the residual of the Yarmouk to Jordan and the residual of the Jordan to Israel. That Dulles had required that Israel accept a fixed allocation of water was overlooked. In fact, both Jordan and Israel found this formula acceptable because it appeared to give either state a free hand to develop its portion of the basin. This 'free hand' proved, however, to be the case only for Israel, which immediately developed its interests. It became only very partially – and very slowly – true for Jordan. Why was this so?

The main reason for this unequal outcome was simply the power of Israel, both hard military power and diplomatic manoeuvrings. By these means, Israel proved capable over subsequent decades of preventing all upstream development of the Jordan by any other party and also of long delaying development of the Yarmouk. By contrast, the weaker party, Jordan, was prevented for many years from its planned development of the Yarmouk by both upstream and downstream riparians – Syria and Israel – and could do nothing to restrict the development of the Yarmouk by Syria. During all this time, Israel not only enjoyed most of the water of the Jordan as the residual beneficiary but also had access to the Yarmouk water that Jordan could not use.[40]

The second shift was that the amount of water needed within the Jordan Valley was reassessed and found to be very much less than previously assumed. A February 1955 study by Baker & Harza increased the area in the Jordan Valley available for cultivation but reduced the total amount of water needed to irrigate those lands. It was on this basis that Johnston reduced the proposed allocation to Jordan from 1,047 million cubic metres as proposed by the Arab League – and from the 829 million cubic metres that had been proposed in the first draft of his plan – to 720 million cubic metres.[41]

At the same time, the ambition to settle 100,000 Palestinian refugees in the valley was quietly shelved. Part of the allocation to Jordan under Johnston's final plan included 100 million cubic metres for a West Ghor canal to benefit refugees. This canal and the irrigation networks have never been constructed. The water allocated by Johnston to the West Bank of the Jordan has never been delivered and the West Ghor irrigation scheme has been completely elided from discussion.[42]

In 1967, Jordan laid claim to this water on the grounds that the country was having to absorb yet more Palestinian refugees. However, by then it was neither in the interests of Israel nor in those of Jordan to maintain the notion that this water was for resettlement of refugees in the Western Ghor. These lands fell under Israeli control in 1967 ,and Israel briefly maintained a claim to the 100 million cubic metres in question (see Chapter 6 later). However, this soon fell away and the idea of developing irrigation in the Jordan Valley specifically for refugee resettlement disappeared into the mist of history. Jordan did settle some refugees on the East Ghor schemes but this was never the main purpose or result of that development.[43]

US, Israeli and Arab reactions

Although the Plan was far from fulfilling its original policy objectives, the US initially concluded that its mediation had enabled 'the community of technocrats . . . to arrive at a technical solution'. In the US view, the Johnston Plan was seen as a successful de facto water-sharing agreement. It provided a framework for the two major riparians to achieve key objectives: Israel to take water out of the basin for the purposes of national development, and Jordan to develop the East Ghor, with US finance. However, it quickly proved that the 'community of technocrats' were not sovereign over water resources.[44]

The Arab League rejected the plan. The conclusion of Johnston's mission came at a time when the United States was no longer the only great power in the region. When Johnston was putting his plan on the table, the USSR had gained a foothold in the Middle East, and the Arab states were consequently becoming less dependent on US aid. This undermined one premise of the Johnston mission – that US project finance could induce the riparians to cooperate. In the new environment, the Arab states were freer to take an independent view of the proposal.[45] Although the plan would have brought some benefits to the Arab states, it was clear that Israel would be the main beneficiary and that Israel intended to transfer Jordan water out of the valley to irrigate and settle the Negev. This led the Arab League Council to adjourn its decision and to effectively refuse to accept the plan. When Israel moved in February 1956 to renew its works at the B'Not Yacov Bridge, President Nasser of Egypt spoke[46] for the Arab League to clarify that Arab governments would not accept the Johnston Plan because it was being taken as a licence for out-of-basin transfers. [47]

In the event, the United States put pressure on Israel to postpone the development of its out-of-basin transfer. The month following Nasser's statement, on 28 March 1956, Secretary of State Dulles urged Israel not to resume work at the bridge. Implicitly the Americans recognized that out-of-basin transfers were unacceptable to the Arabs, whatever Johnston had been induced to propose. Israel consented to put off the works for two years – but only if the United States granted a $75 million loan to finance other water resource development projects. The United States agreed to this arrangement as it would at least for the moment avoid new conflict over Israel's diversion plans.[48]

The Arab states had freely cooperated with Johnston and it is clear from their serious consideration of his proposals that they were generally in favour of a comprehensive development plan for the Jordan basin. In particular, Jordan was more interested in water security than in continuing friction with Israel and was keen to benefit from the offer of US financing for development of the lower Jordan Valley. Syria stood to benefit less and was not politically aligned with the US sponsor. The main concern of Damascus was to maintain the integrity of the DMZ and so not to lose the chance of territorial control over the east bank of Tiberias. The critical factor that led to the rejection of Johnston's plan was the Arab view that Israel would unduly benefit. The allocation of the residual water in the Jordan to Israel gave the Israelis the opportunity to proceed with out-of-basin transfer. This the Arab states hotly rejected, even in Zeitoun's phrase, considering it 'outright water theft'.

Preventing out-of-basin transfer rather than integrated development thus became the central policy goal of the Arab states. Arab counterproposals were devised. First, Nasser came with a proposal for two separate programmes loosely framed within the Johnston Plan. However, under this proposal, Jordan would have lacked access to storage in Lake Tiberias for the Yarmouk winter floods. As a result, there would not be enough water for the West Ghor canal, affecting the plans for refugee resettlement.[49] The alternative Arab plan – the 'Damascus plan'– on which see the section *The Arab water plan* in what follows – would divert the two Jordan tributaries that rise in Syria and Lebanon: the Hasbani in Lebanon and the Banias in Syria.[50] This plan was not accepted by the Arab League Council at the time but it showed the risk that Arabs might also take matters into their own hands.[51]

Conclusion on the Johnston Plan

Johnston never had any formal authority or mandate. Trying to win consent with the inducement of US project finance largely failed. The arrangements that followed mostly suited Israel, and the numerous disputes that arose contributed to the causes of the Six-Day War, which in turn resulted in the consolidation of Israel's control of the Jordan River system. The ultimate irony was that a water plan originally conceived to help Palestinian refugees simply ended up putting the lion's share of the water into the hands of the Israelis who used it to build a strong state with a compensating weakening of the Palestinians.[52]

The National Water Carrier

Development of the first stage: The Yarkon–Negev pipeline

While the politics and ethics of Jordan Valley development were being debated, the Israelis set about realizing the first part of the masterly plan to build the infrastructure that would integrate all the water resources that the country controlled. The vision was of a national water carrier that would link all sources to all points of demand throughout the country. The initial stage of this huge project was to carry water from the Mountain Aquifer to open up the Negev. The Nahr al

Auja spring, now renamed the Yarkon by Ben Gurion's committee, was the main outlet of the waters of the Western Aquifer.[53] The flow of this natural spring was largely replaced by abstraction from wells on the Israeli side of the border with the West Bank and the water was channelled into the huge pipeline that formed the first stage of the NWC. The switch from spring discharge to abstraction from wells allowed a more complete control. The peak winter flows of the springs no longer rushed to the sea but were fed into the pipeline or simply conserved to recharge the aquifer. The conserved water could be pumped out from the aquifer later when demand was greater.

The Yarkon–Negev pipeline, which was largely financed by US Jews, opened in 1955, conveying water from the Yarkon and the well fields to the northern Negev. The effect of this long-distance transfer of water from the Western Aquifer to the desert south was impressive. It allowed 20,000 hectares of the desert to be brought under cultivation. Again a large part – about two-thirds – of the cost of the development of this irrigated agriculture came from donations by US Jews.

From Negev pipeline to completion of the National Water Carrier

Once a version of the Johnston Plan was on the table, the Israelis rethought the design of the second stage of the NWC. This stage was to bring water up out of the Jordan Valley and integrate it with the Israeli national water grid. It was important that the NWC fit or appear to fit within the Johnston Plan and also that its design should not run up against immediate opposition on the ground over the DMZ as the first attempt had (see earlier, *US, Israeli and Arab Reactions*).[54]

By 1956, Israel had completed a revised design for the NWC, which reformulated the project in a way that Israel argued was in line with the Johnston Plan and did not conflict with the armistice arrangements. The design was presented to the United States for vetting. Israel was seeking not only political support from the United States but also US finance for the project. The United States responded cautiously, requiring that the project meet certain conditions if it were to qualify for US financing: it should be economically sound, should not conflict with the armistice arrangements and should respect the allocations of the Johnston Plan. A final condition was the most stringent of all – *that the project should not convey water to the Negev.*[55]

To meet at least part of these conditions, the Israelis decided in October 1958 to move the diversion offtake away from the original location. The new location was Eshed Kinrot, further south and outside of the DMZ, at the northwest corner of Lake Tiberias. Water would be pumped from Tiberias 212 metres below sea level to a reservoir 40 metres above sea level, a lift of over 250 metres. From there it would flow through the extended NWC to join the Yarkon–Negev system.[56]

From an engineering point of view, the new site was plainly inferior as it lay at a considerably lower elevation and would not generate any hydropower to contribute the energy needed to pump the water out of the basin. In addition, the water was of lower quality as it would be mixed with the more saline Tiberias water. Yet, from the point of view of political expediency, and given US pressure to avoid confrontation in the DMZ, it was the only solution. Construction began on 4 March 1959.[57]

This fully realized version of the NWC was a massive and costly engineering project to lift water out of the Jordan basin and flow it down the length and breadth of Israel to provide water for 3 million people and to meet the nation's agricultural water needs. The capital and operating cost of the NWC were – and are – very high. One estimate is that in these early days Israel used fully one-fifth of its total electricity supply just to pump water.[58]

The United States proved hesitant initially to agree to Israel's request to finance the NWC. It appeared that the design would allow Israel to extract 100 million cubic metres more from the basin than was provided for in the Johnston Plan. However, in 'technical talks' in Washington DC in November 1959, Israel apparently persuaded the United States, and the United States 'quietly approved' a $15 million loan for the main conduit of the NWC. The US team requested 'no publicity' and specified that the money was to finance the part of the project that would carry surplus groundwater from the Coastal and Mountain Aquifers rather than Jordan River water. As the whole purpose of the NWC was to unify water management, this distinction was, to say the least, disingenuous. In fact, it was clear to all that 'behind the scenes, the US accepted that later the coastal waterworks would become part of the larger NWC and take Jordan water to the Negev'.[59] The United States also allocated separate financing for a pipeline from Tiberias to provide irrigation water in the Beit Shean area.

Development of the second stage

The NWC was constructed by the national water company Mekorot, with planning and design done by Tahal, a government-owned engineering and water planning company. The construction gave a huge boost to Israel's economy and employment and the continuing effect on jobs and economic growth has been incalculable.[60] Four large pumps were constructed on Tiberias to lift water up to the level of Israel's coastal plain and to flow it into the NWC. Further pumping was required to distribute the water within Israel. Tiberias water might, in fact, be lifted from Tiberias more than 200 metres below sea level right up to Jerusalem which is 1,000 metres above sea level, a massive total lift of some 1,200 metres. Once the water was pumped up from Tiberias into the reservoir it flowed into a canal section and then into a 3-metre-diameter (108") pipeline 100 kilometres long which connected to the Yarkon–Negev pipeline. Part of the line was directed through tunnels in the rock for both topographic and security reasons. The NWC can convey 450 million cubic metres of water each year.[61] Many secondary pipes branch off, bringing water from local wells, despatching water to recharge groundwater aquifers and supplying the majority of Israel's population, industry and agriculture.[62]

By 1964, the diversion project was complete and the NWC was fully operational. With extensive laterals feeding points of demand throughout the length of the country, the NWC was the backbone of a fully integrated and unified national water grid unique in the world at the time.

The NWC and water management

The NWC is key to the integrated management of water in Israel. But it was also a key part of the building of the new state, its economy and its national consciousness. It has been the vital component in establishing an integrated physical bulk water network throughout the country. In hydraulic terms, the NWC brought together into a single network under state control all the water resources within Israel, together with the bulk of the waters of the adjacent Jordan River and Mountain Aquifers. In terms of water management, the NWC was the main artery which allowed integrated management of the entire water resource, transferring water from the very north of the country right to the Negev in the south and allowing distribution throughout Israel's territory. There was a hydrological equity to this beyond the appropriation of Jordan water – the pipeline allowed water to be transferred from the relatively water-rich north to the dry south where the desert could be 'made to bloom'. Multiple sources of surface and groundwater from different hydrological regimes were integrated and could be despatched to any point throughout the system. The network allowed water to be permanently available, and it proofed consumers and the economy against short-term deficits.

This full integration of all national water resources in a single system also took pressure off coastal wells and wadis and allowed water to be managed between seasons and between locations. It allowed conjunctive use of surface and groundwater at any point throughout the system, so that dependence on local water sources was eliminated and water was constantly available everywhere in predictable quantities. Where any source was in short supply, it could be replaced, for example, the temporary replacement of groundwater by surface water and vice versa, thus essentially mitigating the effects of any drought.

The NWC also largely solved the problem of storage. There was no need to build expensive reservoirs at the point of origin of the water, or to leave water in Lake Tiberias between seasons where evaporation losses would be very high. The NWC allowed water to be stored at multiple points along its whole length. In particular, by using techniques of 'injecting' water from the NWC into groundwater aquifers, surface water from Tiberias could be stored underground in the aquifers of the coastal plain.

The NWC's role in the building of the new state, its economy and its national consciousness

The NWC opened with great fanfare on 10 June 1964. Israel's old advocate Lowdermilk was there to see part of his dream for the land realized. In *Let There be Water*, Siegel argues that the NWC is more than just a pipe. He asserts that planning and construction of the NWC unified the nation while transforming the country.[63]

The most significant effect was on the security of the new state. With scant internal water resources, Israel's economy was very vulnerable. By unifying the nation's water systems and allowing rational water management throughout the country, the NWC brought a large measure of security of water resources to Israel.

Connecting Tiberias in the north with all of the coastal plain and cities and so on down south to the Negev, the NWC created a strong infrastructural backbone and skeleton binding the country physically together. Reliable access to good-quality water for all uses throughout the country created an assurance of physical water security. A unified water system, all under Israel's control, created 'water independence' to match political and territorial independence.

The NWC was also key to developing Israel's agricultural economy. Just as Ben Gurion had dreamed, the NWC 'made the desert bloom'. The extension of irrigated agriculture to the rainfed lands around Beersheba and into the Negev desert drove the rapid growth of high-value agriculture and the valuable export of fresh fruit and vegetables. This expansion of the economy also opened up the south to more extensive settlement – the population of the Beersheba metropolitan area today is nearly 400,000.[64]

Siegel goes further. His understanding is that the NWC was transformative for the Israeli nation. It provided a strong sense that challenges could be overcome and security strengthened, a feeling that the NWC was not just an infrastructure project successfully accomplished, unifying the country in terms of water infrastructure and services, but that it was also an inspiration that helped Israelis feel part of a larger common cause. The NWC helped to bind the country together and unify it.

The fact that this was a public resource and a public project, conceived to bring water equitably to all, contributed to a sense of Israeli identity. The NWC was seen as a force that helped build a nation in which all could rise together. In this way, the NWC did much to counter the economic, social and political fissures that ran through Israel at the time.

Arab views

The NWC brought about a significant shift in the allocation and management of water in the region – and resulted in a shift in regional water politics. It effectively altered the water balance in natural basins by transferring much of the water of the Jordan basin to Israel's coastal plain. In so doing, the NWC set a new pattern of water allocation amongst the riparians.

In terms of regional water resource management, Israel defended the NWC as a form of cooperative water management in the region within the vision and the terms of the Johnston Plan. In the view of the other riparians, the NWC was seen as the very opposite of a cooperative management approach. It was essentially viewed as a fact on the ground that accomplished two grand water thefts. One theft was of the regional resource of the Jordan basin shared by Lebanon, Syria, Jordan and the West Bank Palestinians; and the other was the consolidation of the appropriation of the bulk of the water from the Mountain Aquifer that underlay the Palestinian West Bank.

Unsurprisingly, Arab opposition to the NWC was very strong. When the NWC was completed in 1964 and Israel was preparing to pump Jordan water out of the basin, Arab criticism was intense. The United States tried to prove that 'adherence to the Johnston Plan was resulting in an equitable division of Jordan water'.[65] Seen from an Arab viewpoint, the integration of all the water resources Israel controlled into a single system within its borders was the water equivalent of the conquests of 1948. The irony of this 'zero-sum game' was not lost on Israel's neighbours. They looked on sadly at what they saw as the appropriation of a regional resource to strengthen the new state at their expense – and at the expense of the Palestinians, both refugees and West Bank residents.

Concerned that Israel's plans were not, in fact, in line with Johnston, the United States despatched Wayne Criddle to the region on a confidential mission to check, and to develop measures to compensate Jordan for the fact that its allocation under Johnston could only be realized if the Maqarin Dam were constructed. Israel and the United States then met together to agree to the 'Criddle Formula' which was designed to deliver 100 million cubic metres of Jordan River water to Jordan.[66] Sharing in the general Arab hostility to the out-of-basin transfer and hence the NWC, Jordan rejected the formula. However, Jordan was a poor, weak state and Jordanian opposition was dulled by the fact that it was dependent on the United States for finance to construct the East Ghor irrigation works. This allowed Jordanian opposition to the NWC to be silenced by an opposing Israeli quibble about 20 million cubic metres of Yarmouk water.[67]

The Arab water plan and the Six-Day War

The Arab water plan

In opposition to Israel's out-of-basin diversion of the Jordan, the Arab states devised their own 'Arab Water Plan'. When Israel announced in November 1959 that it was intending to proceed with out-of-basin transfer and to pump Jordan water to the Negev, the Technical Committee of the Arab League came up with the 'Damascus Plan' to divert the Upper Jordan tributaries, the Hasbani and the Banias (see earlier, *US, Israeli and Arab reactions*). Essentially, the logic was that if Israel was going to take unilateral action to appropriate and use Jordan water outside the basin, then why should the Arab states not take similar action? The Arab League Council decided that it was 'necessary to utilize the waters of the River Jordan in the interest of the Arab countries and the Palestinian Arabs'. However, no actual steps were taken by the Arabs at this time.[68]

Throughout the early 1960s, the Arab states maintained their opposition to Israel's plans, arguing that they had never approved the Johnston Plan and that Israel's unilateral actions compromised the Arab states' riparian rights and harmed water quality and environmental flows. Behind these points were two political motives. One was that the Arab countries were aghast at the growing strength of Israel in the region and understood that the diversion would increase the scope for settlement within Israel, allowing the build-up of the population in this energetic and aggressive state. The other was that the understanding all along had been that settling Palestinian refugees, and not a new wave of Jewish immigrants, would be given priority in the use of Jordan water.

However, this was a time of turmoil and weakness in the Arab world. The early 1960s saw Syria withdraw from its United Arab Republic union with Egypt, while Egypt itself was embroiled in a brutal civil war in Yemen. As a result there was no action until 1963–4 when Israel was completing the NWC and preparing to start pumping the water out of the basin. Arab criticism grew, despite valiant US efforts to try to calm matters with the Criddle Formula (see earlier). As Israeli plans for the out-of-basin transfer were about to become a reality, Arab opposition strengthened. Matters came to a head at the 1964 Arab summits which headlined the water diversion as the first issue and decided on actions to counter the NWC project. These same summits established a unified Arab military command and set up the multiparty Palestine Liberation Organization.[69] On the first day of the following year, 1 January 1965, Fatah carried out its first-ever major attack, infiltrating Israel and placing explosives alongside the NWC. In the event, the device failed to explode but the action had a symbolic significance of opposition to Israeli water plans.

As Israel began test-pumping, the Arab states came back to the idea of diverting the headwaters of the Jordan. The plan was that Lebanon would divert the upper Hasbani, with 40–60 million cubic metres going to the Litani and 20–30 million cubic metres to the Yarmouk, while the Banias in Syria would be diverted to the Yarmouk where the combined flow would be regulated by a Jordanian dam at Mukheibah. The diversion plan for the Banias called for a 73-kilometre-long canal to be dug that would link the Banias with the Yarmouk, carrying the Banias's flow plus the water diverted from the Hasbani. The diverted water would then have entered the Jordan Valley within Jordanian territory south of Lake Tiberias. The engineering and economic logic of this purely political project was considerably less than that of the NWC, but nonetheless a $30 million fund was set up to finance it. The Soviet Union publicly supported this Arab plan.[70]

Israeli reaction to the Arab plan was extremely hostile and belligerent. Although neither Israel nor the United States believed the plan would ever be realized, they saw that if it ever did see the light of day it could reduce the water available to the NWC by one-third and increase salinity in Tiberias. The Israeli government called it a 'spite diversion' without economic justification that would give Lebanon and Syria 200–250 million cubic metres of Jordan water, whereas they had been allocated only a total of 77 million cubic metres under the Johnston Plan – see the table *Allocations in the Johnston Plan* earlier. Prime Minister Levi Eshkol said in the Knesset on 16 January 1965 that 'any attempt to deprive Israel of its share of the Jordan river system under the Johnston Plan would be considered an encroachment on our borders'. 'Jordan water,' he said, 'is as precious to us as the blood in our veins. We shall act accordingly.'

Eshkol was both knowledgeable and particularly involved in the question as he had been a lead negotiator of the Johnston Plan. Much earlier, under the Mandate, he had also been one of the founders of Mekorot, the Israeli water company, as well as an executive of the Jewish Agency's agricultural planning section. As a classic Labour Zionist, he placed great importance on the twin development vectors of immigration and agriculture. For him, water was vital to Israeli development, even to its existence, and he was perfectly willing to fight to protect it. Moshe Dayan was equally belligerent, urging Eshkol to regard any attempt to 'divert Israeli water as an act of war'.[71]

US role

Throughout this period the United States made efforts to maintain some balance, particularly by helping Jordan develop the Yarmouk. Despite the essential failure of the Johnston Plan to bring its expected fruits or even to attain a more balanced regional cooperation on water, the United States continued to finance projects within the plan. In the period between 1955 and 1963, these mainly benefited Israel as we have seen earlier. The United States provided $50 million to Israel for water in this period, but only $13 million to Jordan. The United States nonetheless continued to try to redress the balance by supporting the development of the Maqarin Dam which would give Jordan winter storage for Yarmouk water. The September 1964 Arab summit had brought agreement between Syria and Jordan on the project and the summit approved the dam. Supporting the project as 'not inconsistent with the Johnston Plan', the State Department encouraged the World Bank to share in financing the estimated cost of $65–85 million. However, the bank turned it down, questioning the economics. Nonetheless, Jordan went ahead with preparations, contracting with a Yugoslav firm for a feasibility study and detailed engineering, to be completed by 1965. Construction was slated to begin in January 1967. However, two problems arose. The United States cooled to the idea when it emerged that Soviet and Yugoslav contractors were being considered. And second, Israel threw the usual spanner in the works by demanding a share of Yarmouk water for the Triangle farmers. In the event, Jordan was still seeking finance for the dam when war came in June 1967 – and the region changed forever.[72]

In any case, by this stage the United States was moving away from its more neutral 'honest broker' stance of the 1950s. Once the issue of the Arab diversion flared up, the United States straightforwardly supported Israel. In 1964, President Johnson wrote to Prime Minister Eshkol, 'We stand behind you in your right to withdrawal [of water] in accordance with the [Johnston] Plan.'[73] In fact, the United States did not see the Arab plan as practical but was nonetheless concerned not to push the Arabs too hard into the Soviet camp. Dean Rusk wrote to LBJ that the United States has 'been trying to maintain an even keel in our Near East relations in the backwash of Arab reaction to Israel's completion of its Jordan River diversion project. The Arabs have equated the diversion with the establishment of the state of Israel in Arab territory and Nasser has used their emotional reaction to forge a solidarity.' Nonetheless, the United States emphasized that it would not 'condone or support the use of force' by Israel in relation to the Arab plan and constantly warned Israel that US arms deliveries were conditional on Israel refraining from pre-emptive strikes against Lebanon, Syria or Jordan.

By 1965, concerns were deepening as Lebanon and Syria were starting attempts at diversion and Arab coordination was improving. Despite US attempts to mediate on the issue, the risks of violent conflict increased. Israel attacked the works on the Banias first with tank fire and then, as the Syrians shifted the works further eastward, with airstrikes. By February of that year, US, Israeli and Arab diplomats believed a larger violent conflict was imminent over the water issue. Johnson sent Averell Harriman as special ambassador to mediate. Questions of possible UN intervention were raised but roundly rejected by both sides. Both Israel and the Arabs urged the United States to rein in the other side.

At the same time water was becoming an issue in Israel's ever-turbulent internal politics. Eshkol had to appear strong in a difficult election campaign, and he pleaded with the United States to give public support on the water issue. When this was not forthcoming to the extent that Eshkol desired, Israel began to take unilateral action, ignoring Harriman's attempts to defuse the situation. Israel attacked and destroyed Syrian equipment in the Dan and Doka areas. The United States publicly condemned these attacks but privately the State Department thought they could be effective and provided they remained limited they could be considered 'normal' border incidents.[74]

The road to war

By 1966, the situation was confused. Israel had managed to halt the implementation of the Arab plan by air and artillery attacks. In any case, Egypt was attempting to quieten things down and was not at this stage supporting the diversion scheme. However, these more pacific Arab moves were counterbalanced by more extreme Syrian positions. A coup in Syria in February 1966 brought a more radical regime to power which supported increased Palestinian attacks and skirmishes in the DMZ. A massively punitive raid by the Israelis in November 1966 on Al Samu and other Jordanian towns killed eighteen and destroyed many buildings, bringing international condemnation.

The Arabs were quite disunited, with President Nasser clearly trying to avoid conflict, even when Israelis conducted a huge demonstration of air power, shooting down six Syrian MiGs and buzzing Damascus. In April 1967, Palestinian guerrillas succeeded in blowing up a water pump station in the north of Israel. And at last, Egypt was stung into action. In May 1967, in an attempt to save face and preserve Egypt's position as leader in the Arab world, Nasser mobilized the Egyptian Army and closed the Gulf of Aqaba. And so began the war, which was over in just six days with a crushing victory for Israel on all fronts.[75]

Was the Six-Day War a water war?

From Suez in 1956 up until the early 1960s, the Arab–Israeli conflict had been largely dormant. Only when Israel's plans to divert the Jordan became a reality did frictions grow. In fact, many view Israeli actions against the proposed Arab diversion project as the start of the war. This was certainly the view of Ariel Sharon, the general who later became prime minister. Sharon said: 'people generally regard June 5th, 1967 as the day the Six Day War began . . . but in reality it started two and a half years earlier on the day Israel decided to act against the diversion of the Jordan.'[76]

In this sense, the war was about water security but, of course, the larger questions of security of the states of the region were at stake. Contingent political factors also played a key role: Nasser's need to assert leadership and deflect attention from the domestic economy; the typical populist, aggressive strutting of an Israeli election cycle; the instability of Syria under a new autocracy which lacked legitimacy. For all concerned, except perhaps the Jordanians who had the most to lose, belligerence was the preferred posture and a card for national leadership to play. The US role, too, was important. The Americans had been arming Israel to the teeth with sophisticated and highly effective weaponry, yet failed to give them the diplomatic support they requested on the water diversion issue. The conclusion was clear. Essentially, the tacit message was: *We cannot support you but we have given you the means to sort the problem out for yourselves.*

The water outcome was in any case decisive. A still vulnerable Israel entered a war and less than a week later emerged with a secure water inventory and absolute mastery over watersheds and water management. It was clear that one of Eshkol's priorities on the Syrian front was control of the water sources.[77] On 10 June 1967, the last day of the Six-Day War, the Golani Brigade occupied the Golan Heights, securing complete Israeli control of Tiberias and of most of the Upper Jordan watershed and resources. Israel's quick, decisive victory gave it control of the Banias River and new frontage on the lower course of the Jordan by occupation of the West Bank. Israel also won an extended frontage on the Yarmouk by occupying land up to the 1922 international boundary of Mandate Palestine. In addition, Israel now controlled the Golan Heights up to Wadi Ruqqad, a major channel of winter floods into the Yarmouk.[78]

* * *

The two long decades that lay between Israel's independence and the Six-Day War saw the rapid development of all the water resources which the new state could put its hand upon, and the construction of a nationwide, integrated water system that could provide Israelis with exemplary security of water resources and sure access to water services. Building on the early Zionists' understanding that water security was vital to state security and to economic growth, Israel took over and developed the lion's share of regional water resources, including much of the transboundary resources of the Jordan Valley and the Mountain Aquifers. The Six-Day War set the seal upon this, giving Israel control over all the catchments of the water resources it had acquired for its inventory.

That this took place unilaterally, without the agreement of the other riparians and outside of the kind of cooperative framework that characterizes much of the management of shared resources nowadays, was a source of bitter dispute at the time, and – at least for the Palestinians – remains so to this day.

In fact, this chapter in water history marks a decisive stage in the Palestinian itinerary of loss. Where they had lost most of their land and the water within that land in 1948, in the subsequent twenty years they also lost control of the water in the aquifers beneath their feet as well as access to the region's largest water resource, the Jordan River. And where it seemed for a while that a possibly well-intentioned world was willing to allocate some small share of that Jordan water for the relief of West Bank Palestinian refugees, in the end the water went elsewhere.

And Palestinian loss was Israeli gain. With secured access to the waters of the Upper Jordan and of Lake Tiberias, the Israelis were able to fructify the desert and to provide water for their fast-growing population. The Zionist dream of peopling the land was being realized. Where Jews in Palestine at the end of the Mandate numbered only some 700,000, only half of the Arab population, by 1967 the Jewish population had risen fourfold to nearly 2.4 million, outnumbering by half the entire Arab population of the territory.[79]

The Six-Day War also brought Israel control over the West Bank and the Gaza Strip. Already, Israel was exploiting the great majority of the resources of the aquifers. Now the victor gained complete control of the land above the resource and of all the development and uses of water within that land. How Israel was able to use this power we shall see in the next chapter.

Chapters 6 and 7 complete this contentious history of water up to the present. In the companion volume we shall explain the extent to which this history resulted in a wide disparity of water outcomes for Israelis and Palestinians. And we shall suggest what may be done to close the gap and build water security for both Palestinians and Israelis.

Chapter 6

WEST BANK PALESTINIANS UNDER OCCUPATION

POLITICS, POWER AND WATER, 1967–93

Israel's stunning victory over its neighbours in the Six-Day War brought not only military dominance and strengthened national security. The victory also heightened Israelis' sense that history was on the side of the new nation. The outcome was extended and defensible borders with Syria and Jordan, together with control over most of the watershed of the Jordan River and mastery of the productive aquifers that underlay the hills of the West Bank.

Many believed that a Greater Israel had arisen in all the old biblical lands. But as old Eshkol said 'we like the dowry but we don't like the bride'. He meant the Palestinian Arabs who lived within the lands Israel now controlled. In the tradition of Israeli politics, every solution was ceaselessly debated but the underlying history of the twenty-five years between the Six-Day War and Oslo lay in the progressive Israeli takeover and settlement in the new lands. By 1993 more than half the West Bank had been formally taken over by the Israeli state as military zones, settlement areas, farms and parks, and more than 100,000 Jews had settled all through the West Bank, not counting the 150,000 who had moved into East Jerusalem. Deep wells had been drilled for settler use. The West Ghor, the West Bank of the Jordan, long intended to settle Palestinian refugees, was, instead, essentially barred to Palestinians and was being irrigated in high-value Israeli settler agriculture.

The Palestinian Arabs lost all civic and many human rights. They suffered dispossession, expulsion and arbitrary arrest. The attempts of the PLO to alter things from the outside by armed struggle and terrorism brought only more severe repression within the Occupied Territories. And yet, after a fashion, the Palestinian Arabs prospered: incomes and employment shot up, many families acquired household durables for the first time, running water came to most homes. The question remained, however: *At what cost was all this acquired?*

In the end, the humiliation and the arbitrary abuse was too much. As in 1936, so in the 1980s, the people simply rose up in an *intifada* or general 'shaking off' of the oppressive regime which left them helots in their own land. The Israeli repression was brutal. Even water supplies were cut off. But the Palestinian Arabs persisted – and in the end, as we shall see, they won the right to their day on the world stage.

In the wider region, Israel used its newly established dominance and emerged the clear gainer. The earlier attempts to get agreement on the Jordan basin through the American Johnston Plan had failed because of conflicting interests and shifting regional politics. Now both Syria and Israel essentially renounced the Johnston Plan in favour of gaining the maximum water possible for themselves. With the land captured in the Six-Day War, Israel controlled the Upper Jordan and its confirmed military superiority gave it the decisive say in what happened throughout the Jordan basin. In this, Israel first argued for a share of Jordan River water for West Bank Palestinians and then forgot the claim. In the end Israel acquired access to far more water than Johnston had allowed.

*   *   *

Water resources and their management

All through this story, water has been a political issue, but after 1967, water begins to play a more central role both in Palestinian life and economy and in the struggle for self-determination. The Jordan Valley continues to be both a national and a regional issue, and in the West Bank, the politics of groundwater become more and more a part of the larger territorial issues of the struggle between Palestinians and Israelis. Throughout the period, there is intense controversy over the way in which the Israelis come to control, develop and use water resources the Palestinians regard as entirely their own. Some Israelis begin to argue that the acquisition and control of water are security issues which make it impossible for Israel to ever give up the West Bank.

*   *   *

Water policies

Water policies for the West Bank under Jordanian administration, 1949–67 In the period between 1949 and 1967, the need to develop West Bank water resources had been clear. A 1955 study[1] of the prospects of developing the economy of Jordan, including the West Bank, concluded that 'nothing is more important . . . today than judicious development and exploitation of water resources'. The study recommended development of groundwater, with a water resources board to regulate development and ensure that water extraction remained within sustainable limits. The study also recommended the improvement of the use of springs where the outlet was too often 'a puddled swamp which domestic users share with cattle and mosquito larvae'. Protection of the spring, drinking troughs, night storage tanks and the lining of canals were simple infrastructure improvements available. The study also considered that the Jordan Valley was a massive resource awaiting full development which would require a regional and partnership approach. The possibility of a West Ghor canal irrigated by a siphon from the Yarmouk would be 'no more than marginal economically' – but as we have seen in Chapter 5, irrigation development on both banks of the Jordan was seen by many as a vital project to settle Palestinian refugees.[2]

During the nearly twenty years that Jordan administered the West Bank, there was some new development of water resources. A 1959 law set up the East Ghor Canal Authority to develop irrigation infrastructure on the east bank of the Jordan Valley, in line with that part of the Johnston Plan (see the section on the Johnston Plan in Chapter 5, *Distribution systems*). In the same year a Central Water Authority was established to develop a drinking water supply.[3] Agricultural water use remained largely traditional both in Jordan proper and in the West Bank, although some go-ahead farmers began to develop more advanced irrigation systems for market gardening. Urban water supply was largely from wells drilled near the cities, while village water supply was predominantly from springs or drawn from cisterns or shallow wells. Tube well technology was only just coming in, and the depth to the water table across most of the highlands of the West Bank was considerable, making drilling of deep wells both expensive and technically challenging. Modern water drilling on the western slopes to exploit the deep groundwater of the Western Aquifer began only in the mid-1960s under a project to bring water to Jerusalem and Ramallah. However, the project – financed in part by the World Bank – was suspended in 1967 when Israel occupied the West Bank.[4]

The relatively slow pace of water development in the West Bank accelerated in the 1960s but was interrupted by the 1967 war. When Israel occupied the West Bank, it concluded that much more could have been done. Early Israeli assessments claimed that Jordan had invested little in West Bank development, 'choosing to spend most of its scarce development resources on the East Bank'. In the Israeli view, West Bank agriculture remained 'primitive and primarily rainfed'. What irrigation existed was considered inefficient – it was largely flood irrigation in which 40 per cent of the water was lost either to seepage in unlined canals or to evaporation from the flooded fields. Lack of storage meant that irrigation must take place when water was available, not when the plants needed it.[5]

A further strand of Israeli discourse was that, during the period 1948–67, Jordan had never challenged Israel's growing use of the West Bank aquifers. As we shall see, this observation was later to be used by Israel to assert rights of use over the lion's share of these aquifers, a position to be set out in the Oslo Accords. In fact, this Israeli position still governs the use of these waters to date. In 1967 it was estimated that Palestinians used about 100 million cubic metres of groundwater and surface water resources arising in the West Bank[6] – and 100 million cubic metres is about the same amount which West Bank Palestinians are able to use even today, more than fifty years later.[7]

Israeli dominance in regional water resources after 1967 With the occupation of the West Bank and the Golan Heights, Israel effectively controlled all the waters of the coastal plain, the Mountain Aquifers and the Jordan Valley. Israel occupied both banks of the Upper Jordan, the headwaters of the Banias, the west bank of the lower Jordan, and the Western, Northeastern and Eastern Aquifer basins.[8] This gave Israel complete command over all the waters within the territory of the state of Israel and of the lands it had conquered.

The Six-Day War also completely changed the hydropolitics of the Jordan river basin. Israel's frontage on the Yarmouk grew and its control of both the Golan watershed and the entire west bank of the river together with its military ascendancy gave it decisive control over the whole length of the river, from headwaters to the Dead Sea. This control in the Jordan Valley brought two significant gains. First, Israel was able to exploit more of the Jordan water – Israel's use of Jordan River water rose from the 400 million cubic metres provided in the Johnston Plan to 550–600 million cubic metres.[9] Second, water resources became a bargaining chip in the same way as land, and Israel was to play this chip very astutely, both in relation to the Palestinians of the West Bank and Gaza, and in international relations, particularly with Jordan.[10]

A new legal framework for water Israel lost no time in taking control of the water resources it now controlled, moving to extend Israeli water law within days of the military takeover and passing a multitude of military orders which essentially defined the legal framework in the Occupied Territories, including for water. Almost the first legal act Israel took after the Occupation was to nationalize West Bank water resources. Proclamation No. 2 declared these resources to be the property of the State of Israel. This was in line with Israel's 1959 water law, which had similarly made all water resources within Israel itself public property to be managed and controlled by the state.[11] Alongside this proclamation came Military Order No. 92 of 15 August 1967, *Concerning Powers for the Purpose of the Water Provisions*. Under this order, the military commander of the West Bank Area could appoint an Officer in Charge to hold definitive power in all water-related decision-making for the territory. Any previously existing water provisions became null and void unless permitted to continue under the officer in charge's directive. The application of the order was backdated to 7 June 1967, the day following the end of the war.[12]

Military Order No. 158 placed all water production facilities under Israeli control. Licences were required for further construction or operation of water facilities. Those who owned water installations such as wells prior to the Israeli occupation had to apply for new licences under this order. Additionally, Military Order No. 291 suspended and repealed aspects of Jordan's Land and Water Settlement Law No. 40, allowing real estate transactions to take place for land or water for which the registration process had not yet been completed.[13]

Israeli policy on water in the West Bank There was ambiguity in Israel's political intentions in the West Bank after 1967. In the first decade, to 1977, the Labour-led coalition appears to have seen the Occupation as a necessarily temporary situation. The expectation appears to have been that Israel would, in time, trade land for peace. This would have included some measure of surrender of Israel's newly acquired control of the region's water resources. The first evidence of this is in the apparently liberal approach to both administration and the economy – Defence Minister Dayan's 'Open Bridges' policy; the continuation of the Jordanian administrative apparatus together with its personnel, law and law enforcement; the encouragement of continued local government; and, above all, the new freedom of movement for Palestinians both to Jordan and to Israel itself.[14]

During this decade of Labour-led government, the Israeli policy towards water and agriculture contained elements of good practice, despite the high-handed imposition of the new legal and regulatory framework. The approach combined public control of the allocation and use of water through regulation with promotion of potable water supply and of water saving. As we shall see, water saving and water-use efficiency measures in agriculture were encouraged in order to increase production and incomes while moderating water consumption. The narrative accompanying this approach was essentially that both Israel and the Palestinians expected that 'land for peace' would ultimately work, and that support to Palestinian economic development and to the modernization of agriculture would lay the groundwork for a peaceful agreement and subsequent cooperation.

Good practice water regulation was introduced – although this was seen as a two-edged sword by Palestinians. The regulatory measures that Israel brought in certainly had the effect of increasing water productivity and water-use efficiency in agriculture, so that production and incomes went up while water use remained at pre-1967 levels. Israel also promoted the development of infrastructure for water supply to municipalities, industry and rural communities. Priority for any new allocations was rightly given to potable water supply.

The downside was that regulations limited both water development and water use. There was a ban on further drilling except for some domestic needs. Drilling permits had to be obtained from the Civil Administration[15] after the agreement of the two Israeli water institutions, Tahal and Mekorot. All pumping was to be metered and monitored. These measures conserved water within sustainable limits but also constrained supply below demand and consolidated Israel's existing predominant use of the water of the Mountain Aquifers. In the longer run, Palestinian demand for water increased both with the population and with agricultural profitability, and this led to unmet claims and apparent water shortages.

Some innovative technology on the supply side increased the yield of the Eastern Aquifer. The Israelis drilled wells above some existing springs and wells to extract fresh water before it was affected by the high concentration of salt at lower elevations. This effectively increased the yield of the aquifer from 58 million cubic metres to 100 million cubic metres. But even this became a source of contention when the Palestinians saw most of the increase in the water abstracted being allocated to Jewish settlements in the Jordan Valley. Of the extra water, 35 million cubic metres went for irrigation by Jewish settlers on 7,200 hectares and 7 million cubic metres was allocated for domestic use by both settlers and Palestinians. Palestinians also saw the yield of their own wells in the Eastern Aquifer decline, and they naturally linked this to the extra pumping by the Israelis upstream in the aquifer.

Seen as water resources management, much of this could count as good water conservation practice but viewed from a Palestinian perspective, Israeli controls were seen as oppressive, despite the benefits that also arose. The Palestinians saw regulation as a self-interested act by Israel, designed to limit Palestinian use of the water resources of the West Bank to pre-1967 levels, with a resulting highly skewed and inequitable allocation of a common resource. Controls on Palestinian water use were seen as mechanisms to protect the aquifers for Israeli use. These negative perceptions were sharpened when Palestinians saw that Israel was overdrawing the aquifer resources prodigally for use within Israel, and also developing water wells within the West Bank for the use of the growing number of settlements and settlers.

A harsher face of Israel's water policy in the West Bank was shown when the 'liberal' approach was subordinated to 'security' concerns. From the outset, Israel secured the right bank of the Jordan River and the foothills above it. Palestinians claim that 'early in the Occupation' the army destroyed water pumps along the Jordan and closed 30,000 dunums (3,000 hectares) of agricultural land.[16] Palestinians were effectively excluded from this area, and their farms were replaced over time by settler agriculture. Ironically, it was the development of these very lands in the Western Ghor that had been intended in the 1950s for the resettlement of Palestinian refugees (see Chapter 5 *passim*).[17]

And then in 1977, a Likud-led government came to power in Israel. Policy towards the West Bank hardened, and the proliferation of settlements convinced Palestinians that a 'creeping annexation' was underway. Ever stricter controls were applied to Palestinian water use and deep wells drilled within the West Bank for Israeli use multiplied. In 1982, the Israeli water company Mekorot was given responsibility for managing West Bank water systems and it began to integrate West Bank water resources more comprehensively into the Israeli water network. As shortages grew, West Bank Palestinians were obliged to buy water from Mekorot – and had the understanding that they were 'buying back their own water'. In fact, as Palestinian demand for water grew and tight restrictions on Palestinian development of West Bank resources were maintained, Mekorot began to pump water from the NWC back up to West Bank Palestinians. By the early 1980s, 3 million cubic metres a year were being pumped back up in this way.[18]

Palestinian water use under the Occupation, 1967–91[19]

Water use overall Estimates of the volume of water used by the Palestinians in the West Bank in 1967 vary between official Israeli sources (42 million cubic metres) and the less politicized estimates made by the West Bank Database Project (80–100 million cubic metres) – see the table *Water use in the West Bank*. The main discrepancy is in agricultural water use, with Israeli official sources indicating very low usage in 1967 and a large increase over the period.[20] For urban water supply, the story is different. Both sources agree that domestic and industrial water use in the West Bank shot up over the twenty-five-year period by a multiple of five times.

Estimates of Palestinian water use in the West Bank in 1990–1, shortly before Oslo, show much less variance – just over 130 million cubic metres. Most

Palestinian water use was in the agricultural sector – by the end of the period, 95–100 million cubic metres or about 70 per cent of the total water available was being used for irrigation, the rest for domestic and industrial purposes.

The remainder of the resource originating in the West Bank was used by Israel. In 1991, Israeli settlers were using about 43 million cubic metres, four-fifths (81 per cent) for agriculture. The rest – upward of 800 million cubic metres – was being abstracted and put into the NWC, most of it from wells and springs beyond the Green Line in Israel proper.

The effective demand for water by the Palestinians, given their per capita income level, was almost certainly higher than the low usage levels indicate. Israeli regulation of water use by quotas, combined with pricing practices that had scant relationship to economic costs, make it hard to establish real levels of demand at economic prices but the constant complaints of Palestinian farmers combined with real shortages experienced in both agriculture and potable water supply suggest that demand was well above availability in this period. Water use per capita was certainly only half that of Jordan and less than one-third of levels in Israel (see Tables 6.2 and 6.3).

Table 6.1 Water Use in the West Bank, 1967–91 (million cubic metres)

	1967		1990–1	
	WBDP	**Israeli sources**	**ESCWA 1990**	**Israeli sources 1991**
Palestinian use				
Agricultural	75–95	35	95	100
Domestic and industrial	6.5	7.2	38	32
Total Palestinian	**80–100**	**42.2**	**133**	**132**
Israeli settler use				
Agricultural				35.0
Domestic and industrial				8.0
Total settler				**43.0**
Total water use				**175.0**

Sources:
WBDP – The West Bank Database Project, the *Jerusalem Post*/West View Press, 1987.
ESCWA – Land and Water Resources in the Occupied Palestinian Territories. The Centre for Engineering and Planning. Report for ESCWA, 1992.
Israeli sources: Data Obtained from Civil Administration, Mekorot and Tahal in 1993.

Table 6.2 Total Water Use in the Occupied Territories, Israel and Jordan in 1990

	West Bank	**Gaza**	**Total OT**	**Israel**	**Jordan**
Total water use (in million cubic metres)	**118**	**97**	**215**	**1,890**	**879**
Agriculture	84	68	152	1,300	657
Domestic	29	27	*56*	480	179
Industry	5	2	7	110	43
Population	937,000	730,000	1,666,000	4,690,000	3,453,000

Was water development in the West Bank after 1967 unfair?[21]

Increasingly unequal shares of the groundwater of the Mountain Aquifers During this period, Israel developed and used a larger share of the groundwater of the Mountain Aquifers than prior to 1967, while maintaining strict controls on Palestinian water development and use. The recharge range of these three aquifers is estimated at 620–890 million cubic metres annually.[22] As we have seen, during the period between 1967 and 1993, West Bank Palestinians were using about 15–20 per cent of this resource.

There was scant new Palestinian water development permitted. Over the period between 1967 and 1990, the Civil Administration issued forty-six drilling permits to Palestinians, of which ten proved unsuccessful. Most successful wells – twenty-eight in total – were for municipal and industrial supply, yet even for this priority use, drilling permits became increasingly hard to obtain under the Likud regime. For example, when the large town of Tulkarem ran short of water in 1986, the mayor's request for a new well was turned down. Yet, in the same period, five new wells were drilled for settlers in the already stressed Western and Northeastern aquifers.[23] Agriculture fared the worst. Over the whole of the period between 1967 and 1993, there were just eight permits issued to Palestinians for agricultural purposes, all but one in the difficult drilling conditions of the previously underused Eastern Aquifer.[24]

At the same time, Mekorot developed a number of new wells. The Mekorot wells were reported to have accessed deeper aquifers and, by 1993, to be producing about 52 million cubic metres – nearly half (47 per cent) of all water discharged from West Bank wells.[25]

Not only did Israeli abstractions increase, but they also affected Palestinian abstractions. The drilling of new deep wells dried up historic springs and wells. In the Jordan Valley, average water tables dropped 16 metres between 1969 and 1993, causing twenty-six Palestinian wells to dry up – see the case of the Jordan Valley village of al-Auja discussed later. Overpumping also led to salinization of Palestinian wells. Total chlorine concentration increased by 50 per cent between 1982 and 1991, to about 440 mg/L in the northern section, and up to 1,700 mg/L near Jericho.

The implications of this unequal development are threefold. First, under the Occupation Israel moved from its previous method of exploitation of the Mountain Aquifers through wells drilled within Israel to a new approach of abstracting increasing quantities within the territory it was occupying, to the extent that by

Table 6.3 Per Capita Water Use in the Occupied Territories, Israel and Jordan in 1990

	West Bank	Gaza	Total OT	Israel	Jordan
Per capita use (m³/capita/year)	126	133	129	403	255
Domestic Use (m³/capita/year)	31	37	34	102	52
Domestic use (litres/capita/day)	85	101	93	280	142

Source: World Bank 1993.

1993 Israeli abstractions within the West Bank accounted for practically half of West Bank water production. In the eyes of Palestinians, exploiting the natural resources of an occupied territory was contrary to common justice and to international law. Second, Israel was able to use this water as it saw fit, including for settlements, without any Palestinian knowledge or control over the resource or its use. Third, as Palestinian demand rose and Palestinian water production was restricted, Palestinians became dependent on water purchases from Mekorot. In the eyes of Palestinians, it looked like Israel had taken Palestinian water and was selling it back.

Water supply to settlements From the beginning of the Occupation, Israel began to develop West Bank water resources for the benefit of settlers. By the late 1980s, Mekorot had thirty-six wells in the Jordan Valley for twenty-eight settlements. These Jordan Valley settlements housed only about 2,000 Israelis, and the bulk of this water was for agriculture. This was allowed by the rules the Israelis laid down – settler use of West Bank wells was permitted, but Mekorot was not allowed to pump water from these wells to Israel. Under this mechanism, by 1991 settlers were using a quarter of total water resources within the West Bank – 43 million cubic metres out of a total use of 175 million cubic metres (see the table *Water use in the West Bank* earlier). Not only were Palestinians excluded from the benefits of new water development, but some of it also affected their historic water rights. Sosland cites the case of the Al-Auja spring, which had irrigated the village fields for more than 150 years. The spring dried up because the water table had been lowered by wells drilled for the nearby Jewish settlements.[26]

Not only did settlers use the water of the West Bank aquifers within the West Bank, but they also overused the water the Israeli administration allocated to them, while Palestinian use remained tightly regulated. Reporting on water use in the West Bank in 1987, Israel's State Comptroller found that Arab water use was closely monitored and any overuse penalized but that the settlers were systematically overusing their quotas, in some cases by up to nearly half – see *Water stewardship* in what follows.[27]

Higher prices paid by Palestinians The Comptroller's 1987 report also recorded that Palestinian farmers were paying five times as much as Israeli settlers for water. The settlers were paying Mekorot 15 agorot per cubic metre (about 5 US cents) for agricultural water while Palestinian farmers paid 70 agorot per cubic metre (about 22 US cents) to the Civil Administration. The difference was even more glaring for domestic water where West Bank Palestinians were paying NIS 1–1.60 per cubic metre (29–46 US cents) while Mekorot was charging settlers only 23 agorot per cubic metre (7 US cents).[28]

The unequal impact of groundwater regulation[29] The Israelis introduced regulation of groundwater abstractions from agricultural wells. Metres were installed on individual wells in 1972 and in the following year individual well quotas were set at rates slightly above 1972 water abstraction levels. Between 1973 and 1975 well-owners were informed of the quotas and of their right to appeal. The quotas became effective from 1975. In 1987, due to drought conditions, water quotas in the Occupied Territories and Israel were cut across the board by 10 per cent, and the quotas remained unchanged at that lower level thereafter.

Israel also limited new groundwater development in the West Bank. As we have seen, only forty-six permits for new wells were issued to Palestinians; the issue of permits was restricted largely to refurbishment of existing wells, with 100–120 licenses issued to Palestinians for well-rehabilitation during the period from 1967 to 1990. The World Bank reported that 'virtually no actual work has been done as engaging excessively expensive Israeli drilling contractors is a condition of the permit'.[30] In fact, both routine maintenance and refurbishment appear to have been limited. It is reported that out-of-date engines and pumps were not replaced and piped distribution systems deteriorated, with conveyance losses increasing. By 1993, about fifty of the wells that had been in use in 1968 had gone out of service and had not been refurbished or replaced.[31]

In general, Palestinians resented this regulatory framework, in part simply because it was imposed by the Occupier but mainly because it was seen as unfair and designed to favour Israeli interests rather than a shared and agreed interest. This unfairness was most glaring in the fact that different rules applied to Mekorot, the Israeli water company, which drilled about thirty-two new deep wells in the West Bank during the period to supply settlements, which housed at most 100,000 people. By contrast, Palestinian municipalities were allowed to drill only twenty-eight new wells, for municipal water supply for a population of nearly 1 million. In the Palestinian view, this was not only unfair and abusive of power but also illegal. They argued that the supply of West Bank water to settlers was specifically ruled out by the international law of occupation, while the use of West Bank water for settler agriculture when Palestinian agriculture was denied any more water was an outrage.

Water stewardship, the water crisis and the intifada

The 1980s saw a big change in Palestinian attitudes, from grudging endurance of the Occupation in the hope that it would soon end, to a resentful but hopeful activism intended to accelerate Israeli withdrawal. After more than a decade without any real sign of Israeli disengagement, Palestinians decided that it was time for more coordinated and resolute action. This was not purely a reaction to the Occupation and to the multiple humiliations and infringements of human rights the Occupation had brought. It was also a reaction to Likud policies and to the growing neglect of the economic and political needs of the Palestinian population. Israeli indifference to the rising need for water seemed part of this pattern. The *intifada* provided both hope and leadership for Palestinians. It also had an influence on Israeli public opinion, by beginning to erode support for the status quo.[32]

Israeli management of the water resources of the West Bank was an important part of this change in Palestinian attitude. Effectively, over time, water became an

Occupation issue.[33] Rising unemployment and the settlement policy intensified Palestinian awareness of the inequity of water distribution. With the regional economic downturn in the 1980s and the return of many Palestinians to the land, water emerged as a binding constraint to agricultural growth. Palestinians became aware that their water use was rigidly and sometimes violently constrained, while settlements enjoyed abundant water, and even swimming pools. By 1990, the Civil Administration was reporting that while West Bank Palestinians were consuming 119 m^3 of water per capita each year, settlers were consuming almost three times that amount.[34]

This emerging understanding amongst Palestinians in the West Bank joined a growing concern in Israel about the management of all the water resources to which Israel had access. In 1990, the Israeli Comptroller reported: 'the [1990] water crisis is not the result of natural factors but of actions of man.'[35] According to the Comptroller, the crisis was caused principally by uncontrolled exploitation influenced by Israel's agricultural lobby.

The Comptroller reported that the level to groundwater in the Western Aquifer had dropped 'during the period beginning in the early 1970s to 1990s by about 4 metres – each metre is equal to approximately 100 million cubic metres'. Not only was this overabstraction unsustainable but, according to the Comptroller, it risked destroying the aquifer altogether as depletion brought the water level to approach a 'red line' where saline water would mix with fresh water. Decades of overuse coupled with a three-year drought had led to a cumulative overdraft of 1.6 billion cubic metres, equivalent to more than Israel's water use for an entire year.[36] In addition, because the stocks of water stored in the aquifer were depleted, there were scant reserves that would help weather a dry year, which is one of the main advantages of groundwater in a dry climate. As a consequence, every dry year now brought a crisis. In fact, the three recent dry years – 1979, 1986 and 1990 – had been years of serious shortage. The worst was 1990, as storage was exhausted and the risk of salinization from overpumping was high.[37]

The Comptroller provided independent confirmation that many settlements had been exceeding their water quota (see the section *Water supply to settlements* earlier), thereby contributing to the unsustainable overdraft of the aquifer. In the drought year of 1986, settlements in the Jordan Valley had exceeded their quotas by over one-third (36 per cent) and settlements in the southern district of the West Bank had overdrawn by almost half (45 per cent). Taken altogether, Israeli settlements had exceeded their allocations in the Eastern Aquifer by nearly 10 million cubic metres in that year.

At the same time, the Comptroller reported, sewage and pesticides were polluting the environment with risk to the quality of aquifer water. With high levels of water use in the settlements came high levels of wastewater. Without treatment facilities, sewage was discharged directly into the environment, typically into wadis where it ran down and polluted downstream areas and infiltrated into groundwater. Settlements polluting the Western Aquifer included Qalqilya and Kfar Saba, and Tsofin and Alfei Menashe along the western ridge. In addition, Palestinian towns developed piped water systems under the guidance of the

Occupier but there was almost no attention paid to the accompanying sewage collection, treatment and disposal systems.[38]

From the early 1990s, Israeli water policy changed, partly as a result of the Comptroller's critique but largely because politicians and society at large understood that the situation was unsustainable. Israel's Ministry of Agriculture acted decisively, making drastic cuts to agricultural allocations and introducing deep structural changes in water resources management. The situation eased, helped along by the abundant rains of 1991–2. This would have a beneficial effect on the Mountain Aquifers and went some way towards restoring Israel's 'stewardship role' of the resources which it controlled. However, it did not bring any greater fairness to the Palestinians or any easing of the restrictions on Palestinian water development or use.[39]

The Jordan Valley, 1967–93

After 1967, Israel successfully used its dominance to rewrite the Johnston Plan in its own favour, effectively frustrating Jordan's attempts to develop its own allocations of Yarmouk and Jordan water. Syria, too, proceeded with the development of the Yarmouk quite outside anything foreseen in the Johnston Plan. One loser was certainly Jordan, which was continually stymied in its efforts to get storage of the Yarmouk winter flood flows or access to water from the main Jordan River. The Palestinians lost too, elided from the story, with hopes of their allocation under Johnston first casuistically advanced by Israel and then forgotten altogether.

New realities on the Jordan

The story of the Jordan River in the period between the Six-Day War and Oslo was driven by new realities. First and foremost amongst these realities was Israeli military dominance, and an acceptance in the Arab world that Israel could not be defeated by military means. This dominance was reinforced by the strengthening identity of Israeli and American policies and the growing cooperation between the two countries.

Second was the territorial reconfiguration that the war had brought about. Israel now controlled not only the West Bank aquifers but also the Golan Heights, which gave control of most of the Upper Jordan, as well as a longer stretch of the north bank of the Yarmouk. It was now Israel, not Syria, that the Jordanians found opposite to them at Adasiya, the proposed site for the offtake for the canal that was to irrigate Jordan's East Bank, the East Ghor. Third, the Jordan River valley was now effectively the frontier between Israel and Jordan, and both sides saw the valley not only in economic terms but also as a strategic zone where a combination of development, population and military bulwarks were needed to strengthen national security.

In practical terms, there were immediate effects as the Arab riparians struggled to come to terms with the outcome of the Six-Day War. The Arab Plan to divert the upper tributaries of the Jordan (Chapter 5) came to an abrupt halt. In November 1967, both Syria and Lebanon suspended their diversion projects. Jordan still wished to develop the Jordan Valley fully but its concerns were now limited to the East Bank. After 1967, interest in developing the western side for the benefit of the Palestinians or in recognizing any rights of the West Bank Palestinians to Jordan River water faded from political considerations. It was now Jordan and Israel that were to tussle directly for their own reshaped national interests. If there was any memory at all of Johnston's proposals for refugee resettlement in the basin, this was folded into Jordan's desire to settle the Jordan Valley with as many people as possible. That some of these would be Palestinians was a secondary consideration.

Jordan Valley development

In the years immediately after 1967, Palestinian resistance to Israeli occupation provoked conflict that impeded development on the Jordanian side of the river. Immediately after the occupation, Fatah and others began resistance both through violent attacks and by civil disobedience. Israel reacted decisively, deporting over a thousand Palestinians from the West Bank, eliminating Fatah cells and demolishing homes. By 1968, Israel had effectively crushed Palestinian resistance in the West Bank – and by 1970 in Gaza, too.

The PLO decamped to Jordan, which it used as a base for many attacks on Israeli targets. In the summer of 1969, *fedayeen* attacked new Israeli settlements in the Jordan Valley. The *fedayeen* also blew up the old Rutenberg turbine house at the confluence of the Yarmouk and the Jordan, disturbing the flow of Yarmouk water to Israel for three weeks. Israel responded robustly, attacking Jordan in the valley and moving armour up the hills towards Amman. Some 55,000 Jordanians fled. Between 1968 and 1970 Israel attacked Jordan's East Ghor canal project eight times, leading even a complaisant State Department to 'weakly question'[40] whether a US-financed East Ghor canal was an appropriate target for armaments provided and financed by the United States. Under these circumstances, Jordanian plans to extend the East Ghor canal had to be shelved. It was not until King Hussein expelled the PLO to Lebanon in 1970 that the setting became calm enough to begin planning for further development of the valley on the Jordanian side. After 1971, however, any idea of development in the Jordan Valley for Palestinian refugees was downplayed and progressively faded from discourse.

With the PLO removed, Jordan was able to resume planning for development of the valley, and the 1970s saw the extension and expansion of its Jordan Valley scheme on the East Bank.[41] In 1972, King Hussein appointed his brother, Crown Prince Hassan, to take charge of the rehabilitation and development scheme. In 1973 the Jordan Valley Commission, which was to become the Jordan Valley Authority in 1977, was established to plan, implement and subsequently manage development projects. The King Talal Dam was constructed on the Zarqa tributary, which rises near Amman and lies entirely within Jordanian territory.[42] The dam was completed in 1977, and an 18-kilometre extension of the East Ghor canal was completed the following year, 1978.

The Jordan Valley Authority (JVA) transformed the landscape with the introduction of high-technology irrigated agriculture for the market together with village infrastructure and social services. It was a model of what might have been a comprehensive and integrated resettlement project for Palestinian refugees. This programme was reputed to be one of the most expensive per capita development projects in the world – 'gold plated', one World Bank official said.[43] The investments allowed Jordan to settle 100,000 people in the valley, giving a significant boost to the Jordanian economy, providing employment – and setting up a human shield against Israeli incursions.

The original intention of the scheme had been the settlement of Palestinian refugees either of 1948 or of 1967, creating 'a community of owner-operators, self-supporting and productive'. However, most of the land was, in fact, assigned by the Jordanian government to large owners, who were often absentees. 'The main beneficiaries were Jordanian big-wigs, government officials and merchants, often living in Amman. In 1974, 55 per cent of the owners of plots on the scheme were living outside the Jordan Valley.'[44]

Although few landless Palestinian refugees acquired ownership of the new farms, many found work there as labourers or sharecroppers. Later most of the farms were leased by their owners – 61 per cent of the total units in the Jordan Valley were let in this way in 1994. Many Palestinians acquired these leases and developed high-value greenhouse agriculture. Their experience in modern irrigated agriculture helped develop the high-value horticulture that characterizes the valley today. One Jordanian witness commented: 'Palestinians had agriculture experience and were cultivating since a long time. It was Palestinians who brought for the first time a *bait al plastic* (plastic house) in the Ghor.'[45]

Development on the Yarmouk 1: The Maqarin Dam

There still remained the question of regulating the Yarmouk and capturing the winter flood flows for the Jordan Valley scheme (see Chapter 5). Despite its 'entitlement' under the Johnston Plan to all the residual of the Yarmouk, Jordan was constrained on two sides. On one side, Syria was developing infrastructure upstream which would reduce Yarmouk flows. On the other, Israel was now a dominant and assertive riparian, benefiting from the water that Jordan could not take and insisting vigorously on its 'rights'.

These constraints became clear in 1974 when Jordan proposed to build a storage dam at Maqarin, the project that Mills Bunger had identified as long ago as 1952 and which was specifically written into the Johnston Plan (see Chapter 5). The Maqarin Dam proposal stemmed from the fact that although the Johnston Plan had allocated the residual of Yarmouk waters to Jordan, storage was necessary to enable Jordan to hold over the bulk of the winter floodwaters to the summer when the water would be needed. As long as there was no storage, Jordan was unable to use all the floodwaters – in the meantime, the beneficiary of this was Israel which had built the Beit Shen pipeline from the Yarmouk to Tiberias in the late 1950s on US finance and was pumping the excess Yarmouk winter floodwater to the NWC. In the 1970s, Israel was helping itself to 60–70 million cubic metres of Yarmouk winter floodwater in this way, far more than the 25 million cubic metres provided for in the Johnston Plan.[46] At the same time, once Syria had abandoned its nugatory attempts to divert the Jordan headwaters, it turned its attention towards development of the Yarmouk and, from 1970, began the construction of many small dams upstream. Jordan's 1974 plan for Maqarin thus competed with both Israeli and Syrian vested interests and it gained little support or cooperation from these rival states.

One problem was that the 1978 Harza feasibility study proposed a storage dam larger than that foreseen in the Johnston Plan – or, indeed, in Bunger's initial proposal.[47] The new proposal was for a 178-metre rock-filled dam to hold 486 million cubic metres – together with a low (5 metre) weir to divert the water at the East Ghor canal intake at Adasiya. The total cost of the project was estimated at $1.13 billion, including $642 million for the dam structure.

Despite Syria's initial opposition, political events in the region induced a change in attitude. Put out by Egypt's breaking of the Arab ranks to make a separate peace with Israel, Syria was seeking closer ties with Jordan, and the Maqarin Dam provided a practical field for political cooperation. In 1978, Jordan and Syria signed a Maqarin Dam agreement and by 1980 financing had been mobilized.

However, Israel again raised 'concerns' as it had about earlier versions of the Maqarin project. These concerns included water shares – with Israel now claiming 40 million cubic metres as its share of the Yarmouk, against the 25 million cubic metres in the 'US version' of Johnston (see Chapter 5), and also hydroelectricity rights. This latter claim was greeted with general astonishment, even by the Americans. Israel again asserted, as it had in its opposition to the Bunger plan in 1953, that it was the sovereign successor to the Palestine Electricity Corporation and the Rutenberg Concession (see Chapter 4) and thus had the exclusive right to exploit the Yarmouk for hydroelectricity. The matter was referred to the old Mandatory power, Britain, which replied vaguely. Israel also raised 'environmental concerns' about the ecological impact of the dam on the lower Jordan and on the Dead Sea. These concerns were widely regarded as disingenuous. They had, nonetheless, to be taken seriously as Israel was by now the dominant power in the region and was quite ready to back up its claims with force.

Perhaps most oddly in the light of subsequent events, Israel insisted that provision must also be made for West Bank water needs. The Israeli government became strident on this issue of water allocations to the West Bank, writing officially that 'the water issue allocations for both the Yarmouk Triangle and the West Bank are of such pressing importance that they could not be deferred'. The Carter White House saw that heads needed to be knocked together and despatched Philip Habib as special ambassador to sort out the problem. In May 1980, Ambassador Habib met Menachem Begin and King Hussein to try to thrash out water shares – both the Yarmouk Triangle question and the issue of Yarmouk water for the West Bank.

The issue of water for the Yarmouk Triangle was resolved by an agreement that 25 million cubic metres of Yarmouk water would be allocated to Israel in summer as provided for in the Johnston Plan. The issue of water for the West Bank proved less tractable. Habib reported that 'without an agreement on West Bank water, Israel was unwilling to accept the Maqarin Dam'. He went on to record Israel's argument that West Bank Palestinians were entitled not only to the 100 million cubic metres allocated to Jordan for this purpose in the Johnston Plan but also to an extra 40 million cubic metres, a quantity based apparently on an old Yugoslav report on Maqarin (see Chapter 5). According to Sosland, Begin's reasoning was that Israel would provide for West Bank settlements from its own resources but could not accept responsibility for the water needs of the Palestinians. This approach could, of course, be interpreted either as a far-sighted planning for the water needs of a future Palestinian state – or as an attempt to secure yet more Jordan water for Israel itself. In any case, it was at the least disingenuous as Israeli settlers were already exploiting West Bank water resources and there was no reason to believe that any further access to regional water was intended to benefit the Palestinians of the Occupied Territories.[48]

Jordan refused to reopen what it saw as the Johnston Plan allocations. It also argued that it had never received the 100 million cubic metres from the Upper Jordan which was allocated to it under the Johnston Plan (see the table *Allocations in the Johnston Plan* in Chapter 5). As for the allocation to the West Bank, Jordan washed its hands of any responsibility, refusing to become a negotiator for West Bank interests when the West Bank was under illegal occupation. This approach could also be seen as disingenuous in that it avoided reducing the water available for Jordan itself by an allocation to the West Bank. Jordan also considered that it had absorbed large numbers of Palestinian refugees from the West Bank and that therefore any allocation previously considered for the West Bank should be diverted to its scheme east of the river.

Of course, the principal losers in this tussle were the West Bank Palestinians, whose faint claims to any water from the Jordan or the Yarmouk were effectively extinguished at this time. Subsequent events confirmed that whoever got extra out of these deals over the Jordan basin waters, nobody had the slightest interest in giving up any of it to the West Bank Palestinians.

In the event, Syria withdrew its support for the Maqarin Dam. Although the project was beneficial to Syria, providing both hydropower and irrigation water, Syria's primary motivation had been to improve relations with Jordan in order to get King Hussein to join a new anti-Israel coalition, the Tripoli bloc. When King Hussein refused to join, relations deteriorated and by 1981 Syria no longer supported the project. USAID, which had been putting together the financing, concluded that 'it is not fruitful to pursue [the Maqarin] project'.[49]

The Yarmouk forum

With the Maqarin Dam project thus shelved, Jordan and Israel settled down to a period of public sabre rattling and informal cooperation over management of the Yarmouk. Tensions persisted and were very publicly played out, with troops mobilized on either bank on occasions in 1979, 1986 and 1987. Yet, from July 1979, the two sides tacitly began a period of secret practical cooperation dubbed the 'Yarmouk forum' which lasted for the next fifteen years. Because the talks were often held *al fresco* around a picnic table, they received the sobriquet of 'the picnic table talks'. The achievement was considerable – to agree on flows and flow management and on an equitable summer sharing of water, and even on water loans in periods of surplus or deficit. All this worked well for Israel and for Jordan. Both states could satisfy their own interest without letting on to their own citizens or to the wider world. The interests of the Palestinians in the West Bank were completely forgotten, apparently no longer of concern or even of relevance.

Development on the Yarmouk 2: The Unity or al Wehda Dam

The decade 1979–90 saw increasing Syrian abstractions upstream on the Yarmouk. A Syrian master plan of 1981 proposed developments that would by 1990 divert and use nearly three-quarters of the water available in the Syrian part of the basin – 250 million cubic metres from the total 346 million cubic metres. Implementation proceeded rapidly and by 1988, Syria was already abstracting 172 million cubic metres (see the table *Syrian depletion of the Yarmouk*), and the stream flow at Adasiya that remained for Jordan and Israel had dropped by more than one-third (37 per cent) from its 1947 level.[50]

Jordan's development ambitions were once again caught between Syrian and Israeli interests – but now the quantum of water under discussion was shrinking fast. Jordan moved to meet this new challenge by proposing a new, smaller dam project very favourable to Syria. To secure Yarmouk water before Syrian development was complete, Jordan entered into a treaty with Syria in September 1987 for a Unity Dam (*al Wehda* in Arabic). This treaty provided considerable benefits to Syria. The 100-metre dam was to be a dual-purpose structure – irrigation water and hydropower. Syria was to get 75 per cent of the hydropower together with 140 million cubic metres of water, considerably more than the 90 million cubic metres allocated to it in the Johnston Plan. Jordan was to pay all the capital and operating and maintenance costs. In addition, Syria was to be able to build twenty-four more small dams upstream.

The agreement seemed to promise peaceful cooperation and the United States supported it, working with the World Bank to put together a $440 million financing package. The project looked set to go ahead – and then Israel once again raised objections. The US secretary of state James Baker sent out a senior official,

Table 6.4 Syrian Depletion of the Yarmouk (million m³ annually)

	Syrian abstractions	Stream flow at Adasiya (for Jordan and Israel)
Pre-1947	-	454
1954	20	434
1984–8	172	282

Source: Sosland 2007: 102.

Richard Armitage, who shuttled back and forth between the capitals for an entire year, from September 1989 to August 1990, at the end of which Israel informed the United States and the World Bank that it needed additional 'project detail'.

Israel claimed Yarmouk winter water which it had been using but to which it had no entitlement. The particular claim was that Israel needed to be 'no worse off' as a result of the Unity Dam. This, as we have seen, represented a claim way beyond Israel's 'entitlements' under the Johnston Plan as Israel had been for years pumping 60–70 million cubic metres annually from the Yarmouk winter flood flows up to Lake Tiberias, well in excess of its 25 million cubic metres allocation under the Johnston Plan.[51] In fact, according to the Johnston Plan, all of Yarmouk winter water belonged to Jordan. The US ambassador wrote: 'the winter flow of the Yarmouk to which Israel has access and has made use of in the past is not an allocation to which it has a legal right.' Nonetheless, Israel demanded a guaranteed winter water allocation of 50–70 million cubic metres and a guaranteed 25 million cubic metres in the summer. Later the Israelis reduced their winter demand somewhat – but only to 42.5 million cubic metres.

The Americans concluded that, in fact, Israel had benefited from the status quo of a river without a dam and had little reason to make major concessions on the issue. They also recorded that Israel acknowledged 'as a point of fact that [it] controls 100 million m³ of Jordan water beyond that originally allocated to it' under the Johnston Plan. Essentially, Israel was negotiating from a position in which it was getting an extra 100 million cubic metres of Jordan water, and 60–70 million cubic metres of Yarmouk water rather than 25 million cubic metres, a total of some 150 million cubic metres beyond its Johnston Plan allocation, a sizeable share of its total annual water budget.

Yet it was not this issue that fatally undermined the project but the evolution of the political situation.[52] An increase in regional political problems began to fracture chances of consensus on the dam. Within Jordan, a new parliament was elected in 1989 with thirty-one Islamists out of a total of eighty members. Pressure not to deal with Israel mounted. At the same time, Syria and Jordan fell out over the First Iraq War in which Jordan supported Iraq, the arch-enemy of Syria. Policy in Israel changed, too, as the country prepared to receive a huge influx of new immigrants following the crumbling of the Soviet Union. Prime Minister Yitzhak Shamir began talking about the need for Greater Israel and for extra land and water resources to absorb the new arrivals. At the same time, protracted drought and resulting water shortages across the region made for scant willingness to negotiate away any water resources.

As politics changed, the United States began to abandon Johnston in pursuit of solutions more favourable to Israel. In a bizarre volte face that greatly favoured Israel, the United States performed an abrupt about-turn from its previous position that water allocations were to be determined by the Johnston Plan. This shift came at a time when Johnston solutions no longer favoured Israel and when Israel stood to gain more by its de facto control of regional water resources and by its ability to impose new facts on the ground through military might. By contrast, Jordan, which like other Arab states had never adopted the Johnston Plan, now clung to the provisions of the plan as a protection against Israeli power. But the United States did not buy this. Essentially siding with Israel, Armitage wrote derisively in February 1990: 'The Johnston Plan has become, within Arab political circles, a mindless incantation.' In any case, these events were on the eve of the First Gulf War in which Jordan's pro-Iraq stance led to withdrawal of American support across the board.

The United States also appears to have glossed over the question of Jordan or Yarmouk water for the Palestinians in the West Bank. No party had any interest in raising it other than the Palestinians themselves, who had no seat at the table. In a weak statement, the United States sought to make clear that any Unity Dam agreement would not 'prejudge [West Bank] water issues that will need to be addressed in any overall peace settlement'.[53]

Water for people and business

Water supply services to the West Bank[54]

During the Occupation, network water supply was extended to many West Bank towns and villages for the first time. By 1993, almost all people in urban areas and about 70 per cent of the rural population had access to piped drinking water through house connections. In fact, for many West Bank Palestinians, one of the most striking memories of the Israeli Occupation was that for the first time they were connected to piped drinking water.

Initially the military and later the Civil Administration had legal responsibility for water supply, working in cooperation with the Israeli water institutions. In practice, the responsibility for providing water and sewerage services was delegated to the Palestinian municipalities and village councils in the West Bank and Gaza. Bulk water was supplied by the West Bank Water Department (WBWD). Originally established under the Natural Resource Authority of Jordan, the WBWD was taken over in 1967 by the Israeli military and later transferred to the Civil Administration. Under Israeli Army officers and with Palestinian technical staff, the WBWD was responsible for bulk water distribution, for connections to the Israeli (Mekorot) system, for projects outside of municipal jurisdictions and for provision of assistance to municipalities. However, it had little power. It had no decision-making abilities and did not participate in water planning. Effectively it was there to execute the water plans devised by the Israelis. Although the WBWD made a material contribution to the improvement of conditions for West Bank Palestinians, it received little thanks. In fact, as the Occupation continued, the WBWD became for Palestinians both a symbol and an instrument of direct Israeli control over Palestinian water resources and their use.

Urban water supply

Urban water suppliers Two large conurbations were served by independently constituted water utilities. In Ramallah and its environs, the *Jerusalem Water Undertaking*, which had been set up under Jordanian rule, supplied water to the municipalities of Ramallah, al Bireh and neighbouring villages, as well as to a large part of East Jerusalem; the *Bethlehem Water Authority* provided water to Bethlehem, Beit Jala and neighbouring villages. Most other towns delivered water supply services through their municipal water department, which formed an integral part of the municipality administration. The two largest of these were the *Nablus Municipality Water Department*, supplying water to Nablus and neighbouring villages and refugee camps, and the *Hebron Municipality Water Department*, providing water to Hebron and also to nearby villages and refugee camps.

Many water departments and utilities had their own wells but as demand rose, these wells proved inadequate and suppliers had to buy water from Mekorot, from the Israeli grid. Residents of the refugee camps usually received their water from wells administered by UNRWA.

In addition to the water utilities, municipal departments and the Civil Administration (and, in rural areas, village councils – see later, *Rural water supply*), several Palestinian non-government organizations (NGOs) were involved in executing water supply and sewerage projects. They included the Palestinian Hydrology Group, the Land and Water Institute and the Agricultural Engineers Association.[55] Many of these organizations had international support – as was the case with Oxfam in the Zababdeh project described later. There were also a number of engineering firms dealing with water projects. Water quality analysis was carried out at the Universities of Bir Zeit and Al-Najah.

Urban water supply While most of the urban population had access to piped drinking water, the service levels were quite low. By the 1990s, domestic water supplied (including network leakage and unaccounted-for water) in the West Bank and Gaza was about 93 litres per capita per day (lcd), compared to 142 lcd in Jordan and 280 lcd in Israel (see the table *Water Use in the Occupied Territories* earlier in this chapter). However, the average water actually received at the tap by consumers was little more than half the water theoretically supplied – about 50 litres per capita per day (see the table *West Bank Urban Water Supply in 1993*).

The main problem – and what accounted for the huge difference between raw water supplied and water actually delivered to people's homes – was the massive losses in the distribution systems – up to 50 per cent or more in the worst cases. Many supply mains and distribution lines needed to be repaired or replaced to reduce the appalling level of leakages. Distribution networks also needed to be repaired as systems had been extended in a random manner, connecting groups of houses where needed, but often without regard to a rational plan. Other problems included the actual shortages of raw water which most municipalities faced. Wells, the main sources of water, needed rehabilitation. In many towns, supply was intermittent, sometimes only for a few hours once or twice a week, often rotated between districts on a schedule. With poorly maintained networks and intermittent supply, water quality suffered.[56]

Issues of costs and finances One classic challenge for the water service providers was how to generate enough revenue to cover costs. In fact, during the Occupation, most West Bank suppliers did fairly well in covering their recurrent costs of operation and maintenance, but few generated enough revenue from tariffs to cover investment spending (see the table later, *Income Generation, Capital Investment and Operation and Maintenance Costs*). In some cases, tariffs were set too low to cover costs and the shortfall was made worse by high levels of non-payment of bills. Thus, some municipalities were running their water supply operations at a deficit. For example, the average rate for water paid by consumers in Nablus in 1990 was US$0.68 per cubic metre. This covered only about 40 per cent of the operation and maintenance cost of supplying water. Several municipalities were, however, doing better. In and around Ramallah, consumers paid their supplier, the Jerusalem Water Undertaking, much more than in Nablus – an average of twice as much, US$1.13 per cubic metre. These higher tariffs covered the operation and maintenance cost of delivered water with a healthy margin of more than 50 per cent. Generally, problems grew worse during the *intifada*. Cost recovery deteriorated, with high levels of non-payment of bills in some towns – up to 60 per cent in Bethlehem, for example.[57]

Water charges differed substantially from municipality to municipality. One factor in this was that there was a considerable difference in the cost of water in different localities. The fragmented nature of water supply and variations in the topography of both the supply locations and the demand centres, as well as the physical conditions of the distribution networks, all contributed to these differences. The biggest difference was between towns that could supply their needs from their own wells and those that were obliged to buy in water from Mekorot.

The weak finances of the service providers made it impossible for them to raise market finance, and public finance was limited – contributions from the Civil Administration for water investments were small. Most investments were, in fact, financed by donors and NGOs.

Table 6.5 West Bank Urban Water Supply in 1993

Municipality	Population served	Average water supply (m³/day)	Leakage (%)	Water actually supplied per consumer (l/cap/day)	Water demand estimated by municipality (l/cap/day)
Jerusalem/ Ramallah	179,000	12,590	26	52	
Nablus	140,000	15,840	50	57	
Hebron	220,000	12,000	60	44	
Refugee camps	55,000	[2,000]	[50?]	[18]	
Tulkarm	60,000	6,000 + 90 in summer	40	60	
Bethlehem	80,000	5,880 + 6,000 m³ from Mekorot in summer	45	40	140

Source: World Bank 1993.

Table 6.6 Income Generation, Capital Investment, and Operation and Maintenance Costs by Municipalities in the West Bank and Gaza Strip Potable Water and Sanitation, 1987–8 (in 1,000 NIS)

				Potable water		Revenue as percentage of	
Area	Income generated	O&M cost	Capital investment	Total expenditure		Current O&M cost	Total expenditure
West Bank	8,295	8,660	2,281	10,941		96%	76%
Gaza Strip	4,330	2,662	1,237	3,899		163%	111%
Total	12,625	11,322	3,518	14,840		-	-
			Sanitation				
West Bank	614	1,631	574	2,204		38%	28%
Gaza Strip	321	149	518	668		215%	48%
Total	935	1,780	1,092	2,872		-	-

Source: World Bank 1993, based on data derived from the government of Israel. Judea, Samaria and Gaza Area Statistics, Vol. XVIII, No. 2, Jerusalem: Central Bureau of Statistics; 1988, pp. 196–222; and Haddad, M. Potable Water and Sanitation in the West Bank and Gaza Strip. Report Prepared for Policy Research Incorporated, Clarksville, MD; 1992.

Institutional issues The institutional capacity of the municipal water departments and water companies was generally very weak. These weaknesses were in part due to the structure of the sector – the model of water departments embedded in municipalities can weaken incentives for efficiency and financial performance, and the small size of the typical West Bank department left no scope for economies of scale. At least 20,000 house connections are typically required for a water supplier to be viable and efficient, but only a handful of towns in the West Bank were of this size – Ramallah, Nablus and Hebron.[58]

The sector was fragmented and lacked policy guidance and planning and coordination functions. With no agency to help coordinate plans for water supply, each town or village was basically left to find its own solutions – in terms of water resources, technology, business planning, etc. There was no mechanism for planning across the West Bank as a whole that could, for example, have developed a regional approach to bulk water supply or have promoted economies of scale by encouraging pooling of resources and joined-up infrastructure.

There was also a shortage of professional and technical skills. It was reported that in 1993 there were 'only six to eight water supply and sanitary engineers with a BS degree, or higher in the West Bank and Gaza' (World Bank 1993). With such limited professional resources, the municipalities and utilities had extreme difficulty designing, implementing and operating water supply and sewerage projects. Capacity in management and in accounting and financial management was also said to be weak. Palestinian universities were not at this time offering courses in water supply and sanitation.

Regulatory constraints The most important regulatory constraint was the control of the volume of bulk water available to the Palestinians. Simple lack of enough water was a major impediment to adequate water supply to towns. This control was seen as particularly unfair by the Palestinians who could not fail to see the high levels of use of water by Israelis and settlers (see the table *Water Use in the Occupied Territories*). Nor could the Palestinians be unaware of the rising levels of abstractions from the Mountain Aquifers beyond the Green Line.

Regulatory constraints also reduced investment efficiency. The bureaucratic constraints cited by the Palestinian utilities include delays – or simply no response – in the approval of urgently needed water supply and sewerage projects. Lack of access to essential water data also constrained planning and management of water supply infrastructure.[59]

Perhaps most importantly, the growing fragmentation of the West Bank, divided by settlements, roads and military areas, made the development of a rational water supply grid – along the lines of that in Israel – impossible. Not only was water scarce and constrained, but the Palestinians also did not have the opportunity to convey water between points of supply and demand in a rational and economically efficient manner. Every town, every village, was obliged to be its own little water supply area – unless it was hooked up to the Mekorot grid.

Water sources and purchases from Mekorot The lack of joined-up infrastructure and the paucity of the water resources permitted to the Palestinians led to another burning issue. Where local resources were inadequate, recourse had to be had to purchase from Mekorot – politically unpalatable, expensive and, worst of all, essentially seen by Palestinians as their buying back their own water and becoming dependent on the occupier. Several municipal water suppliers were obliged to purchase a large percentage of their water from Mekorot at a price (US$0.65 per cubic metre) almost double what they would pay for water from local wells.[60] And the share of water purchased rose as demand grew: the largest West Bank supplier – the Jerusalem Water Undertaking (JWU) – was purchasing only 10 per cent of its water in 1974. By 1990 the JWU was purchasing two-thirds of its water.

Sanitation and wastewater Most sanitation facilities for West Bank Palestinians were at the household level. Septic tanks were typically used, although some municipalities – Bethlehem, for example – were investing in sewage collection systems. But even where sewage was collected, there was essentially no satisfactory treatment system either in the Palestinian towns or in the Israeli settlements.[61] What wastewater was collected was generally being discharged by both municipalities and settlements directly into seasonal streams or wadis. According to the Israeli State Comptroller in a 1987 report, the limited wastewater treatment capacity that existed 'appear[ed] to be poorly designed and operated'. Pollution was already creating serious problems, and farmers were using untreated wastewater to irrigate their fields.

Policy conclusion The policy conclusion from a World Bank review in 1993 was that autonomous, commercialized utilities should be established for both water supply and sanitation. The review, conducted in preparation for the Oslo negotiations, found that the sector 'suffered from a general institutional weakness . . . exacerbated by the limited access to funds to finance improvements and rehabilitation works'. The recommendation was for 'the establishment of autonomous water and wastewater utilities with clear commercial and service objectives . . . . The large rehabilitation programme which was needed requires an appropriate institutional structure for the water agencies and agreements on the basic principles for project selection, preparation and implementation.'[62]

Rural water supply

In the rural areas of the West Bank, village councils were usually the water suppliers. Many villages received piped water for the first time under the Occupation and by 1993 half of the rural communities by number – and about two-thirds of rural households in total – had access to piped water. During the 1970s, for example, the Palestinian village of Zababdeh got its first-ever water network and running water piped right into people's homes. The network was established by Oxfam in 1979.

> I remember those days. I was ten years. I remember when they started to put the pipes the first time, in Zababdeh . . . . I remember . . . . I was a little boy . . . . I was standing with them, [and they were] digging beside the street.[63]

Julia Templin, the researcher who collected many such stories, continues:

> But the supply of water to Zababdeh was not completely reliable. [Villagers]
> remembered 1985 and 1986 to be especially dry years, so most of the water
> from the well was used by the Israelis [settlements and a military camp] before it
> could come to Zababdeh . . . the Israelis also often cut water to the village when
> people had not paid for it . . . and during the years of the first *intifada*, from 1987
> until 1993, the water to the village was often cut for days or weeks. When water
> to the village was cut, people relied on their backup cisterns that used to be their
> primary source of water. These dried up during the hot Palestine summers, at
> which time Zababdeh's inhabitants had to purchase the contaminated but very
> expensive water brought to the village in water tankers.

Other villages and households still depended on unprotected water sources.[64]
Reports at the time cited problems of water quality and contamination: septic
tanks, located above the spring source of water supply, lack of chlorination, water
contaminated through fluctuating pressure in the distribution pipes or during
transport of water from standpipes to houses. The high rate of dysentery – an
incidence of 246/100,000 was reported for the West Bank in 1991 – illustrated
some likely problems arising from poor water quality.

An emerging environmental crisis

There is a price to be paid for everything and the price for Israel's rapid development
and use, even overuse, of the entire water resource of the territory defined by
Mandate Palestine was a range of environmental impacts that had a severe effect
on the ecology and the human environment. In addition to the overpumping of the
aquifers and the consequent risks of depletion, salination and seawater intrusion,
these effects were felt in the natural watercourses that arose largely in the West
Bank and ran west into the coastal plain and east into the Jordan Valley. Problems
also arose in the wider Jordan basin system. There were particular consequences
of the draining of wetlands, notably the Huleh valley.

Streams and the environment

In the rocky valleys that ran west and east from the highlands, the streamflow,
which used to course down after the rains, began to dwindle to negligible levels
as Israel progressively developed the groundwater and surface water. The natural
ecosystems of these seasonally flowing streams are, by their intermittent wet/dry
character, already under considerable stress. These vulnerable systems largely
disappeared in Israel in the 1950s and 1960s as flows began to be diverted for
irrigation. The dry channels were filled with untreated municipal sewage and
household and industrial refuse. Less water entered the system anyway as Israel's

aggressive pumping from the upstream Mountain Aquifer dried up springs and depleted the headwaters. The Yarkon River, for example, which flows through Tel Aviv, shrank to just 2 per cent of its natural flow.

Where water did flow or ponded, it was contaminated by nutrients and bacteria. The vegetation either disappeared or took on a new character adapted to the polluted environment. Streams like the Kishon and the Na'aman that flowed through industrial zones carried a toxic cocktail of untreated factory effluents. Often more than half of this melange of water-borne contaminants percolated to the water table and polluted the aquifer.

As often with environmental deterioration, few were aware of the degradation of the riverine environment until it was well advanced. Only extremes made people sit up and take notice – for example, the death of Australian athletes who fell into the Yarkon during the Maccabiah Games in 1997, and cancer amongst veterans who had dived years earlier at the mouth of the heavily polluted Kishon River. And corrective action took much longer to emerge.[65]

Wastewater treatment and irrigation

As early as the 1960s, Israel began to reuse wastewater in agriculture and from the 1980s this took off on a massive scale, so that today more than 95 per cent of wastewater is treated and reused. Treated wastewater now accounts for two-thirds of the water used in agriculture. Initially the quality was poor as treatment was only at the primary level and the water contained a large range of biological and chemical contaminants. As a result, boron from laundry detergents and industrial solvents entered the soil profile and passed from there to aquifers and water bodies. Streams and groundwater were contaminated for years, and wells were closed when high levels of nitrates were discovered. Over time, increasing levels of salt remained in the soil – a threat to soil health and agricultural production. Progressively, wastewater treatment improved and the risks diminished. Yet, doubts remain. The distinguished Israeli scholar, Alon Tal, reflects that 'it is not clear whether this is a Faustian deal that will be paid for by future generations'.[66]

The draining of the Huleh wetlands

As we saw in Chapter 5, by 1958 the pioneering settlers had drained the entire Huleh valley, both the 14-square kilometre lake and the extensive wetlands that spread out alongside. Agriculture grew apace – but then declined as the environmental consequences of draining these peatlands quickly emerged. In the centre and south of the valley the peat soils, exposed to air for the first time, degraded. Beneath the surface, the peat caught fire and great caverns formed. The soils turned to black infertile dust. By the end of the last century, the area was largely abandoned.

A further negative side effect of the draining of the wetlands was the deterioration of water quality in Lake Tiberias and the Jordan River. The Upper Jordan was canalized through the valley and therefore bore directly to Tiberias all the impurities and contaminants that had previously been absorbed within the wetlands.[67]

The Jordan River system[68]

As a result of developments since Israel's independence – and particularly since the 1960s – all three of the principal components of the Jordan River system have suffered extreme environmental decline. The three components are connected: Lake Tiberias in the north is connected through the lower Jordan River with the Dead Sea in the south.

Israel pumps out virtually all of the water that flows into Lake Tiberias to feed its National Water Carrier (NWC) for transit over the length of the country as far as the Negev desert. The only exception is the water of the saline springs which are diverted around the lake and discharged into the lower Jordan River. In recent years, heavy pumping combined with dry winters that reduced the inflow caused the lake water level to drop. It fell by about 27 metres between 1960 and 2013. This brought the water level close to a danger point, the Red Line, below which saline springs beneath the surface would begin to mix with freshwater, causing irreversible damage.

Water flows from Tiberias to the lower Jordan are controlled by the Degania dam, originally built by Rutenberg in the 1930s to regulate flows to the hydroelectric scheme at the confluence with the Yarmouk (see Chapter 4). Until the mid-1960s, the flow of the Jordan River between Tiberias and the Dead Sea averaged 1.5 billion cubic metres a year, most of which ended up in the sink that is the Dead Sea. From that time, the three lower riparians – Israel, Jordan and Syria – have appropriated almost the entire flow, both of the main river and of the tributaries and side wadis. For many years, all the rainfall and run-off entering Tiberias has been pumped out to the NWC.[69] At the same time, virtually all the flows of the Yarmouk, the Zarqa and the smaller side wadis are diverted by Syria and Jordan for irrigation and water supply, reducing the flows in the lower Jordan River to an average of 10 million cubic metres a year. As a result there remains only a tiny fraction of the previous flows – less than 1 per cent – to support the riverine ecology and to sustain the extraordinary biophysical environment of the Dead Sea.

The cultural and religious values of this world-famous river have been severed. The flora and fauna have been damaged and the role of the valley as one of the world's most important crossroads for migratory birds has been devastated. Virtually no water reaches the Dead Sea today except for some low-grade wastewater and agricultural drainage water. The Dead Sea has been a resort and health spa since biblical times and the source of a wide range of unique, specialized and exotic products. Today, the level of the sea is dropping by about one metre a year, and many installations built for access are now stranded on a constantly receding shore.

*   *   *

There is said to be an arc in a modern economy and society of about three decades from the first depredations on the environment to the beginning of effective remedial and conservation action. Plainly, many negative effects are irreversible, but palliative measures can be applied, and these have begun in recent years. Israel is now wealthy enough to be able to afford the high cost of these measures, and some rather limited progress is being made. This is described in our companion volume, where we also look at the transboundary environmental issues – of how Palestinian actions affect the environment in Israel and vice versa. And we also look at how these issues, and others like climate change, are a reminder to Israelis and Palestinians that they share a common home, a reminder that can give impetus to cooperation on environment and on water.

Attitudes and sense of loss

> My grandmother like Jewish so much. You know, because Israel, they came here, they make everything for Palestine, but especially for Zababdeh. They give electricity, they give it water, they kill the mosquitoes, she said that. When they came here, the life became better.[70]

The first twenty years after 1967 proved something of a boom time for much of the West Bank population. Many traders and businessmen profited from the new and rich markets. Many workers benefited from employment opportunities. A measure of modernization occurred. As we have seen, safe piped water came to many for the first time.

Did these new amenities and advances in prosperity make Palestinians accepting of or comfortable with, the Israeli Occupation? Was it akin to a return to the acceptance of foreign overlordship that most Arab subjects of the Ottoman Empire had given? Was there somehow a consent to be governed by an alien power in return for a modicum of comfort and prosperity? Of course, we have no clear or democratic answer to the question as the people were never consulted, just as they had never been consulted by the Ottomans or by the British.[71] But there is, in fact, no evidence that there was any current of opinion that would have opted for life under Israeli rule. There is no testament to a choice to trade subjugation and humiliation and loss of civic and human rights for material well-being. In fact, quite the opposite – the *intifada* is testament to that.[72]

Overall, the picture is a mixed one – of resistance, survival and adaptation. Many West Bankers, both professionals and workers, voted with their feet, leaving for a new life in the Gulf or elsewhere. Those who stayed began to proclaim their love of liberty through the largely non-violent *intifada*.

Any positive feelings about the Israeli Occupation did not last, of course. Julia Templin, whose excellent thesis provided the grandmother's thoughts cited earlier, quotes another villager from rural Zababdeh, who summed it up. '*Israel is a curse and a blessing in the same time, because [we are] getting better with money now, and a curse because it's an occupation.*'[73]

*   *   *

The period between the Six-Day War and Oslo brought a contradiction in water security for the Palestinians. Water services undoubtedly improved – although with scant credit to be given to the occupier – but, overall, despite the rise in living standards and the better access to domestic water supply, the era is one which consolidates and intensifies Palestinian loss. The limited access to the water of the Jordan River that the Palestinians had enjoyed before 1967 was annulled. The Palestinians' riparian status on the river and their presumed right to a share of Jordan water appeared to be slipping from their grasp. Their access to the water of the Mountain Aquifer that lay beneath their feet was strictly controlled while Israel pumped out more and more. The growing number of settlers in the West Bank enjoyed plentiful water both for domestic use and for agriculture. For the Palestinians, the only way to obtain more water was to buy it from the Israeli network, setting off a pattern of dependency that was as politically unpalatable as it was economically inefficient.

Meanwhile, the natural environment began to deteriorate, with the groundwater level dropping as the aquifers were overpumped. The dry wadis began to fill with untreated sewage and household refuse. With the massive abstractions upstream that Israel and the other riparians were making, the Jordan River was well on the way to becoming a foul drain. The Dead Sea continued to shrivel.

And at the high level of Palestinian aspiration for self-determination and control of their own land and water, the hopes in the early years after 1967 of 'land – and water – for peace' dwindled and seemed close to expiration.

But then the largely peaceful insurrection of the *Intifada* brought renewed hope and the path to Oslo. Water resources and water security were to become a key topic in the negotiations. The Palestinians hoped to secure water rights and the ability to develop water resources and services that would serve in state-building and economic development for them just as they had for Israelis. The negotiation of these aspirations and the results that followed are the subject of the next chapter.

Chapter 7

OSLO AND AFTER[1]

The decade of Oslo and what followed Oslo began with high hopes, higher perhaps in the wider world that dreamed of an equitable 'peace' than amongst Palestinians and Israelis who faced the daily issues of Occupation and the deep-seated problems that arose from 1948 and 1967. Nonetheless, there was a momentary conjuncture, a brief alignment in which Palestinian hopes for sovereignty and Israeli demands for security appeared as though they might just be reconcilable with the establishment of a Palestinian state.

Oslo was a very complicated arrangement in general and nowhere more so than in the elaborate provisions on water contained in Article 40 of the 1995 Interim Agreement. At first sight the stage seemed set for exemplary cooperation over shared water resources. But quite quickly this view dimmed.

The amount of water allocated to Palestinians at Oslo was scarcely more than they had enjoyed in 1967. The agreement formally excluded the Palestinians from the lion's share of the water beneath their feet. And it ignored the rights they claimed on the River Jordan. The way in which the Article 40 provisions for development of water and water infrastructure were carried out led to huge delays in investment and ultimately to such meagre levels of new infrastructure and services that West Bank Palestinians in 2020 had access to less groundwater than they had in 1995.

This was also a time of water crisis in the region. As resources dwindled and the population swelled, Israelis experienced a halving of their water resources per capita. However, through technology and good management they emerged with better water services and a rapidly growing economy. The Palestinians also suffered a drop in water availability per head but there was no comparable improvement in services or prosperity. Water production fell, water infrastructure remained fragmented and the environment suffered as raw sewage from Palestinian communities and Israeli settlements alike flooded the West Bank wadis.

The Palestinians concluded that Article 40 was in essence yet another instrument of Israeli control, confining them to a meagre water ration, preventing development of a water carrier that would rationalize water distribution as Israel had long since done, and blocking investment in modern and efficient water and sanitation infrastructure.

The institutional effect – or lack of it – was palpable, too. The Palestinians set up a Water Authority on best practice lines but its authority was only over scattered fragments of territory and gave no power to manage the water resource for sustainability or efficiency. The authority's standing was fatally compromised in the eyes of the population it was intended to serve by its obligation to enforce strict limits on water use and to collaborate with the Israelis in repressive action. At the same time, Palestinians saw Israel far exceeding the water ration it had agreed to, Israelis enjoying first-class water and sanitation services, and settlers in the West Bank bathing in swimming pools while West Bank schools went without water.

Article 40 on water was part of a larger agreement on a five-year transition to a Palestinian state. Yet, when the five years expired at the turn of the millennium, little had been done. The provisions of Article 40, increasingly seen as highly constricting, remained in place, as they do to this day more than a quarter of a century after Oslo.

Disappointment on the water front was paralleled by that on the political front. Ultimately, 'peace' seemed to the Palestinians to offer little more than a continuation of the status quo – no statehood, a fragmented land, and permanent occupation and settlement on most of their remaining territory. From 2003 frustration boiled over in the *al Aqsa intifada*, ruining any shreds of hope remaining from Oslo. 'Cooperation' on water lingered on for a few years, but in the end the Palestinians withdrew from that, too.

*   *   *

This chapter tells the story of the West Bank water sector in the years after Oslo when Article 40 and the institutions and practices that sprang from it governed water investment and management and determined the quality of water services to Palestinians. Our analysis is based on a large literature review and on our own personal experience and the data we gathered during our visits to the West Bank and Israel in 2008 and 2009, and again in 2016 and 2017.

The road to Oslo

The Occupied Territories at the time of Oslo[2]

You never had it so good . . . As we saw in Chapter 6, there is no doubt that there was an increase in prosperity in the West Bank during the period of the Israeli Occupation from 1967 to 1993. This is borne out not only by income data but also by figures for household goods like radios and television sets, gas cookers and refrigerators, and for car ownership. The biggest boom was in the construction sector, which contributed to improving incomes and standards of living.

However, this rise in the standard of living should not be exaggerated. Over the whole period from 1948 to 1983, the Palestinian economy had grown less fast than that of other Arab countries in the region. In 1948, GDP per capita for Palestinians had been above that of Transjordan, Syria and Lebanon. By the 1980s, Palestinians in both the West Bank and Gaza had fallen to the bottom of the list (see the table *Economic and Social Data*). In other aspects of living standards, Palestinians did

Table 7.1 Economic and Social Data for Arab Countries (1983)

	West Bank and Gaza	Jordan	Syria	Lebanon
GNP per capita in USD	$687	$1,640	$1,760	$1,010
Primary and secondary school enrolment	81%	92%	79%	82%
Life expectancy at birth	72 years	64 years	67 years	65 years
Population per hospital bed	566	1,711	2,236	260
Daily calories	2,861	2,882	3,040	3,000

Source: Sayigh 1993.

not fare badly. Life expectancy was well above that of neighbouring Arab countries, nutrition was on a par with – although no better than – countries of comparable levels of income, and provision of health services was good. School enrolment was average for the region, although surprisingly, Palestinians had fallen behind Jordan.

. . . but at what cost? With the possible exception of the more conciliatory policies practised early in the Occupation, there is no evidence that economic growth in the West Bank was an objective of Israeli policy. Rather, the improvements that took place were a by-product of a 'skewed' economic system under which the West Bank economy was partially integrated into the Israeli economy as a largely captive market for Israeli goods and as a source of cheap labour, raw materials and produce, which were welcome in the Israeli economy provided they did not compete with domestic employment or production.

The main policy influences on the economy of the Occupied Territories that produced this 'skewing' were fourfold. First, an asymmetrical trade relationship – Israel was increasingly an open economy and its exports to the Occupied Territories were unrestricted while trade in the opposite direction experienced multiple barriers. The Palestinian economy was also hobbled by the regulatory regime of multiple licensing and taxation which cumulatively increased the cost of doing business, imposed barriers to entry, and discouraged investment, longer-term planning and innovation.

A second influence was in the labour market, where the Occupied Territories benefited from access to Israel but became a pool of low-cost labour where there was little premium on skills and where changes in the political and security situation created large shifts in demand and access. By 1983 there were 87,000 Palestinian workers employed in Israel – one-third of the West Bank workforce (33 per cent) and nearly one-half of the Gaza workforce (46 per cent). Almost all of these workers were employed in casual, unskilled, even menial jobs.[3] Poignantly, half of those crossing from the West Bank into Israel to work were refugees from 1948, returning to their homeland as poorly paid migrant workers.[4] At the time of the *intifada*, from 1987, different influences began to reduce employment. In agriculture, shrinking markets and restrictions on access to land and water reduced opportunity. The decline in the tourist trade reduced employment in handicrafts. The end of Jordanian payment of civil service salaries and the replacement of striking Palestinian civil servants by Israelis reduced public sector employment.[5]

Low public spending was a third consideration, with total public spending in the Occupied Territories[6] amounting to only 24 per cent of GDP, against 37 per cent for both Israel and Egypt. The result was very low provision of public services and very little development spending – just 3.5 per cent of GDP was allocated to public investment. There was scant road building (at least for the benefit of Palestinians) and little investment from the central budget in water and sanitation. The contrast with the heavy investment in world-class services in the Israeli settlements was not lost on the Palestinians.[7]

The final factor was the primitive financial system. With no currency of their own and no trusted banking system, the Occupied Territories had taken a step back towards an economy in which cash was the dominant means of exchange.

Under the influence of these factors the Occupied Territories' economy had developed in a very lopsided way. Integration with Israeli markets contributed to high rates of growth, with GNP more than doubling between 1970 and 1987, but also to a position of dependence on Israel. In 1983, the Occupied Territories were Israel's second-largest single market for the export of goods ($680 million out of a total of $5.6 billion). Goods from Israel accounted for over 90 per cent of the Occupied Territories' imports in that year. Three-quarters of exports from the Occupied Territories were going to Israel. Part of this was an import and re-export business as Israeli firms took the opportunity of finishing goods in the low-cost Palestinian economy. But the main reason was that Palestinians encountered difficulties in importing or exporting from or to other markets.[8]

This dependence made the economy highly vulnerable to changes in Israel. Patterns of saving and investment were distorted by the high rate of inflation in Israel and by the frequent devaluations of the Israeli currency in the 1970s and 1980s. The arrival of immigrants into Israel in the 1980s reduced the demand for Palestinian labour, and it sufficed for Israel to limit access to labour markets during the *intifada* for the economy of the Occupied Territories to veer back towards recession. The economy was vulnerable to external shocks, too, particularly within the region – the collapse of oil prices in the early 1980s, the Iran–Iraq war, the Gulf War – all had adverse consequences for the Occupied Territories. Although remittances provided ample capital finance, investment patterns were distorted by fears of arbitrary policy changes affecting land tenure and the business environment. By 1993, not only had growth slowed to a halt but the skewed pattern of trade and investment had also left the economy with inadequate infrastructure and a depleted productive base.[9]

The moral factor – human rights and contempt The period up to Oslo in 1993 saw not only the denial of sovereignty but also the destruction of thousands of houses, the deportation of thousands of Palestinians, the closure of schools and universities, the suppression of newspapers and the widespread use of detention without trial. Many Palestinians simply quit. Between 1967 and 1982 it is estimated that up to 700,000 people left and the population shrank, only to rise again with the large number of returnees at the time of the First Gulf War.[10]

And the attitudes towards Palestinians that underlay the Occupation? It is not surprising that they were largely the contemptuous attitudes of the conqueror towards the conquered, of the strong towards the weak. A combination of fear and a sense of superiority led to general day-to-day rough handling which was as bad for the eternal soul of the young Israelis sent to carry out policies as it was for the physical and moral well-being of the subjects of the ill-treatment.[11]

Intifada The situation changed dramatically with the first *intifada* ('*shaking off*'). This protest movement began for the first time to make direct Israeli–Palestinian dialogue a possibility. The *intifada* began in late 1987, at a time when glasnost and seismic shifts in the USSR and Eastern Europe were changing the face of the world and the fate of its peoples, when openness and approaches to democracy were sweeping Africa, when apartheid was crumbling, when dictators and juntas in Latin America were toppling one after another. Oppressed peoples across the world were experiencing liberation. The times looked propitious for change in the Middle East – not least for Israelis and Palestinians. It was not lost on either the Palestinians or the Israelis that after decades, no solution had been found either to the refugee problem or to the Occupation.[12]

The *intifada* was driven by the persistent aggravations of the Occupation. Palestinian grievances had grown sharper. There had, in fact, been a process of 'creeping annexation' consisting of the piecemeal incorporation into Israel of territory: Greater Jerusalem, the settlements which were multiplying, the large military areas, the nature reserves. Alongside this was the practice of docile 'home rule' in other areas. But the persistent denial of civil liberties and basic freedoms, and the fugitive lure of real autonomy were a constant source of friction. These grievances and the 'creeping annexation' were too obvious sores in this small territory. Inevitably, these impairments of fundamental rights were a daily torment to the Palestinians.[13]

Economic dependence was a constant aggravation too in the lower salaries, the higher taxes and the more challenging procurement processes which Palestinians faced in the Israeli economy. 'The *intifada* was a universal outburst of anger against economic exploitation, land expropriation, daily harassment, Jewish settlements.'[14] It was grounded in the profound sense of deprivation and injustice all Palestinians felt at the events of 1948 and 1967 and at the daily humiliation of an occupation.[15]

A leading cause of the *intifada* was the more oppressive policies of Likud. The 'shaking off' began in the camps of Gaza where the average age was twenty-seven – this very young population had lived much of their lives under oppressive conditions and with scant hope. Palestinians determined to use every means possible, largely peaceful, to 'shake off' the Occupation. The *intifada* both in towns and in the countryside was organized through a network of popular committees. Workers and rural people were the main participants, although workers were less resilient, being dependent on their employers. It was a popular action, with the middle classes largely absent. Women participated fully – one-third of casualties were women. Children and youths participated – and paid dearly. Ironically it was the harm done to youngsters more than anything that alerted world opinion to the nature of the Occupation. The international media for the first time since 1948 presented matters more from a Palestinian perspective.[16]

From intifada *to political gain* Stone throwing, strikes, picketing – but how to transform this into political gain? In fact, the protest movement began for the first time to make direct Israeli–Palestinian dialogue a possibility. The PLO took advantage of the *intifada* successes and in November 1988 the Palestinian National Council set out its Declaration of Independence with the Palestinian agenda – the return of refugees and a Palestinian state.[17] The Declaration recognized that partition was necessary for ending the conflict and the PLO followed up with various declarations about ending armed struggle and recognizing the state of Israel. The momentum, however, for the time being remained with the popular movement in the Occupied Territories. The leadership on the ground set up a kind of government-in-waiting in Orient House in Jerusalem, forming 'teams' to plan for the government of the future state.[18]

Oslo and after

Oslo

Oslo I – the Declaration of Principles On the Israeli side, domestic politics offered, for the moment, some softening of approach. With the Zionist left supporting talks with the PLO on the basis of some form of partition, the 1992 elections opened up for the new Labour-led government the possibility of at least partial evacuation from the West Bank and Gaza. Mid-level contacts were made and with the help of the Norwegians, the Oslo process got underway. On the Palestinian side, the PLO quickly took centre stage as the negotiating partner. At Oslo, the organization came with a clear enough position: recognition of Israel and acceptance of a two-state solution, full independence for Palestine with Jerusalem as its capital, and no settlements.[19]

The September 1993 Declaration of Principles was signed with much fanfare on the White House lawn. There would be an Israeli withdrawal from Gaza and Jericho, followed by transfer of civil administration in those areas to the PLO. Progressively the Israelis would quit all Palestinian towns and population centres. If, and only if, this Interim Agreement was successfully carried out, negotiations could begin on three 'final status issues' – Jerusalem, Palestinian refugees and Jewish settlements. The agreement also allowed both parties to add further issues. For the Palestinians this would be the issue of statehood. Pappé comments tersely that the list of unresolved issues 'shows clearly why the document does not so much end the conflict as expose its true nature'.

In this view, the list of the thorny issues that would have to be resolved later on – Jerusalem, refugees, settlements – simply postponed the inevitable disappointment of Palestinian hopes as these were the very issues on which the Israelis were intransigent. Nonetheless, the Palestinians signed up, lured by the prospect of one dazzling prize – statehood. And Israel after 1948 had shown just what was achievable if only a people could achieve statehood. Anything and everything seemed to be possible if only Palestine could become a sovereign power.[20]

Oslo II – the Interim Agreement Two years after 'Oslo I', the initial Declaration of Principles which initiated the peace process, Palestinians and Israelis signed the 1995 Interim Agreement, usually referred to as Oslo II. The Israeli approach to the negotiations of this very detailed arrangement was very cautious and risk-averse. Their delegation was extremely well prepared and able, and they achieved a veto on change by making their further participation in future negotiations conditional on 'successful and peaceful' implementation of the Interim Agreement. This was a condition which was essentially as long as a piece of string. The Israelis could invoke it almost at will. Nonetheless, both sides signed the Interim Agreement in September 1995.[21] A division of the West Bank into three areas of differing governance and control – Areas A, B and C – was agreed on. Areas A and B where the Palestinians had some control comprised 165 separate units with no territorial contiguity. This fragmentation was to end through the progressive transfer of territory to Palestinian jurisdiction. Part of the agreement was Article 40, which laid down interim rules for the Palestinian water sector. Although intended to last for just five years, during which time a final status agreement would be negotiated, this Interim Agreement essentially remains in force today. In particular, the ABC mosaic is still in place, little changed from 1995.[22]

Acute observers felt at the time that all the responsibilities and downside risks were on the Palestinian side. An early indication was that during the negotiations and thereafter, Israel continued its settlement process. The Israeli governments of the period, both Labour and Likud, took steps which appeared to 'change the status of the West Bank and Gaza Strip' in contravention of the agreement. And 'massive land confiscation and settlement expansion marked the period 1992–6'.[23]

In fact, Israel had long since created a joined-up Jewish West Bank with a dense infrastructure of settlements, roads and pipes – as early as 1984 the stunningly detailed *West Bank Data Project* had laid this out with extraordinary transparency.[24] The Israeli West Bank was, in fact, more joined up than the Palestinian one as Israelis could move seamlessly amongst settlements and in the two-thirds of West Bank land that Israel controlled, and could commute back and forth to and from Israel proper. The Palestinian West Bank was fragmented not only into the 165 separate units in Areas A and B but also into a further 532 islets within Area C. Moving between these units entailed crossing Israeli-controlled Area C. Checkpoints multiplied and movement was more constrained than ever. It seemed to many Palestinians that they enjoyed less freedom than before, not more.[25]

As events unfolded and people began to understand the implications of Oslo and the way the Israelis interpreted it in practice, the Palestinians came to see that the devolved functions were limited to the running of daily life in small scattered fragments of land. Many began to call the agreement a lot of *salata* (honours) without *sulta* (authority). 'Jobs for the boys' in the new administration created a big vested interest but brought little benefit to the people.[26]

Politics from 1996: Likud and Shamir Matters then took a decisive downturn. On 4 November 1995 Yitzhak Rabin was assassinated by a Jewish extremist. When Likud returned to power in the summer of 1996, Israel's stance changed. The new prime minister, Netanyahu, argued that Palestinians might have 'self-government' – but never sovereignty. This was the essence of Netanyahu's May 1997 final status proposal under which Palestinians would control less than 40 per cent of the territory, Israel would control the rest and the Palestinians would be forever excluded from the Jordan Valley.[27]

Amongst Palestinians, there was widespread disappointment and frustration – and some furious violent opposition. After 1996, the Palestinians basically despaired of Oslo, looking on it as another form of occupation – worse in a way as it gave the occupier legitimacy and laid down rules that the occupier could police.[28] Oslo turned Gaza into a huge prison. Hamas and Islamic Jihad began to oppose the accord with bombings, relations deteriorated and Israeli repression and retaliation grew fiercer.[29]

The end of Oslo hopes By the end of the century the process looked moribund, lingering on largely because it remained popular with the hopeful segments of the Israeli public and the international community. But it had not brought any kind of peace and the Palestinian people were paying a high price for illusions. Essentially, the Palestinians saw the whole process as unfair. There was scant reward for decades of suffering. The Declaration of Principles and the Interim Agreement were interpreted harshly by the strong party and the process was brokered by a partial and biased United States. Palestinian views were that Israel, as by far the stronger actor, had simply been able to impose its own version of an agreement. The Palestinian entity was seen as structurally emasculated, administering some limited state functions under the domination of the powerful party. Jewish settlement was proceeding rapidly without check and no solution was likely either on the refugee problem or on Jerusalem.

The PLO, which had briefly looked like a state actor, emerged weakened, bound by rules to which it had agreed but which kept it subordinate. It was widely seen by Palestinians as having squandered the advantages brought through sacrifice during the *intifada*. The continuation of the settlement process was seen as the ultimate bad faith and the integrity of Israel's intentions was seriously undermined when both Labour and Likud ran in the 1996 elections on platforms that promised *no* dismantlement of settlements and that most or all of them should come under Israeli sovereignty.[30]

Camp David 2000 Nonetheless, two factors coincided to revive some hope. The return to power of Labour in 1999 under Barak brought some measure of renewed commitment to the process while in the United States, Bill Clinton, mired in the impeachment process, sought a legacy foreign policy achievement. However, the substance for an agreement was lacking. At Camp David in the summer of 2000, the Palestinian leadership was presented with a take-it-or-leave-it choice: sovereignty over 73 per cent of the West Bank – about 16 per cent of the area of

Mandate Palestine, with a possible expansion 'after 10–15 years' – and sovereignty over all of the Gaza Strip. Palestinian lands would be split into three blocks, and the main Jewish settlements would remain and be incorporated into Israel. Israel would retain rights to bring its military into Palestinian territory, there would be no access to Jerusalem, and the 'right of return' would be limited to 100,000 refugees on 'humanitarian grounds'. The Palestinian leadership refused such limited territorial sovereignty and circumscribed powers.[31]

Zeitoun records a cack-handed attempt at a 'deal' on water, when a US facilitator in the water talks scribbled a note on the whiteboard saying '*US = $*'. Zeitoun says that the implication was that the water issue could 'be resolved because water can be manufactured and the US would pay for this'. In the event, the Americans did agree to pay for a desalination plant and for a north–south transmission line in Gaza, but both projects were halted after the killing of three US bodyguards in Gaza in 2003. Like much development assistance, particularly from the United States, the projects fell foul of attitudes towards the rise of Hamas and were abandoned after 2006.[32]

That there was almost no popular support for the Camp David deal became clear when the second *intifada*, far more violent than the first, erupted in September 2000 after Ariel Sharon made his visit to the al Aqsa mosque. There were high numbers of casualties caused by Palestinian suicide bombings and Israeli shootings and tank and air attacks – about 3,000 Palestinians and 1,000 Israelis were killed. Dreadful acts were committed on both sides and Israel essentially reoccupied all of the West Bank. Talks continued into 2001 but by February 2001 Clinton was out and the new president, George W. Bush, went for a 'hands off' policy, 'ready to assist, not insist'. In Israel, Sharon was in as prime minister. He quickly withdrew from any Israeli commitments made at Camp David and the process died a second death.[33]

The Road Map and the quartet By 2002 Bush had been persuaded to backtrack on his 'hands off' policy, declaring on 24 June of that year that US policy was to support the creation of 'a viable Palestinian state'. Then in 2003 Britain agreed to follow the United States into Iraq on condition that the Palestinian peace process be revived. This produced the Road Map supported by the quartet of the United States, EU, Russia and the UN. The map was to result in an independent Palestinian state by 2005. This, however, led strictly nowhere.[34] Palestinian bombings and attacks and Israeli reprisals continued. Settlement proceeded apace. The Israelis built a wall around the West Bank to complement the one they had already erected around the Gaza Strip in the mid-1990s.[35]

The violence eventually fell away. Israel's security measures proved effective and at the Sharm el-Sheikh Summit on 8 February 2005, Abbas and Sharon agreed to halt violence and recommit to the Road Map process. Sharon also agreed to release 900 Palestinian prisoners of the 7,500 being held at the time and to withdraw from West Bank towns. There was essentially a return to the *status quo ante*, with no improvement in conditions or prospects in the West Bank. In Gaza, Hamas persisted in its opposition to everything.

Article 40: Water in the Oslo II accords

Article 40 In the early morning hours of 18 September 1995, Nabil Sharif for the Palestinians and Noah Kinarti for the Israelis initialled Article 40 of Annex III of the Oslo II Interim Agreement. It was, in fact, the very first portion of the overall Interim Agreement to be concluded between the two sides. Although intended to last for only five years at the most, until the final status talks ended in a comprehensive settlement, this unassuming sounding article entitled '*Water and Sewage*' was to rule the Palestinian water sector from that time up until the time of writing (2021), twenty-five years after Oslo and two decades after the expected end of the interim arrangement.[36]

Article 40 deals only with water within the West Bank, not in Israel, and only in a very limited way with Gaza. The article essentially recognized undefined Palestinian water rights: 'Israel recognizes the Palestinian water rights in the West Bank, to be negotiated in the permanent status negotiations.' It was a struggle for the Palestinians to secure even this recognition, and they accounted it a victory. However, the absence of any specifics left the victory very empty, especially as the permanent status has never been negotiated.

During the interim period, management of water and sewage in the West Bank was to be coordinated according to agreed principles: existing levels of resource use were to be maintained; water was to be managed sustainably; use was to be adjusted in case of climatic or hydrological variations. Principles of protection of water resources and the environment were emphasized, with the parties required to take all necessary measures for the prevention of water quality deterioration and pollution. In particular, sewage was to be properly treated and reused. Each party was to protect water and sewage systems in its own and the counterpart's jurisdictions (Article 40.21–24) as well as to reimburse the counterpart for 'any unauthorized use or sabotage' to water systems under its responsibility (Article 40.24).

Governance arrangements were set up for the five-year interim period, notably a Joint Water Committee (JWC) to deal with all water and sewage-related issues in the West Bank and specifically to coordinate management of water resources, monitor the resource, oversee a joint supervision and enforcement mechanism, license wells and approve water resource systems. Most significantly, all new water development in the area under jurisdiction (i.e. the West Bank) required approval from the JWC from the planning stages onward (see Article 40.1.a–b, 2.d). Decisions were to be based on consensus between the two parties. Where water was to be purchased, the price would be equal to the supply cost at the point of delivery.

The agreement established the enforcement mechanism of the JWC, termed 'Joint Supervision and Enforcement Teams' (JSETs), to be comprised of at least two members from each side, with costs shared equally, to 'monitor, supervise and enforce Article 40'. The JSETs were to have extremely broad inspection and data collection powers (Article 40.17, Schedule 9.5.a–f.).

Specific quantities of the three West Bank aquifers underlying both territories were allocated to each party. Schedule 10 of the Agreement sets out quantities

Table 7.2 West Bank: Allocation of Water Resources of the Three Shared Aquifers under Article 40 (million m³)

Aquifer	Estimated potential	Article 40 allocation		
		Total Palestinian	Total Israeli	Total
Western	362.0	22.0	340.0	362.0
Northeastern	145.0	42.0	103.0	145.0
Eastern	172.0	54.0	40.0	94.0
Eastern (unallocated)				78.0
Total	**679.0**	**118.0**	**483.0**	**601.0**
Percentage of estimated potential		**17%**	**71%**	**88%**

Sources: Article 40, Table 2.

for the 'utilization, extraction, and . . . potentials' of the Mountain Aquifers, which it refers to as the Western, Northeastern, and Eastern Aquifers.[37] Although quantities of the portion of the shared aquifer underlying Israel were included in Article 40, issues related to these quantities or to Israel's use of them were not included in the mandate of the JWC and no rules or sanctions were specified. The share allocated to the Palestinian West Bank was less than one-quarter of the allocation to Israel and the settlements. Of the total 'estimated potential' of the three aquifers, 483 million cubic metres was allocated to Israel (71 per cent), 118 million cubic metres was allocated to the Palestinians (17 per cent), and a quantity of 78 million cubic metres (12 per cent) was left unallocated, 'to be developed' from the Eastern Aquifer (see the table *West Bank: Allocation of Water Resources*).[23]

The largest of the three aquifers – the Western Aquifer – was estimated to have an annual recharge of 362 million cubic metres, of which 340 million cubic metres was utilized within Israel and 20 million cubic metres by the Palestinians. An additional 2 million cubic metres from springs around Nablus was also to be utilized by Palestinians. The Northeastern Aquifer was estimated to yield 145 million cubic metres, of which 103 million cubic metres (from the Gilboa and Beisan springs, including wells) was allocated to the Israelis and 42 million cubic metres was to be utilized by Palestinians (25 million cubic metres by users around Jenin and 17 million cubic metres from the East Nablus springs). The Eastern Aquifer was estimated to have an annual recharge of 172 million cubic metres, of which 40 million cubic metres (from wells) was to be utilized by Israelis, 54 million cubic metres (24 million cubic metres from wells and 30 million cubic metres from springs) was allocated to the Palestinians and an additional 78 million cubic metres was 'to be developed'.

In addition to these allocations to the Palestinians, which totalled 118 million cubic metres, an extra 28.6 million cubic metres was to be allocated to Palestinians for 'immediate needs' during the interim period, 23.6 million cubic metres for the

West Bank and 5 million cubic metres for Gaza. Of the West Bank increment of 23.6 million cubic metres, 20.5 million cubic metres was to come from additional wells. One well, for Jenin, was to be developed by Israeli authorities, the others by the Palestinian Authority (PA). The wells to supply Hebron, Bethlehem and Ramallah were to be in the Eastern Aquifer or from other agreed sources. In addition, an additional 3.1 million cubic metres would be supplied by Israel to the West Bank through Mekorot (in addition to 27.9 million cubic metres already being supplied by Mekorot at the time of the agreement). Total availability to West Bank Palestinians was thus 138.5 million cubic metres from wells and springs within the West Bank, and 31 million cubic metres from purchases from Mekorot.

'Future needs' of the Palestinians were estimated at 70–80 million cubic metres annually (Article 40.6). It has never been clear whether this was an indication of expected future demand over some defined period, or a statement of intent that these resources would be provided from within the water balance.

Some water and sewerage powers and responsibilities in the West Bank were transferred to the PA in spheres 'related solely to the Palestinians, that are currently held by the military government and its Civil Administration' (Article 40.4). However, there was to be no transfer of ownership of water and sewage infrastructure in the West Bank until the final status negotiations (Article 40.5).

The question to be asked Judgement of Article 40 has to tempered by the understanding that it was a temporary agreement. The general expectation was that this Interim Agreement would be revised within a five-year period. However, it has persisted for more than a quarter of a century and still governs the Palestinian West Bank water sector today.

In many ways the agreement sounds exemplary, incorporating many of the principles of cooperative and integrated water resources management, particularly the language on sustainability (in terms of both quantity and quality), the requirements to prevent water quality deterioration (Article 40.3b, f) and to avoid harm (Article 40.3h), the linking of extra water supplies to wastewater collection and treatment, the introduction of wastewater reuse as a principle (Article 40.3f), and the factoring in of inter-annual variability in hydrologic conditions (Article 40.3c,d). There are clear provisions for coordinated operations management, and for development of water and sewage systems.[38] Finally, the agreement incorporates a comprehensive and integrated approach, applying rules to all resources and systems, including those under private ownership or operation (Article 40.3g, i).

The question is whether the principles, allocations and governance structure set out in the 'interim' arrangement genuinely balanced the interests of Palestinian and Israeli stakeholders. And whether these arrangements, still in place, are fair to each party, ensuring the sustainable use of the resource while supporting a viable economy for both Israelis and Palestinians. This is the question which the following sections will seek to answer.

Implementation of Oslo and Article 40

Implementation up to 2000

The germ of Palestinian water governance: Establishment of the Palestinian Water Authority (PWA) Implementation of Article 40 was a challenge for the Palestinians. On the Israeli side, there was fifty years of experience of advanced and competent water management, and powerful, well-staffed and well-endowed institutions. On the Palestinian side there were a few able and competent engineers and planners – recall from Chapter 6 the estimate of 'only six to eight water supply and sanitary engineers' at the time of Oslo. Some of these professionals had taken part in the negotiations of Article 40. The new PA quickly brought together as many of these experts as possible and set up an embryonic water management agency, the Palestinian Water Authority (PWA). Its mandate was grand – to develop water policy and to oversee the allocation, development and management of Palestinian water resources and services.[39]

Implementation of Article 40 The implementation of Article 40 began with some optimism. Palestinian water planners and engineers, few though they were, felt empowered for the first time. The international community was enthralled by the prospects of real cooperation over natural resource management and by the principles of good water management that seemed to be embodied within Article 40. Donors allocated considerable resources to support implementation. The United States backed up its support of the agreement with the promise of almost $200 million for water projects between 1994 and 1998, mostly in Gaza. In 1995, it also allocated $11 million towards a $40 million wastewater treatment plant.[40]

However, from the very outset, implementation of Article 40 proved contentious and problems soon began to emerge. These problems might have been ironed out in the final status negotiations, but, in the event, those negotiations never took place, and the issues inherent in Article 40 and the way it was implemented became more acute as time went by. In particular, dissatisfaction with the JWC as a vehicle for cooperation on water became apparent almost from the beginning. The committee was established under the joint chairmanship of the two people who had negotiated Article 40, Nabil Sharif for the Palestinians and Noah Kinarti for the Israelis. Yet, within a short time of its establishment, we find the PWA complaining that Palestinian projects and requests for drilling permits were being frustrated by Israeli vetoes. The Israelis in turn soon complained of poor Palestinian sewage management and of water theft. As time dragged on, the 'interim' agreement began to look more like a deeply flawed but de facto permanent agreement, and Palestinian dissatisfaction grew more intense.[41]

One factor was, inevitably, the changing politics. Less than a year after the signing of Article 40, Israeli approaches shifted, as we have seen, with the formation of a new Likud-led government. To implement the Israeli side of Article 40, Netanyahu appointed the hardliner, Ariel Sharon, as infrastructure minister. Sharon at once took a tough stance. From 1997 he obstructed US plans to drill three wells at Herodian for Palestinian use. Israel also held up the US-backed Hebron wastewater treatment project when the Civil Administration insisted that the Palestinians first submit a sewage plan. Sharon argued that 'the Palestinians in Hebron are polluting our water sources by directing sewage through the Hebron stream. Our most important aquifer is being polluted by sewage.' At the same time news reports began to appear in the Israeli media accusing Palestinians of water theft, of stealing 10 million cubic metres from Mekorot West Bank pipelines to irrigate orchards.[42]

On the Palestinian side, by 2001 the PWA was complaining that more than 150 projects were being held up, including forty-two wells, sixty-four pipelines and fourteen sewage networks. The total value of these projects was reported to be as much as $200 million.[43] As we shall see, even projects which had got through the JWC could be held up by the Civil Administration.[44]

The five JSETs which were to be set up 'to monitor, supervise and enforce implementation' of Article 40 proved particularly contentious. Two jeeps were provided for each pair of teams – one for the Palestinian team and one for the Israelis. These joint JSETs were to have 'free, unrestricted and secure access to all water and sewage facilities and systems'. JSETs were even supposed to enter settlements although in practice private guards refused entry to the Palestinian teams.

From an Israeli perspective, this was seen as a part of good water regulation and the results were held to be a success. When, for example, early on, in December 1995, the Israelis complained about illegal drilling in the Jenin area, a JSET inquiry was conducted and the Israeli Agriculture Minister Tsur concluded that the problem was solved 'amicably'. He declared himself 'satisfied with Palestinian cooperation'. In the Israeli view, the random drilling and competitive overexploitation that characterized other groundwater economies in the region and led to overdraft and exhaustion of the resource were largely avoided and the quality and quantity of the resource were protected.[45]

From a Palestinian perspective the view was very different. The population looked on these interventions as a continuation of the intrusive aspects of the Occupation. The extent of Israeli abstractions from the aquifers and the huge imbalance with the quantity the Palestinians were allowed to pump were patent to all. Palestinians could see Mekorot pipes crossing Palestinian lands carrying ample water to settlements when water was sorely needed by Palestinian farms and households. Even worse in the eyes of the population was perhaps that these intrusive restrictions on Palestinian water development and use were being enforced by Palestinians working in the JSETs alongside the hated occupier.[46]

In the end, the JSETs failed because it was all too one-sided. This became increasingly apparent to the Palestinian people who came to resent most bitterly this infringement of their supposed new freedoms. With no access to settlements and with limited freedom to enter Area C, where most wells were, the Palestinian teams were in practice excluded from many JSET activities. Israeli JWC counterparts allege another problem: that the Palestinian teams were not willing to continue because they were seen as collaborators. Certainly in the eyes of the Palestinian population, the JSETs, whether Israeli or Palestinian, were unwelcome. For example, at Udalla on the outskirts of Nablus, the municipality built a wall to protect the well. During the *al Aqsa intifada*, the IDF imposed a 24-hour curfew. The guard could not get to the well to open the gate for the JSET, with the result that the Israeli teams could not read the metre – 'so they broke the wall with a tank!', a PWA representative explained.

In 2001, after the start of the *al Aqsa intifada*, the Palestinian JSET teams withdrew, frustrated at taking part in so visible an activity, seen by their fellow Palestinians as collaborators enforcing the unequal laws of the Occupier. After the Palestinians withdrew, the Israeli teams continued to inspect wells, entering Area B as well as Area C. They were entitled to do this under Article 40 but any semblance of a cooperative approach had been abandoned.[47]

Results for the Palestinian population At the outset, there were expectations from Article 40, that secure Palestinian water rights, extra water resources allocated, and donor support for investment would bring new supplies for both households and farming. Yet, these benefits certainly did not appear at first. In 1998, we hear of the deputy mayor of Bethlehem lamenting, 'What kind of peace can there be while we have no water?' In the same year, Isa Atalla, PWA head in Hebron, points to the dramatic – and growing – disparity between water services to Palestinians and those to Israeli settlers. 'Your children are going thirsty', he told the Montreal Gazette in August 1998, 'and you see settlers next door watering their gardens and swimming in their pools'.[48]

Water cooperation after Camp David 2000 As we have seen, the failure of Camp David in 2000 marked a turning point for hopes of a final settlement. Yet, despite the deterioration of the political situation and the outbreak of the *al Aqsa intifada*, cooperation on water stumbled on. Palestinians were aware that cooperation was essential if vital water supplies were to be maintained, and Article 40 and the JWC did at least provide a framework, however unequal it was proving to be. Despite what Mark Zeitoun calls 'power asymmetries clothed in dubious legitimacy', the JWC was one of only two of the institutions established by Oslo which endured (see later).[49]

During the *al Aqsa intifada*, the JWC even managed to make provisions for protecting water infrastructure and services. On 31 January 2001, the joint heads of JWC – Noah Kinarti and Nabil al-Sherif were still in place – signed a *Joint Declaration for Keeping Water Infrastructure out of the Cycle of Violence*, laying down that water and sanitation infrastructure should be spared in any outbreak. In December 2002, Nabil, who was the Palestinian minister of water and head of the PWA, said, 'the only area in which Israelis and Palestinians are continuing cooperation, in spite of 25 difficult months of *intifada*, is water'.[50]

Frustrations on both sides Over time, the Palestinians became increasingly frustrated by the failure of the process to deliver real improvements. They continued to bemoan what they saw as Israeli vetoes on projects in the JWC and the further hurdles to implementation imposed by what Palestinians saw as Civil

Administration obstruction. At the heart of this was the dissatisfaction both of the PA and of the people at the meagre outcomes of the water chapter of Oslo. Palestinians saw a surrender of hoped-for water sovereignty in Article 40 but no compensating improvement in water availability or services. Instead, they saw lack of water both for municipal and household supply and for agriculture. And as settlements multiplied and became ever more populous, Palestinians saw what they considered profligate water use which they suspected came from the resources under their feet, as well as copious untreated wastewater and sewage from the Israeli settlements which began to course down the wadis of the West Bank.

From their side, too, and from their dominant position, the Israelis pointed their finger at a long list of shortcomings of the Palestinians. These included water theft, illegal drilling and Palestinian sewage flowing into Israel. They complained that the PA was not paying Mekorot for water sold to Palestinians. And they faulted the weakness of the fledgling Palestinian institutions – the PWA and the Ministry of Agriculture which oversaw irrigation, as well as the plethora of municipal and rural water supply bodies.

The impact of politics on water cooperation: The PWA and the case of Jenin All this time, the PWA was struggling to gain credibility. Even during the *al Aqsa intifada*, the PWA strove to maintain water services and to develop the 'new' resources that Article 40 had ostensibly brought. Inevitably, such an infant institution had an uphill task, and this was made more difficult both by the limited powers that Article 40 accorded it and by the way in which the implementation of Article 40 became politicized.

A low point came in Jenin, the Palestinian city in the north of the West Bank which played a particularly active role in the *al Aqsa intifada*. Much of the city's water comes from a Mekorot line which draws water from three wells just outside the city. These wells – called Duthan wells 1–3 – were managed by the West Bank Water Department (see Chapter 6), which at that time was still under Israeli control. These wells also supplied nearby Israeli military camps and the Israeli settlements of Sa'nur, Qadim and Janim. In 2001 and 2002 there were three Israeli incursions into Jenin city with heavy armour which resulted in considerable loss of life and destruction of property and water supply infrastructure. Water supplies to many parts of the city were cut for several weeks.

Amidst the upheaval and confusions of this period, Palestinians could not overlook some significant aspects of the Jenin events. When much water infrastructure was damaged, the Mekorot line and the Israeli-controlled wells were untouched. When water was cut to many city residents, Mekorot 'continued to prioritize water delivery to the nearby settlements and military camps, despite the thousands of people in Jenin without any source of water at all'.[51] Beyond that, Palestinians saw the destruction of water infrastructure as a glaring violation of the terms and the spirit of the 2001 *Joint Declaration*. The role of the JWC, which had done nothing either to protect the infrastructure or to restore supplies, was seen as at best feeble, at worst partial. And the PWA was seen to be of no help at all, raising questions of its capacity and legitimacy.[52]

The separation barrier and water – and implications for PWA and JWC Further loss of confidence in the JWC and the PWA occurred with the erection of the separation barrier across the West Bank. In June 2002, the Sharon government approved construction of this 700-kilometre-long wall and fence. When it was completed, it cut off West Bank Palestinians from almost a tenth of their land – some 9 per cent of the West Bank lay west of the wall, including East Jerusalem. Much valuable agricultural land lay on the far side. Close to centres of urban demand and endowed with plentiful water, these lands were of prime value for irrigated agriculture, particularly for market gardening.

The narrow strip of land on either side of the Green Line is, in fact, the area where the groundwater of the highly productive Western Aquifer can be most economically exploited, as is demonstrated by the dense clustering of Israeli wells immediately to the west of this line.[53] The straying of the barrier across the Green Line to the east had the result of not only cutting off the existing Palestinian wells but also precluding any future access to Palestinian groundwater development in the newly inaccessible zone. It is estimated that in this way almost one-third of West Bank water resources became inaccessible to Palestinians.[54]

The failure of the JWC to take any action to protect water rights and water interests was apparent to the Palestinians. And the weakness of the PWA that left it incapable of intervening to prevent existing wells or possible future access to the aquifer being cut off by the barrier further devalued the institution in the eyes of the people it was designed to serve.

More broadly, the implications of the A/B/C mosaic agreed on at Oslo and the consequent truncation and shrinking of the Palestinian West Bank were coming home to Palestinians. With almost one-tenth of their land beyond the barrier, another 8 per cent allocated to settler blocks east of the wall, a further 28.5 per cent of the West Bank under 'settlement jurisdiction' in the Jordan Valley, and much more land under military control or assigned to natural reserves, the area in which Palestinians had sole jurisdiction (Area A) was less than one-fifth of the West Bank area (18 per cent), with a further one-fifth (22 per cent) under 'joint' PA and Israeli administration (Area B). At this stage, even the optimists could see that at best less than half of the West Bank remained under discussion for a possible Palestinian state – and until the final status negotiations much of that area was to remain under Israeli military control.

All this undermined cooperation on water. What looked like a 'creeping annexation', the restrictions on movement and access (M&A), and the generally invasive and often brutal nature of the Israeli and settler presence in the West Bank combined with the political situation and the actual course of water development to reduce Palestinian confidence in water cooperation and progressively eroded any incentives for what looked less like cooperation and increasingly like collaboration.[55]

The story of one West Bank village gives a vivid picture of how these constraints and failures affected the lives of Palestinians at the time. Writing in 2005, Mark Zeitoun relates the case of the West Bank village of Madama, which lies in the Titzah valley up from the Jordan River. Twenty minutes' walk above Madama lay the spring which had been the source of water for the village for centuries. In the

1920s, the Mandate authorities built a brickwork structure to protect the spring and laid pipes to bring water to the reservoir in the village. For one reason or another – probably pumping from the deep Israeli wells nearby – the spring began to dry up in summer, but it still remained the only source of drinking water for the village.

In 1983 a settler outpost, Yishar, was set up on the hill above the spring. Over time Yishar became a full settlement, supplied with water like other nearby settlements from an Israeli well called Beita Azmut, drilled in the West Bank about ten kilometres distant. Soon after the settlement was established, settlers began regularly destroying the pipes that brought water from the spring to Madama and dumping garbage, including soiled diapers, in the spring itself. In a single year, 2000, the pipes were destroyed three times. A team from Oxfam-GB that attempted to bury the pipes was driven off by settler gunfire. An attempt by the PWA to drill a well to bring water to Madama was refused by the Civil Administration, even though it had USAID financing. Without access to the spring water, the villagers' sole coping strategy was to buy expensive tanker water. Sometimes they had to purchase this water from Israeli settlements supplied by wells within the West Bank.

The villagers concluded that they were paying high prices to buy back their own water and that neither the PWA nor any other apparatus or agreement coming out of the Oslo Accords had done anything whatever for them.[56]

Palestinian access to water under Article 40

In 2008, some fifteen years after the signing of the interim accord on water in Article 40, we had the opportunity to assess the workings of Article 40 in considerable depth and to consider its outcomes for the Palestinian people. This is a good point to choose for an assessment because shortly afterwards, the Palestinians concluded that Article 40 was not working and suspended their participation in the JWC. In this section, we summarize and update the analysis and the conclusions we made then.

Water abstractions

Over the years after Oslo, Palestinians abstracted up to about one-fifth of the 'estimated potential' of the aquifers lying beneath the West Bank, each year. Although reliable numbers are hard to find, evidence was that Palestinian abstractions in the West Bank each year were in the range between 113 million cubic metres and 138 million cubic metres, or about 17–20 per cent of the 'estimated potential' of the aquifers. In 1999, for example (see the table *Abstractions from the Three Shared Aquifers* later), Palestinian abstractions were around 138 million m³ in aggregate, almost exactly 20 per cent of the potential and precisely in line with their total allocation under Article 40 of 118 million cubic metres under Schedule 10 and an additional 20.5 million cubic metres from additional wells under Schedule 7. Within the total abstractions, Palestinians had overdrawn slightly on the most productive Western Aquifer and abstracted less than agreed on from the other two aquifers.

From its wells within the West Bank and west of the Green Line, Israel abstracted its own share under Article 40, and in addition regularly overdrew on that share by more than half. The figures for 1999 illustrate this pattern (see the table *Abstractions*), showing an Israeli total abstraction of 872 million cubic metres, an overextraction of 389 million cubic metres (80 per cent) above the agreed Oslo allocation of 483 million cubic metres.[57]

Subsequently, it appears that, contrary to expectations under Oslo II, the water actually abstracted by Palestinians in the West Bank dropped, from 138 million cubic metres in 1999 to 113 million cubic metres in 2007 (see the table *Palestinian Abstractions* later which shows reduced Palestinian withdrawals from all three aquifers over the period to 2007). According to the PWA in 2009, the main causes for this reduced abstraction were a drop in spring discharge and a drop in well production, both of which the PWA attributed to a lowered water table caused by persistent Israeli overabstractions.[58]

The Israelis have been clear that these overdrafts did occur and that overextraction created risks for the aquifers – recall from Chapter 6 the strictures of the Israeli State Comptroller on Israeli overdrafting of the Mountain Aquifers throughout the 1970s and 1980s. Despite improvements in Israeli water management, overdrafts had clearly continued. At a public meeting in Jerusalem on 26 November 2008, the chairman of the Israeli Water Authority stated that abstractions over the last five years have brought aquifer levels 'to the point where irreversible damage is done to the aquifer'.[59]

There is no doubt that this situation contributed to the decline in water available to Palestinian people. In the Western Aquifer, excess abstraction caused water levels in the upper part of the aquifer beneath the West Bank to drop, reducing the amount of water that could potentially be exploited within the West Bank. In the Eastern Aquifer, there is evidence of deep Israeli wells affecting Palestinian wells and springs. At Bardala, for example, in the Northeastern corner of Tubas Governorate, eight Palestinian wells were constructed before 1967 for domestic and agricultural purposes, with depths ranging from 30 metres to 65 metres. After the 1967 war, Israel constructed two deep wells (Bardala 1 in 1968 and Bardala 2 in 1979) a few hundred metres from the Palestinian wells. The water level in the Palestinian wells dropped at the rate of 2 metres a year, and salinity increased. By 2009, the Palestinian wells were dry, as were most of the local springs used by Palestinian consumers for domestic and agricultural purposes.

At Fasayil in Jericho governorate, Israel drilled six production wells. The yield of the single Palestinian well in the area subsequently fell to zero, and the formerly abundant local springs dried up. At Auja, the very productive Auja spring, one of the ancient named springs on the steep eastern escarpment of the highlands, which formerly discharged up to 10 million cubic metres a year (see Chapter 2), began to dry up for months on end through the action of five nearby Israeli production wells. This formerly water-abundant village is now buying back water from local settlements.

Table 7.3 Abstractions from the Three Shared Aquifers within West Bank and Israel 1999 (million m³)

Aquifer	Estimated potential	Abstractions			Excess over Article 40 allocation		
		Total Palestinian	Total Israeli	Total abstracted	Palestinian	Israeli	Total overextraction
Western	362.0	29.4	591.6	621.0	7.4	251.6	259.0
Northeastern	145.0	36.9	147.1	184.0	(5.1)	44.1	39.0
Eastern[a]	172.0	71.9	132.9	204.8	(2.6)	92.9	90.3
Total	**679.0**	**138.2**	**871.6**	**1,009.8**	**(0.3)**	**388.6**	**388.3**

[a]For the Eastern Aquifer, the Article 40 Palestinian allocation was 54.0 million cubic metres (Schedule 10) – see the table *West Bank Allocations* – plus 20.5 million cubic metres for 'immediate needs' under Section 7, making it a total allocation of 74.5 million cubic metres.

Sources: Estimated potential from Article 40. Other numbers from Table 1, Shuval and Dweik: 24 Figure 2.9.

Table 7.4 Palestinian Abstractions from the Three Shared Aquifers 1999 and 2007 (million m³)

Aquifer	Article 40 allocation	1999	2007
Western	22.0	29.4	27.9
Northeastern	42.0	36.9	26.8
Eastern	74.5	71.9	58.8
Total	**138.5**	**138.2**	**113.5**

Sources: Article 40 allocation from Schedule 10 and Section 7. 1999 numbers from Table 1 and Figure 2.9 in Shared Management of Palestinian and Israeli Groundwater Resources by Amjad Aliewi and Karen Assaf, in Water Resources in the Middle East, edited by Hillel Shuval and Hassan Dweik, Berlin, Springer 2007. 2007 numbers from Water Sector Status in West Bank, PWA October 2008.

In 2005, the PWA reported that half of the Palestinian wells in the West Bank had dried up since the start of the Occupation – only 328 Palestinian wells were still operational, compared to 774 wells in 1967. Applications to deepen or replace these wells were typically not approved by the JWC or the Civil Administration. Access to some agricultural and domestic wells was also lost to Palestinian communities due to the separation barrier (see earlier). Effects of the dwindling access to water were particularly severe for the generally more vulnerable population groups living in Area C.[60]

Water availability per capita In 1999, soon after Oslo, water withdrawals per capita (gross water withdrawals divided by the population) were calculated as 190 litres per capita per day (lcd) for West Bank Palestinians, about 1,000 litres per person for Israelis, and about 870 litres for each Israeli settler. By 2007, availability per capita for both populations had declined. The Palestinian population had access to only about one-quarter of the ration *of natural fresh water* of their Israeli counterparts: West Bank Palestinians had about 123 lcd, and Israelis about 544 lcd.[61] The decline resulted largely from increases in population but also, in the Palestinian case, from a dip in resource availability. At the time of Oslo II, Palestinians were using 118 million cubic metres from the West Bank aquifers. By 2007, this had decreased to 113 million cubic metres, while the population had grown by about 50 per cent over the same period.

The Joint Water Committee (JWC)

The workings of the JWC The JWC, which functioned from 1995 up to 2009 when the Palestinians suspended their participation, had an erratic history.[62] Initially one of twenty-six joint committees set up under Oslo, by 2009 – the year when the Palestinians suspended their participation – it was, as we saw earlier, one of just two survivors.[63] This longevity suggests that the committee served some purposes. But how far has the JWC been effective in overseeing management of the shared aquifers, in ensuring that Palestinians receive the extra water promised and in promoting investment in water services for Palestinians?

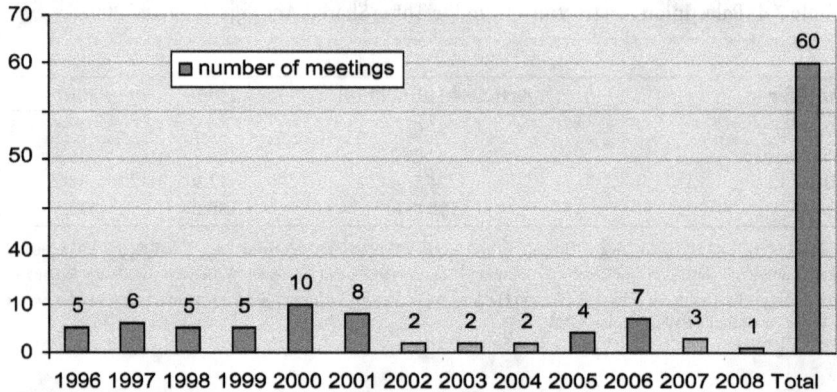

Figure 7.1 Number of Joint Technical Sub-Commitee Meetings 1996-2008. *Source*: World Bank 2009

The first meeting was in November 1995, and the committee met approximately sixty times between 1996 and 2008. It was agreed at the beginning that JWC meetings would be every two months. Although that frequency was maintained only in 1997, 2000 and 2001, the initial rhythm of meetings up to the time of the al Aqsa *intifada* was fairly regular, with a record ten meetings in the year 2000. Reflecting on this early 'honeymoon' period, a PA representative told us when we were in the West Bank in September 2008, 'When relations were warm, in the early years, the JWC worked well, issuing permits to construct wells for more than the 18.6 million cubic metres allowed under Oslo, although with big delays. But by about 1998 there was complete deadlock.'

The JWC survived early challenges partly because USAID joined in. The PA official told us, 'They [the Americans] said *We were partners to Oslo – we demand to be present in the JWC!* After that, 11 wells were approved from Nablus to Hebron. But then things died down again . . . ' When the al Aqsa *intifada* began in earnest, after 2002, the frequency of JWC meetings dropped to generally no more than two or three times a year, with just a single meeting in 2008.[64]

Palestinians assert that the rhythm of meetings and decisions was affected by the political climate. In 2008, PA representatives claimed to us that JWC meetings were irregular because they were called at the behest of the Israeli representatives and much depended on the political situation prevailing at the time. The PA representatives said that

> it became more complicated when the Hamas government was established. Between 2000 and 2005, the JWC rarely met, except informally, without minutes. When the main committee resumed in 2007, the PA had more than 150 projects piled up with the JWC. Israeli counterparts said *Bring the most important projects, those with funding!* In 2007 and 2008 they approved about forty projects.

Fundamental asymmetries A fundamental asymmetry – of power, of capacity, of information, of interest – put in question the status of the JWC as a genuinely 'joint' institution. This asymmetry took several forms. First was the geographical limitation. The JWC's role was to implement Article 40, including water allocation and project approval – but only in the West Bank. Yet, four-fifths of water abstraction and use of West Bank aquifer water is done within Israel outside the purview of the Palestinians or the remit of the JWC. In addition, further Israeli abstraction and use takes place within the West Bank – but outside the ken of the Palestinians. And most importantly, Palestinians had full authority only over Area A, which represented just 18 per cent of the West Bank, and the land where they had any powers at all – Areas A and B together – had no territorial contiguity but was chopped up into 165 separate administrative fragments. This limited and splintered geographical and hydrological access and jurisdiction made it impossible for Palestinians to conduct or even participate in anything resembling integrated water management. Almost all the resource was outside of both their knowledge and their control.

The asymmetry of information worsened once the Palestinians withdrew from the JSETs, as it left them reliant on the Israeli authorities for data. In any case, it had been hard for the Palestinian teams to know what the use of water in the settlements was – and also its source. For this and many other reasons there was an imbalance of information between the partners in the JWC, putting the PWA at a disadvantage for sector planning and management. A salient example was the Israeli overabstraction from the Western Aquifer detailed earlier, of which the Palestinians could have no direct knowledge, still less any control.

Even within the compass of the JWC, the Palestinians wielded little power. Essentially, they proposed but Israel disposed. Israel had veto power over Palestinian projects and could impose conditions – such as the obligation to serve settlements – which forced the PA towards compromise on its basic policy principles.

The Israelis maintain that Palestinians have the same veto power. Yet this power extends only to the West Bank and not to all the other works outside of the West Bank that make use of West Bank water. And within the West Bank, could the Palestinians dare to reject an Israeli project when they knew that this would result in denial of a Palestinian one? Zeitoun describes the case of the Rujeib well project where the PWA was refused permission to drill because they had not cooperated with the drilling of an Israeli well in the Jordan Valley.[65]

The result was loss of trust and poor outcomes. Such an asymmetrical power balance, together with the observed track record of the JWC, contributed to a loss of trust and confidence and to very poor outcomes (for Palestinians), which undermined the rationale for the committee as a joint approach to water sector management.

The JWC not being an effective mechanism for facilitating sector investment A high proportion of the projects proposed by the PA were rejected or long delayed in the JWC. From examination of JWC records regarding Palestinian projects (see the table *Status of Palestinian projects*), it can be concluded that, overall, of the 417 projects presented to the JWC between 1996 and 2008, just over half (57 per cent) were eventually approved.

Amongst these projects, well-drilling projects fared badly, even ones that appeared to be in line with Article 40. Of the 202 well-drilling projects submitted, just sixty-five (32 per cent) were approved by the JWC. Of those, only thirty-eight (19 per cent) were implemented, after receiving the additional approval of the Civil Administration. Amongst the well-drilling projects not approved by JWC or left pending JWC or Civil Administration approval were eighty-two well-drilling projects which were presented by the PWA as part of the agreed quantum under Article 40. JWC approval was systematically withheld for all agricultural water projects presented, even when the request was for simple rehabilitation or deepening. Bizarrely, in view of the emphasis in Article 40 on wastewater treatment, wastewater projects had the lowest rate of approval for any type of project. Of the sixteen Palestinian wastewater projects presented to the JWC, only one had been implemented by 2008 with a further two approved that year.

The process grew more restrictive as time went by. Of the ninety-seven projects submitted between 2005 and 2008, only twenty-eight were approved (29 per cent), with delays in the time from submission to approval varying between two months (one case) to eighteen months. Seventeen projects took a year or more to get approval. During this same period, all Israeli project submissions were approved. Clearly, the process was in general slow and restrictive and the rate of rejection of Palestinian projects was high, particularly for well-drilling and wastewater projects. Agricultural water projects appear to have been simply ruled out. By contrast, the PWA almost never sought to reject Israeli projects – only one was not approved during the entire period from 1995 to the time of Palestinian withdrawal from the JWC in 2008.

Many projects were simply left 'pending', yet all these projects would have brought substantial benefits to the West Bank population. In 2008, the records showed 106 pending Palestinian water projects, some of them dating from as far back as 1999. Four-fifths of these projects were not, in fact, for new water development, which was the main restriction in Article 40. They were for the development of small-scale domestic water supply networks to bring water to

Table 7.5 Status of Palestinian Projects Submitted to JWC up to 2008

Status	Number of projects	% of total
Approved	236	57
Not approved	22	5
Pending	143	34
Approved by JWC/ not approved by CA	7	2
Approved /no possibility for execution	7	2
Withdrawn by Palestinian side	3	1
Total submitted	417	100

Source: World Bank 2009.

Table 7.6 Water Supply Projects Pending in the JWC

Project type	Number	%
Small-scale domestic water supply (largely network construction and rehabilitation)	85	80
Wells for small-scale domestic networks	7	7
Agricultural wells (largely rehabilitation and substitution)	12	11
Small-scale domestic sewerage	1	1
Industrial projects	1	1
	106	100

Source: World Bank 2009.

Palestinian homes, usually for the first time. Records presented by the PWA showed that the pending water supply projects (see Table 7.6 *Water Supply Projects*) would have brought network connections or improved water supply to 1,090,000 beneficiaries, half of the West Bank population. In 2008, PWA also provided lists of twelve large-scale wastewater projects that had been presented to the JWC, most of them in the 1990s, which had either not been approved by the JWC or had been subsequently refused by the Civil Administration. These projects would have created or improved sanitation services for 790,000 people, one-third of the West Bank population, and relieved the environmental problems that were arising from untreated sewage.

As a result, out of the $121 million worth of Palestinian projects presented to the JWC between 2001 and 2008, only 50 per cent by value ($60.4 million) were approved. Both Israelis and Palestinians presented contrasting views on the causes of this shortfall in investment approvals. The Israelis said that projects were rejected because they were poorly prepared, that they breached Israeli understanding of Article 40, or that they did not meet some other policy criterion on the Israeli side (such as connecting settlements or meeting some effluent standard).[66]

The Palestinians considered it entirely unreasonable and against the spirit of Article 40 for the Israelis to impose criteria such as connecting settlements which they knew the Palestinians could not respect. The result was simply less investment, poorer services and unchecked pollution. In addition, the Palestinians alleged that projects may have been judged against other declared or undeclared Israeli criteria related to its policies towards the Occupied Territories. For example, the Palestinians alleged that settlement councils may have been having a say in decisions on projects, either at JWC level or at Civil Administration level, or that small domestic water supply projects were being delayed because the Civil Administration did not particularly wish to improve the living standards of the Palestinian population in Area C.[67]

Particular problems affecting well-drilling, wastewater and agricultural projects Well-drilling projects had a very low rate of approval in the JWC. As a result, water supply projects were often also held up in the JWC because they were dependent on approval for development of the water source. The official Israeli position was that whatever was within Article 40 allocations was accepted – and that Israel had gone far beyond the extra 28.6 million cubic metres of 'immediate needs' provided under Article 40 and had, in fact, approved licences for 55 million cubic metres. The Palestinian position was that not even the 'immediate needs' under Article 40 were delivered by the JWC, which appears to be correct – see the table *Palestinian Abstractions, 1999 and 2007* earlier. Moreover, population growth and rising demand in both municipal and agricultural water use in the years since Oslo had made the development of extra resources an imperative. The fact that Palestinian water abstractions in 2007 were 20 per cent lower than in 1999 (see the table *Palestinian Abstractions* earlier) suggest that, whatever the licences approved, the Palestinians had not been able to develop the water resources to which they were entitled, and that the yield of their existing sources was declining.

As we have seen, wastewater projects suffered the lowest rate of approval and the longest delays in the JWC. Although both Israelis and Palestinians gave nominal priority to these projects, there were key issues that led to a very low rate of approval and very low investment. One political issue was that the Israeli authorities insisted that Palestinian projects should also serve adjacent settlements. While this may have made some sense from an economic and technical point of view, politically it was a demand that the PA was bound to refuse. The Israelis also required an extremely high effluent quality standard (10:10). Although this was in line with the latest Israeli regulations, the requirement was considerably above the internationally recommended WHO norms, and well beyond the capacity of the PA and Palestinian people to afford.

Given the need to locate wastewater treatment plants away from cities, and to reuse effluent further downstream, there were almost inevitably investments to be made in Area C, which triggered a whole set of Civil Administration issues and requirements which generally proved almost impossible to surmount, especially once the *al Aqsa intifada* started and a pipe came to be seen as a weapon of war.

Financing sources were also an issue. The high cost of wastewater treatment plants made the PA dependent on a handful of donors, and hence on the politics of bilateral aid. Much of the investment was promised by USAID but the close engagement of the United States with Israeli policy orientations led to a series of moratoria and cancellations that followed the rhythm of politics rather than need.[68]

After years of delay and disagreement, the Israelis agreed only in 2008 to move forward on wastewater projects because of environmental and health concerns. Within Israel, there were mounting worries about the lack of effective wastewater treatment, both amongst those concerned about the environment and health, and at the political level. Ariel Sharon raised the notion that there was a 'sewage intifada'. As sewage flowed down the West Bank wadis into Israel, pressure was brought to bear, including by Israeli environmentalists, and two additional wastewater treatment plants – Hebron and Nablus West – were approved by the JWC and the Civil Administration. Following this start, the Israeli government wrote to the PWA in 2008 listing a further seven wastewater treatment projects and putting the onus on the Palestinian side in each case – either to present applications to the JWC or to the Civil Administration, or to proceed to implementation where permissions had been given.

These new Israeli positions on wastewater treatment were, however, met with scepticism. Whatever the shifting position of the Israelis, the experience of the PA and of donors and NGOs with the JWC and Civil Administration on wastewater treatment had demonstrated how problems cropped up in practice. One involved donor told us in 2008, 'On sanitation, our discussion was on Wadi Nar. The discussion was pending for a long time. It was about politics, including issues of whether it should be a joint project including settlements, or should it be a plant in Area C and run by an Israeli company.' In the case of the Ramallah/ Betunia wastewater treatment plant, the JWC gave its approval but the project ran into problems at the hands of the Civil Administration – see the discussion on this later.

Any request for wells for irrigation water was flatly rejected. Whether linked to drilling of new or replacement wells or mobilization of surface water streams, applications for extra water for agriculture were not approved, even where the request was for renewal or deepening of existing wells or where ancient sources had dried up as a result of overabstraction of groundwater.

Existence of a gap between what was approved by the JWC and what was implemented Of the 236 projects approved overall by the JWC between 1996 and 2008, only 151 (64 per cent) were implemented. Seven projects were rejected outright by the Civil Administration (see later), and seventy-eight were not implemented because of lack of Civil Administration approval, or lack of finance, or implementation problems. By value, of the $60.4 million worth of investments approved between 2001 and 2008, sixty-five per cent ($39.1 million) were implemented (see the figure *Status of projects submitted to the JWC*). This compares with target sector investment of about $180 million *per year.*[69]

A further Palestinian concern: Some water-related actions and decisions taken unilaterally by Israel, without consultation in the JWC Where sewage ran untreated towards Israel, Israeli authorities took to treating it and charging the PA. From 1996 to 2008, NIS 170 million ($47 million) was deducted by Israel from Palestinian tax revenues to pay for construction and for operation and maintenance of plants treating Palestinian sewage. There was no formal billing. The Palestinian Ministry of Finance was simply informed of the decision and respective charges.

Another example of these unilateral actions was the proposal to extend sewage treatment for Tulkarem. On 13 November 2008 Moshe Garazi of Israel's Ministry of National Infrastructure wrote to the PWA to inform them that the Yad Hannah Treatment Plant, which serves Tulkarem, 'has to be expanded to deal with higher flows, and to be upgraded to deal with the low quality of effluent, particularly during the olive season. The cost of upgrading is NIS 50 million ($13 million) and this will be charged to the PA by deduction from tax revenues.'

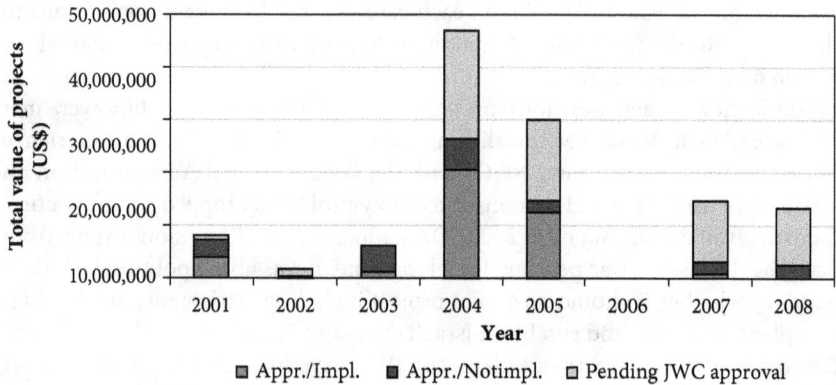

Figure 7.2 Status of projects submitted to the JWC: by value in US$. *Source*: World Bank 2009.

This kind of action was seen by PWA as an unjustified unilateral decision, and one made necessary only by the positions which the Israelis took in the JWC. Already in 2002, the PA had been charged NIS 18.5 million (US$ 5.5 million) for upgrading at Yad Hannah. PWA told us in 2008, 'We didn't see the investments in advance, they just deducted the money.' This was perhaps slightly disingenuous as PWA officials had, in fact, visited the plant, at least to see the problem of the olive discharges. They had, however, never seen any project proposal, let alone approved one. The basic point remains: 'They charge for capital and operation and maintenance costs that are not approved by PWA. And they take the wastewater at zero value – 5 million m³ a year.' According to PWA, 'since 1996, they have postponed all our wastewater projects, so the problem is their fault!'[70]

The Civil Administration and movement and access (M&A) restrictions

Additional constraints placed on planning and investment by Civil Administration rules From the outset, certain water projects approved by the JWC required a second approval by the Civil Administration. Under the 1967 Military Order that required permits for all water structures, permits from the Civil Administration were required even after Oslo for any Palestinian water infrastructure that touched on Area C, which covers nearly two-thirds of the West Bank. This included wells, water conveyance and distribution works, and wastewater treatment and reuse infrastructure. Given that Palestinian-controlled areas (A) or partly controlled areas (B) are, on the whole, small fragments surrounded by Area C territory – as we have seen, 165 disconnected and often small fragments – almost all water infrastructure impinged on Area C and fell under this requirement. Thus the Civil Administration represented a second screening of Palestinian water projects, quite separate from the JWC. As a result the anomaly arose, as we saw earlier, that a number of projects were approved by the JWC for which detailed planning permission was then not granted by the Civil Administration.

The rules that the Civil Administration applied to Palestinian water infrastructure development and management bore some resemblance to regular physical planning applications in Israel itself. However, the planning approval process was done by the Civil Administration in Area C without public participation or representation by Palestinians, and as though the land and water resources were the property of the Israeli state.[71] Palestinian accounts of the experience of the process reported that it was slow and, Palestinians believed, arbitrary and aligned with Israeli and settler interests rather than with those of the Palestinians.

An example of how the process worked against Palestinian interests was the Civil Administration's screening of the few sorely needed wastewater treatment plants that had finally made it through the JWC. One example was the case of the Ramallah/Betunia plant. The need for this project was never in dispute. Both Palestinians and Israelis were fully agreed on it and it received the approval of the JWC. On 24 June 2008, the PWA requested approval from the Civil Administration. The Civil Administration responded with some standard requirements: detailed plans to be submitted for approval, a full environmental assessment report to be prepared, the project not to impinge on three archaeological sites. These requirements, although galling for the Palestinians on whose land the project was to be constructed, were not unreasonable and could have been imposed by the Palestinians themselves had they been fully in charge. The sticking point, however, was the requirement that 'The plans should take into account the possibility of connecting the community of Beit Horon to the plant'.[72] This stipulation was plainly unacceptable to the Palestinians – it would have meant not only providing services to one of the hated settlements but also implicitly recognizing its 'right to exist'. The project was well and truly stalled.

Whatever the project, the Civil Administration was generally seen as a major constraint to good development. One donor commented in 2008:

> First thing we request is a letter from PWA approving the project. Then we go to the JWC. But then we have to go to the Civil Administration – and there delays of 2–3 years are normal. In fact, we have no positive outcomes for Area C. For example, the Jiflik project was approved by PWA and then by the JWC, then we pushed it – only to fall foul of the archaeology Catch 22.[73]

Often the restrictions imposed appeared arbitrary. Comments from project staff and donors who tried to implement water infrastructure investments in Area C show the difficulties encountered.[74] One donor commented: '*In Area C we are not allowed to build any field structure such as ponds, we cannot bury a conveyance system . . .*'. A project manager said, '*Household cisterns are destroyed even though you don't need a licence. They say this is because in Area C water is considered "property of the Israeli state"*'. Sometimes the restrictions seem to run counter not only to good water management practice but even to common sense – '*Even the smallest rehabilitation project needs a licence in Area C . . . but it is very difficult to get any licence in Area C – even for reducing unaccounted-for water.'* Reducing unaccounted-for water requires repairs or replacement of networks of water pipes – and pipes are a strictly controlled security item.

And again, in respect of essential repairs: *'In Tulkarem, the water connection was damaged, the Civil Administration would not give approval to repair it. Water had to be trucked in.'* Sometimes the decisions seemed to be connected to a desire to reduce Palestinian use of water, as when the PWA wanted to increase the efficiency of groundwater extraction but was refused – *'Refusal to allow the connection of wells to electricity reduces efficiency and increases costs. This applies to most wells in Salfit, Qalqilya, Tulkarem.'*

The administrative constraints imposed by the Civil Administration were backed up by force. There was frequent use of military control in Area C to enforce Israeli authority over water resources. The case of the village well at Arrabona discussed later is a case in point. Even rainwater harvesting cisterns have been destroyed by the IDF – see the case in our companion volume of the six cisterns demolished in 2019 at Mount Tamoun.[75]

Overall, the result has been very low levels of development and loss of donor funds. Donors and NGOs have avoided Area C because 'you can't get a permit'. Or long and costly delays have been incurred. For example, if changes were required by the Civil Administration, perhaps that a pipeline be relocated from Area C to Area B, the request had to go back to the JWC. Rational water planning also became impossible. One Palestinian official said: 'When we asked about a long-distance water carrier route, the answer came: *"You cannot have a line from Bethlehem to Hebron because in 2020 there will be an Eastern Wall."* They just show maps indicating future settlements – this was the reason why the [Palestinian] National Carrier Project was frustrated.'[76]

Beyond that, too, the uncertainty about the final status and the future of the settlements made large-scale planning impossible. A Palestinian official said, 'We have a fear of building white elephants – it is hard to plan when you have 400,000 settlers who have to leave.'[77] Which is one way of putting it. Another way of putting it would be that it is hard to plan when most of the territory for which you want to plan is occupied by a state whose actions suggest a permanent occupation and progressive appropriation. Although some of the Civil Administration restrictions on water investment in Area C in this period clearly related to security concerns, there was considerable suspicion that, overall, the intended outcome was to make life difficult enough for the Palestinians who still lived there that they might prefer to leave.

Arrabona's failed coping strategy We saw examples of the problems when we visited the northeastern corner of Jenin governorate in 2018. In this part of the West Bank, the JWC did not license further wells and coping strategies became extreme. In one village, Arrabona, residents ran out of all alternatives for access to safe water at a reasonable cost and they dared to drill an unlicensed well for drinking water

Arrabona lies right on the separation barrier, and 2,000 dunums (200 hectares) of its land are, in fact, on the other side of the barrier. Although the village itself is in Area B, it is surrounded by Area C. For years the village had been very short of water. It was using what rainwater it could collect in cisterns, and buying in tanker water, paying up to 14 NIS per cubic metre (US$ 4 per cubic metre). The quality was very poor and there was water-related disease.

The villagers had long tried to get a licence to drill a well, but without success. They tell us that they got no clear reply from the PWA, no written answer, only an unhelpful verbal message that 'the Joint Water Committee has not met for a long time now'. So in early 2007, the villagers pooled their financial resources – it came to NIS 90,000 ($25,000) – and they started to drill an unlicensed well for water supply.[78] The study for the well was done by the representative of an NGO, the Palestinian Hydrology Group, in nearby Jenin. When they got to 100 metres they received a notice from the Civil Administration. Nonetheless they continued drilling. They received a second notice, in Hebrew, from the Planning and Construction Department of Beit Il, the headquarters of the Civil Administration. Attached were other notices saying that certain houses were to be demolished, as being 'outside the zoning' of the village.

Yet they continued drilling and reached 274 metres. A villager explained: 'The contractor was drilling day and night. But he was afraid. He left, and another came.' Then, one morning soon afterwards, '40 to 50 military vehicles came with a bulldozer. The IDF surrounded the village and called a curfew. They bulldozed two houses and filled in the well.'

The villagers have turned the well site into a small play park, with a dry fountain in the middle. They told us, 'We spent 90,000 shekels for nothing. All we wanted was safe water for our children. Now we have a very expensive play park – and the same contaminated expensive water.'[79]

The bitterest thing for the villagers is not that the Israelis behaved as they did, although that was bitter enough. It was that their own Palestinian institution, the one charged with bringing them safe water, let them down. Not only did the PWA never help, but shortly after the incident, the PWA also came and confiscated all the drilling equipment.

*   *   *

The result of Oslo and all that followed was a significant shortfall in development and services. Taken together, the operation of the JWC, Civil Administration rules, the physical M&A restrictions, the institutional weaknesses in the PA and the shortfalls in aid effectiveness reduced the development of water resources and services for the Palestinian population well below levels expected at the time of Oslo. The impact on the Palestinian economy and on well-being is significant.

LAST WORD

THE DIVERGENCE OF TWO PEOPLES – ISRAELI GAIN AND PALESTINIAN LOSS

The history of water is at the heart of the development of the land once called Palestine. From the beginnings of modernization, it was the harnessing and use of water in late Ottoman times that drove the development of the domestic economy and the export trade. Over the course of the last century, water has turned from a constraint to a vital motor of development. As a result, a land which experts at the start of the Mandate said could support a scanty population of a million or at the limit two, today sustains more than 13 million people, many of them living at a standard not even imagined by their forbears. Much of this extraordinary change has been due to the development of natural water resources and to their clever use. More recently, innovation has created new resources – wastewater cleaned and reused, and desalinated water made from the limitless resource of the Mediterranean Sea.

Alongside this change in water and water use in the century that has passed since the end of the Ottoman era have come other changes that an observer from 1918 would scarcely credit.

Demographic change, with more than three-quarters of the territory inhabited by a people 7 million strong who a hundred years ago numbered no more than 100,000, and alongside this people the descendants of the former Arab majority, who have also multiplied to be around 6 million within the boundaries of Mandate Palestine (and many more millions around the world). Those Arabs who live in the West Bank and Gaza – more than 4 million – are locked into hundreds of islets of land that make up no more than one-tenth of their former territory. Others are citizens of a Jewish state, or spread across the region and the globe in a new diaspora.

Political change, with the state of Israel, once little more than a dream of Zion restored that was held by a few visionaries and refugees, utterly transformed into a powerful modern state dominant in the region and bound up in a partnership of equals with the world's only superpower. And crammed in beside them, the Palestinians of the West Bank and Gaza, stateless and, these days, virtually unsupported by the world in any of their aspirations to building a state as Israel has, living in little enclaves with limited home rule, often seen in the shadows as pariahs or terrorists, and constantly under threat of correction by the powerful occupier.

Social and economic change, one of the two peoples confident, prospective, pioneering, affluent, thoroughly at home in the modern world, the other at best suppressing bitterness at perpetual failure and loss, generations growing up poor and jobless, the hapless youth prepared to offer themselves to hurt or even death because they have no hope and so no longer give a damn. The water is a part of all this, both symbolic and illustrative of the larger whole.

The Palestinians see that the people who came to share their land and were expected to go forward together with them into the modern world have taken not only nine-tenths of the land but almost all the water resource. *Water is life* is a truism of the Middle East. The appropriation of water not only symbolizes a larger, more general appropriation but is also a confiscation of the means of life, a means of fructifying the land, a means of developing healthy and prosperous communities and a growing economy, a means even – as the case of Israel so well shows – of strengthening the polity, reinforcing the sense of nationhood and consolidating national pride and an identity rooted both in the land and in history.

Where Israel has won water independence, the Palestinians must now buy their water in a market where there is only one seller, at a price determined by the marginal cost of production – the high price of desalination – with the extra cost of pumping water back up to the highlands, when there is water at a fraction of the cost beneath their feet.

Where Israel has developed a national grid that stores water and dispatches it seamlessly throughout the country, the Palestinians are denied such a connectivity and, if they are not dependent on water from Israeli sources, must live within little water islands, unconnected to the next Palestinian town.

Where Israel supplies to its citizens enough water to meet all demands – even water for swimming pools in its settlements in the West Bank – Palestinians scrape by with low quantities, intermittent services and often of poor quality. Where Israel supplies ample water to a prosperous and high-value agriculture, Palestinian farmers must live within a meagre, dwindling ration.

And, it is not only the Palestinian people who suffer this. The environment and the natural resources of the territory have been sadly compromised. For many years, Israel overdrew on water resources, depleting the aquifers at the risk of wholesale saline intrusion, drying up the wadis and filling them with sewage and refuse, drawing down Lake Tiberias perilously close to the point where irreversible salinization might occur, and participating in turning the lower Jordan River into a drain and the Dead Sea into a newly moribund sink.

Today, Israel has the nous and the wealth to begin the arduous process of correcting all this. But where Israel now treats all its wastewater and reuses almost all of it, Palestinian sewage goes untreated, the wadis and groundwater are fouled with it, and reuse is impossible when the water cannot be stored, pipes cannot be laid, and the lands to be irrigated are largely in the no-go zones that extend all across the West Bank.

This book has recounted the history of these two widely diverging water fortunes, the one a triumph, the other a saddening tale of aggravating loss. Our companion volume *Water Security for Palestinians and Israelis* will look at the outcomes within the framework of water security – security of access to water resources, security of water services to people, the economy and the environment, and security against the risks of pollution and environmental harm and of extreme events and climate change. The discussion will show the extent to which the water events of the last hundred years have resulted in a gap, resembling a chasm, between the water security of the two peoples who started from the same point a century ago. And in the final part of that book we will look at practical steps to close the gap.

NOTES

Chapter 1

1 David Ben-Gurion, Diary, 12 July 1937. The Ben-Gurion Archive, Sede Boker, Israel, cited in Rogan and Shlaim, 41–2. The context is a reflection on the Peel Commission report published that month which recommended the transfer of at least 225,000 Arabs out of the lowlands to make way for a proposed Jewish state.

2 The Sibylline Books were the oracular books of ancient Rome consulted in times of crisis. They were 'said to have been obtained in the reign of Tarquinius Priscus, or Tarquinius Superbus, when a Sibyl (Σίβυλλα), or prophetic woman, presented herself before the king, and offered nine books for sale. Upon the king refusing to purchase them, she went and burnt three, and then returned to demand the same price for the remaining six as she had done for the nine. The king again refused to purchase them, whereupon she burnt three more and demanded the same sum for the remaining three, as she had done at first for the nine: the king's curiosity now became excited, so that he purchased the books, and then the Sibyl vanished.' Source: *A Dictionary of Greek and Roman Antiquities*, John Murray, London 1875.

Chapter 2

1 Much of this description is based on *Peake's Commentary on the Bible* by Matthew Black, Harold Henry Rowley and Arthur Samuel Peake (London: Thomas Nelson, 1962). We have tried to give both the historic names of places as they were in late Ottoman times and, where relevant, the modern names used either by Israelis or by Palestinians.

2 In fact, Wales is somewhat smaller, about 21,000 square kilometres (8,100 square miles).

3 Although this fault occurred way back in geological time, some 35 million years ago, geological movement continues and many earthquakes are recorded in history. In the Middle Ages, large quakes occurred in 746, 1016 and 1034. More recently, on 11 July 1927, an earthquake centred around Jericho killed 500 people and caused extensive damage in Nablus and to the Al Aqsa Mosque and the Church of the Holy Sepulchre in Jerusalem.

4 In his moving memoir *Mapping My Return – A Palestinian Memoir* (AUC Press, 2017), Salman Abu Sitta returns to the Wadi Gaza and remembers 'the wheat fields of my childhood', the meadows in spring 'a carpet of green as far as you could see', the abundant cereal production.

5 These valleys lay between the Philistine coast and Israelite Judaea. In each of the valleys prominent cities developed. The Aijalon, the northernmost valley, was guarded by Tel Gezer. The Sorek and Elah valleys were guarded by Beth Shemesh and Azekah, respectively. To the south, the city of Lachish stood over the Lachish Valley.

These valleys, and the strategic cities that overlooked them, were the location of many Old Testament battles.

6   Source: Peake, *Peake's Commentary on the Bible.*
7   See E. Robinson and E. Smith, *Biblical Researches in Palestine, Mount Sinai and Arabia Petraea* (Boston: Crocker & Brewer, 1841).
8   Source: Peake, *Peake's Commentary on the Bible.*
9   The lake was finally drained in the 1950s, although a small part has been restored to wetlands in recent years.
10 Source: Peake, *Peake's Commentary on the Bible.*
11 Source: Peake, *Peake's Commentary on the Bible.*
12 About 30 metres wide and from 1 to 3 metres deep.
13 Source: Peake, *Peake's Commentary on the Bible.*
14 Professor Tony Allan pointed out to us that the White Paper calculations were based on ensuring food self-sufficiency. Clearly the ability to import food needs shifts the water limitation on population considerably.
15 See *The Development of the Water Resources of the Occupied Palestinian Territories: Some Key Issues* (DRC Grey in Isaac and Shuval 1994), 219; Seth M. Siegel, *Let There Be Water* (New York: St Martin's Press, 2015), 337, 21.
16 Source: Society for Austro-Arab Relations, *Development Perspectives for Agriculture in the Occupied Palestinian Territories* (1992).
17 Benjamin Netanyahu, Speech after signing the California – Israel Cooperation Agreement (Mountain View, CA, 5 March 2014), cited in Siegel, *Let There Be Water*, 224.
18 Source WANA 2017, *Decoupling National Water Needs for National Water Supplies: Insights and Potential for Countries in the Jordan Basin.* West Africa–North Africa Institute, June 2017.
19 This description draws on Ward and Ruckstuhl 2017 and on the Report of the State of Israel to the Conference of the Parties (COP) of the United Nations Framework Convention on Climate Change (UNFCCC) on impacts, adaptation and vulnerability to climate change in Israel. https://www.adaptation-undp.org/explore/western-asia/israel.
20 Jeffrey K. Sosland, *Cooperating Rivals: The Riparian Politics of the Jordan River Basin* (Albany: State University of New York, 2007), 141–2; World Bank, *Developing the Occupied Territories: An Investment in Peace* (Washington, DC: World Bank, 1993) Annex 2: Water and Irrigation to Volume 4; Annex IV, Table XIII.
21 Within what is today the Palestinian side of the Green Line.
22 Source: *Water Resources: The Palestinian Perspective*, by Amjad Aliewi, in *Water Wisdom*, edited by Tal and Abed Rabbo, 14.
23 Now within Israel.
24 From the 1930s Zionist settlers farmed the area where the Gilboa and Beit Shean springs discharged and used the spring water for irrigation. Later, wells were drilled. Palestinians use the water from the Wadi Far'a and Bardala Springs, largely for irrigation. Under the Oslo Accords, Israel was allocated 103 million cubic metres from this aquifer, the Palestinians 42 million cubic metres. Source: H. Gvirtzman, *Groundwater Allocation in Judea and Samaria* (Isaac and Shuval 1994), 214.
25 Before 1967, the water of this aquifer was used exclusively by Palestinians, with about 58 million cubic metres used for irrigation. After the 1967 Occupation, Israel drilled wells on the upper slopes of the mountains. The rationale was that the wells would capture more fresh groundwater high up before it reached the natural outlets in the

lower slopes where it became more saline. This allowed use of more groundwater, almost doubling the yield to about 100 million cubic metres a year. Under the Oslo Accords, 54 million cubic metres from this aquifer were allocated to the Palestinians and 40 million cubic metres to Israel. Israel has assigned most of its share to Jewish settlers in the West Bank. Source: Gvirtzman in Isaac and Shuval, 214; see also Mark Zeitoun, *Power and Water in the Middle East: The Hidden Politics of the Palestinian-Israeli Water Conflict* (London: I.B. Tauris, 2008), 116 on this question. Of the extra water developed above the pre-1967 level of 58 million cubic metres, 35 million cubic metres went for irrigation by Jewish settlers on 7,200 hectares and 7 million cubic metres was for domestic use by both settlers and Palestinians – see Chapter 6. At the time of Oslo, it was in the Eastern Aquifer that extra water was allocated to the Palestinians – see Chapter 7. However, years of effort to develop this resource have produced little result. Inevitably the suspicion exists that this 'extra water' was a ploy to divert Palestinians from the productive Western and Northeastern aquifers which were much easier to develop but which were predominantly already exploited by Israel.

26 Source: Grey in Isaac and Shuval 1994, 220–1.
27 Estimates based on *Israel's Chronic Water Problems*. Israel Ministry of Foreign Affairs. https://mfa.gov.il/MFA/IsraelExperience/AboutIsrael/Spotlight/Pages/Israel-s%20Chronic%20Water%20Problem.aspx.
28 See Chapter 13.
29 Source: Zeitoun, *Power and Water in the Middle East*, 48.
30 The description of the river draws on the article on the Jordan River in the Encyclopaedia Britannica.
31 Sources: Arnon Soffer, *The Relevance of the Johnston Plan to the Reality of 1993 and Beyond* (Isaac and Shuval 1994), 108 – see the table and map in Isaac and Shuval 1994, 120; and *Inventory of Shared Water Resources In Western Asia*, ESCWA 2019. https://waterinventory.org/surface_water/jordan-river-basin.
32 These 2017 figures are based on Palestinian access to 109 MCM annually and Israeli access to about 1,000 MCM. Neither figure includes manufactured water or purchased water.

Chapter 3

1 Much of this section draws on Ilan Pappé's *History of Modern Palestine: One Land, Two Peoples* (Cambridge: Cambridge University Press, 2004), 333.
2 Mark Twain, *Innocents Abroad*, cited in Bard, *Myths and Facts* (AICE, 2001), 30.
3 Quoted in the *Report of the 1937 Palestine Royal Commission Cmd.* 5479, 233. On the 'wooden ploughs', Edwin Samuel, the District Officer for Ramallah and later for Nazareth, gives an account in his memoirs of his attempt in the 1920s to substitute iron ploughs purchased from a German firm in Jaffa for the wooden ploughs employed by peasants. 'The iron ploughs promptly and completely broke upon encountering the stony soil of the Ramallah hills.' See Edwin Samuel, *A Lifetime in Jerusalem: The Memoirs of the Second Viscount Samuel* (Jerusalem: Israel Universities Press, 1970).
4 Avnieri provides a description of the topographical and demographic conditions prevailing in the various regions of Palestine immediately prior to Jewish settlement,

basing the study on 'the reports of foreign travellers and early settlers (Oliphant), cartographers (Van de Velde), and foreign exploratory expeditions (Palestine Exploration Fund (PEF))'. Nonetheless, the political motivation and bias of the study are clear even from its title. See Arie L. Avnieri, *The Claim of Dispossession – Jewish Land-Settlement and the Arabs, 1878–1948* (Efal, Israel: Yad Tabenkin, 1982).

5   That Israelis now call the Kishon.

6   Now called the Zebulun Valley by Israelis.

7   Avnieri, *The Claim of Dispossession*, 49–50.

8   An 1874 commentary by C. R. Condor, quoted in Avnieri, *The Claim of Dispossession*, 53.

9   See Edward Hull, *Mount Seir, Sinai and Western Palestine* (London: Richard Bentley & Son, 1885), 139; and W. M. Thomson, *The Land and the Book* (Thomas Nelson & Son, 1911), 556.

10 Pappé, *History of Modern Palestine*, 73.

11 See Julia S. Templin, *Zababdeh: A Palestinian Water History*, May 2012.

12 Pappé, *History of Modern Palestine*, 18, 70.

13 Templin, *Zababdeh*, 44.

14 Twelve dunums is just over one hectare or three acres of land. A dunum was the Ottoman unit of area representing the amount of land that could be ploughed by a team of oxen in a day. The legal definition was 'forty standard paces in length and breadth' but its actual area varied considerably from place to place, from a little more than 900 square metres in Ottoman Palestine to around 2,500 square metres in Iraq. The unit is still in use in many areas previously ruled by the Ottomans, although the new or metric dunum has been redefined as exactly one decare (1,000 square metres), which is one-tenth of a hectare. *Many thanks to Wikipedia for this good information.*

15 Templin, *Zababdeh*, 48–50.

16 *Musha'* nonetheless persisted, to be finally abolished during the Mandate by the British who, schooled in mediaeval English history, saw it as feudal.

17 Pappé, *History of Modern Palestine*, 24, 49; Ruth Kark, *Jaffa: A City in Evolution, 1799–1917* (Jerusalem: Yad Izhak Ben-Svi Press, 1990), 24.

18 Pappé, *History of Modern Palestine*, 25.

19 The source for much of this discussion is the excellent *Jaffa, City in Evolution, 1799–1917* by Ruth Kark.

20 The cultivation of citrus fruit has a long history in Palestine. Hebrew scripture at the time of the Maccabees mentions a citrus fruit which grew around Jaffa and was used for religious rituals. In the days of King Herod, the fruit is said to have been cultivated in the region of Caesarea. The *baladi* orange is thought to have arrived after the Arab conquest in the seventh century. In the documentation of the Crusades, between the eleventh and thirteenth centuries, there are descriptions of large citrus orchards in the Jaffa and Caesarea areas. At the time of Napoleon's invasion of Palestine (in 1799), Jaffa's citrus orchards were already noted. [Source: http://www.jaffa.co.il/main.asp?id =62]

21 Kark, *Jaffa: A City in Evolution, 1799–1917*, 243.

22 Kark, *Jaffa: A City in Evolution, 1799–1917*, 240, quoting Solomon, Mas'a, 108.

23 A case typically contained a gross of oranges, 144 oranges.

24 In 1889, to irrigate one acre (approximately 4 dunums) over a 23-week season or 161 days, 2,300 cubic metres of water were consumed. For a 20 dunum plot (2 hectares) with a crop value of 2,500–3,500 francs, an average of about 800 francs

might be spent on irrigation – in other words, one-third to one-quarter of the earnings. [Kark, *Jaffa: A City in Evolution, 1799–1917*, 242 quoting from *Report on irrigation methods in Palestine*, 29 August 1889, USNA T471].

25 Source: Kark quoting Solomon, Mas'a, 108.

26 *See* Mark LeVine, *Overthrowing Geography: Jaffa, Tel Aviv, and the Struggle for Palestine, 1880–1948* (Illustrated ed.) (University of California Press, 2005). ISBN 0-520-23994-6. ISBN 9780520239944.

27 Kark, *Jaffa: A City in Evolution, 1799–1917*, 245.

28 Where a traditional grove required an investment of just over a hundred francs per acre (107 francs, the equivalent of about US$500 today), a modern grove irrigated by these kerosene-powered engines cost three times as much (317 francs an acre, the equivalent of over $1,500 today). The source is Kark, *Jaffa: A City in Evolution, 1799–1917*, 246 based on Rokal, 96; Ha-Oam, 25, 24 June 1908, p. 337.

29 Aaron Aaronsohn, *Agricultural and Botanic Explorations in Palestine* (1910); Kark, *Jaffa: A City in Evolution, 1799–1917*, 248.

30 Kark, *Jaffa: A City in Evolution, 1799–1917*, 251.

31 Kark, *Jaffa: A City in Evolution, 1799–1917*, 250.

32 Pappé, *History of Modern Palestine*, 31, and the Wikipedia article on Mikveh Israel.

33 In 1954, the remains of Baron Edmond de Rothschild were reburied at Zikhron Ya'akov.

34 As do the huge wine cellars that were carved into the mountain over a century ago. Source: Wikipedia.

35 Six Egyptian piastres was equivalent to about one shilling sterling in 1904. Today's equivalent value is about £4 or $6, so a good wage for those days.

36 Templin, *Zababdeh*, 21: Abu Jilal, interview with author (Zababdeh, West Bank, 8 June 2008).

37 Sources: Dante A. Caponera, *Principles of Water Law and Administration: National and International* (Rotterdam, Netherlands: A. A. Balkema Publishers, 1992), 71; Zeitoun, *Power and Water in the Middle East*, 74; J. W. Eaton and D. J. Eaton, *Water Utilization in the Yarmouk-Jordan* in Isaac and Shuval 1994, 97.

38 Pappé, *History of Modern Palestine*, 29: The draining of the Palestinian marshes continued into the 1950s when the last swamps around Lake Huleh were drained.

39 Most of this description is drawn from Julia Templin, who notes the Masterman quote, from E. W. G. Masterman, *Agricultural Life in Palestine*. The Biblical World 15, no. 3 (March 1900), 189. http://www.jstor.org/stable/3137064.

40 This pool is described in J. M. Barghouth and R. M. Y. Al-Sa'ed, 'Sustainability of ancient water supply facilities in Jerusalem', *Sustainability* 1 (2009): 1106–19. Cited in Amer Marie, Saed Khayat and Muna Dajani, 'Water quality legislation in Palestine over the past century', *Environmental Sciences Europe* 24 (2012): 15.

41 Source: Amer Marie et al. 'Water quality legislation in Palestine over the past century'.

42 Source: *Questions of the Waqf in the Ottoman Period*. Bulletin by Islamic Center for Archive and Cultural Heritage, 2005, Abu Dis Jerusalem, cited in 'Review of water legislation from the Pre-British mandate period through the Israeli occupation', by Amer Marei and Imad Abu-Kishk in the *Palestine-Israel Journal* 19, no. 4 & 20, no. 1 (2014)/ Natural Resources and the Arab–Israeli Conflict.

43 Source: 'The Limits of Separation: Jaffa and Tel Aviv before 1948: The Underground Story, by Nahum Karlinsky', in *Tel-Aviv at 100: Myths, Memories and Realities*, ed. Maoz Azaryahu and S. Ilan Troen (Indiana University Press). Karlinsky cites Shmuel

Avitsur, 'The First Project for the Intensive Exploitation of the Yarkon Waters (The Franghia-Navon Scheme of 1893)', *Haaretz Museum Bulletin* 6 (1964): 80, 88.

44 See Nahum Karlinsky, *California Dreaming: Ideology, Society, and Technology in the Citrus Industry of Palestine, 1890–1939* (Albany, 2005), 96. In fact, the town was renamed Tel Aviv the very next year, 1910, after the Hebrew title of Herzl's visionary novel of 1902, *The Old New Land* (German: *Altneuland*), the translator using *tel* ('ancient mound') for 'old' and *aviv* ('spring') for 'new'. The name Tel Aviv appears in the Book of Ezekiel, where it is used for a place in Babylonia to which the Israelites had been exiled (Ezek. 3.15). The source for this information is the excellent Wikipedia article on Herzl's novel.

45 This section draws extensively on the excellent paper by Vincent Lemire, *Water in Jerusalem at the End of the Ottoman Period (1850–1920)*, Bulletin du Centre de recherche français à Jérusalem. Online, 13 March 2008, Consulted 4 February 2019. http://journals.openedition.org/bcrfj/2572.

46 Source : Lemire, *Water in Jerusalem at the End of the Ottoman Period (1850–1920)*.

47 The Gihon spring or Fountain of the Virgin in the Kidron valley was the main source of water for the Pool of Siloam. One of the world's major intermittent springs – and a reliable water source that made human settlement possible in ancient Jerusalem – the spring was not only used for drinking water, but also initially for irrigation. The spring rises in a cave 6 metres by 2 metres (20 feet by 7 feet). The spring flows from three to five times daily in winter, twice daily in summer, and only once daily in autumn. This peculiarity is accounted for by the supposition that the outlet from the reservoir is by a passage in the form of a siphon. Source: Wikipedia.

48 E. W. G. Masterman, in a treatise on the hygienic conditions in Jerusalem, cites an Ottoman regulation which tied the grant of a building permit to the construction of a cistern on the roof or in the basement of the future building. See the articles by Masterman on the *Palestine Information with Provenance* database.

49 In the early 1920s, the Mandate engineers counted 7,300.

50 Engineer Franghia was a very well-qualified engineer, the president of the Technical Corps of the Engineering School of Istanbul.

51 In the 1870s, Charles Warren reported that 'the Solomon aqueduct was repaired with taxpayers' money … the poor fellahin were forced to bring their own stones and mortar to the site'.

52 Vincent Lemire takes this is as an example of how the image of the late Ottomans became distorted: 'the condescending image of an immobile and complicated East, [characterized by] the long slumber of Jerusalem from 1517 to 1917, and the overblown contrast between the impotence of the Ottoman administration and the golden age of Solomon's rule.'

53 Pappé, *History of Modern Palestine*, 59.

54 Pappé, *History of Modern Palestine*, 58–61.

55 Source: *The Limits of Separation: Jaffa and Tel Aviv before 1948: The Underground Story*, by Nahum Karlinsky.

Chapter 4

1 A. J. Sherman, *Mandate Days: British Lives in Palestine 1918–1948* (London: Thames & Hudson, 1997), 101.

2   Pappé, *History of Modern Palestine*, 71–73.

3   Pappé, *History of Modern Palestine*, 71.

4   See E. R. J. Owen, *Economic Development in Mandatory Palestine, 1918–1948*, ed. Abed (London: Routledge, 1988), 27.

5   Owen, *Economic Development in Mandatory Palestine, 1918–1948*, 13. Professor Owen issues the caveat that data for the economy during the Mandate tend to be patchy and were the subject of constant political intervention and manipulation by both Zionists and Arabs.

6   Owen, *Economic Development in Mandatory Palestine, 1918–1948*, 13–14.

7   See Jacob Norris, 'Toxic waters: Ibrahim Hazboun and the struggle for a Dead Sea concession, 1913-1948', *Jerusalem Quarterly* 45 (2011): 25–42. ISSN 1565-2254. Available from Sussex Research Online: http://sro.sussex.ac.uk/id/eprint/43631/ Norris maintains that as the 1920s wore on, it became increasingly difficult for the old Arab merchant classes to secure government contracts. He cites the Beiruti merchants who had secured the Tiberias Hot Springs concession from the Ottoman government in 1912. Initially, the British Mandatory government extended their concession, but when a Jewish company expressed an interest in the springs in 1925, the government's chief secretary cut short the original concession. In 1932 a Zionist enterprise, the Tiberias Hot Springs, opened to the public.

8   Quotations are from Jacob Norris in *Toxic waters*.

9   This geographical concentration resulted in a particular blow for the Arabs in 1948 when these valuable assets fell into Jewish hands and the Arab workforce either fled or became redundant. See Owen, *Economic Development in Mandatory Palestine, 1918–1948*, 33.

10 Owen, *Economic Development in Mandatory Palestine, 1918–1948*, 17, 25–6.

11 Pappé, *History of Modern Palestine*, 78.

12 Owen, *Economic Development in Mandatory Palestine, 1918–1948*, 27 ff.

13 Pappé, *History of Modern Palestine*, 117–18.

14 Source: *Survey of Palestine*, 391.

15 Which is ironic in view of Israel's later adoption of exactly the same powers in its legislation after Independence. Sources: Eaton in Isaac and Shuval 1994, 97; and *Legal Aspects of Water Quality Management* by Richard E. Laster in *Water Quality Management Under Conditions of Scarcity: Israel as a Case Study* (Academic Press, 1980). Edited by Hillel Shuval.

16 Palestine Gazette 711 (1937).

17 Palestine Gazette 1204 (1942).

18 Dinar 2003, 190, quoted in Zeitoun, *Power and Water in the Middle East*, 65.

19 Trottier 1999, 41 quoted in Zeitoun, *Power and Water in the Middle East*, 65.

20 Herzl's 1902 utopian novel *The Old New Land* (in German, *Altneuland*) is remarkable for its persuasive visionary power and for its depiction of a peaceful, democratic, multi-ethnic society in a land where all citizens live in prosperous harmony at one with nature. The novel tells the story of Friedrich Löwenberg who visits Jaffa in 1902 and finds Palestine a backward, destitute and sparsely populated land. Visiting Palestine again in 1923, Friedrich is astonished to discover a land transformed. A Jewish organization called the New Society has arisen, run by European Jews who have rediscovered and reinhabited their *Altneuland*, reclaiming their own destiny in the land of Israel.

     The founders have obtained the consent of all European powers for their enterprise. They avoid getting entangled in any inter-power rivalry. In fact, the country maintains no armed forces. The country is now prosperous and well populated, boasts a thriving cooperative industry based on state-of-the-art technology and is home to a free, just and cosmopolitan modern society. Arabs have full equal rights with Jews, with an Arab engineer Rashid Bey amongst the New Society's leaders. Most merchants in the country are Armenians, Greeks and members of other ethnic groups.

Rashid Bey explains that the Arabs saw no reason to oppose the influx of Jews, who 'developed the country and raised everybody's standard of living'. Friedrich arrives at the time of a general election campaign, during which a fanatical rabbi establishes a political platform arguing that the country belongs exclusively to Jews and demands that non-Jewish citizens be stripped of their voting rights. The rabbi is defeated. *All of this footnote is based on the excellent Wikipedia article.*

21   Ben Gurion led the Yishuv, the Jewish community, during much of the Mandate period and later became Israel's first prime minister.

22   Siegel, *Let There Be Water*, 15, 101. Emphasis added to Peres's remark.

23   Citation from El Musa and Zeitoun, 266. Also quoted in Committee on the Exercise of the Inalienable Rights of the Palestinian People, *Water Resources of the Occupied Palestinian Territory*, 1992, in UNISPAL, New York: United Nations, url: http://uni spal.un.org/UNISPAL.NSF/0/296EE705038AC9FC852561170067E05F.

24   Zeitoun, *Power and Water in the Middle East*, 65–6.

25   Today the Litani provides a major source for water supply, irrigation and hydroelectricity for the Lebanese people and economy.

26   Eaton in Isaac and Shuval 1994, 95.

27   This did not, however, kill off the idea, which was to resurface half a century later as the state of Israel began to build its water inventory in the 1950s (see Chapter 5).

28   Sharif S. El Musa, *Water Conflict: Economics, Politics, Law and the Palestinian-Israeli Water Resources* (Washington, DC: Institute for Palestine Studies, 1997), 276; Zeitoun, *Power and Water in the Middle East*, 66.

29   Pappé, *History of Modern Palestine*, 95, 98.

30   Pappé, *History of Modern Palestine*, 77.

31   Siegel, *Let There Be Water*, 23–4 describes the role of the innovative water engineer Simcha Blass in the development of the wells in the Jezreel Valley. Blass was encouraged by the pioneering Levi Eshkol who, in the same year, 1935, took part in the founding of Mekorot, the Zionist, and later Israeli, water development agency.

32   Later in 1919, Rutenberg moved to Palestine and at once put his commitment to Zionism into practice. He worked with Jabotinsky to set up the Haganah, the Jewish militia, and led the Tel Aviv unit of the Haganah during the Arab hostilities of 1921. Rutenberg also became the first Palestinian citizen under the British Mandate, after the British had enacted a law creating Palestinian citizenship in 1925. The highly versatile Rutenberg also founded Palestine Airways and subsequently served as president of the Jewish National Council.

33   Rutenberg aimed high here. Reading was Rufus Isaacs. The son of a London East End Jewish fruit importer, Isaacs left school at fifteen and served as a ship's boy. Later he was called to the bar and after a very successful legal career became successively Lord Chief Justice, ambassador to the United States and viceroy of India. Only the second practising Jew to serve in the cabinet, he later became the last ever Liberal foreign secretary.

34   '$1,000,000 Pledged to Harness Jordan; Rutenberg Engineering Project Aimed to Furnish Power for Palestine. Jews Here Contributing; Justice Brandeis Gives $25,000

– Light, Railway and Irrigation Plans', *New York Times* (25 June 1922), https://www
.nytimes.com/1922/06/25/archives/1000000-pledged-to-harness-jordan-rutenberg-en
gineering-project.html. Accessed 18 June 2019.

35   Alwyn R. Rouyer, *Turning Water into Politics: The Water Issue in the Palestinian-Israeli
Conflict* (New York: St. Martin's Press, 2000), 99.

36   An early example of the Zionist practice of 'appropriation by naming'.

37   Other power plants were built in Tel Aviv, Haifa and Tiberias. Jerusalem, where
power was supplied until 1942 under a concession granted by the Ottomans to
Euripides Mavrommatis (see Chapter 3), was the only part of Mandatory Palestine
not supplied by Rutenberg's plants. Under the Mandate, Mavrommatis resisted the
Palestine Electric Company's proposals to build a power station that would serve
Jerusalem. Only in 1942, when his British-Jerusalem Electric Corporation failed to
supply the demands of the city, did the Mandatory government ask the Palestine
Electric Company to take over responsibility for supplying electricity to Jerusalem.
Thanks to Wikipedia for this information.

38   Lowdermilk Department of Agricultural Engineering at Technion University in Israel
is named in his honour, 'the world-renowned American expert on soil conservation,
who supported the development of the State of Israel, and guided and inspired this
Department from its first days'.

39   Siegel, *Let There Be Water*, 29.

40   This idea was a precursor of the conception of Israel's national water carrier, for
which see Chapter 5. The notion of transferring water out of the Jordan basin was
opposed at the time on Christian religious grounds. In 1946 the Church of Scotland
presbytery in Jerusalem submitted a memorandum against the plan, as they feared it
would spoil the sanctity of the Sea of Galilee.

41   Siegel, *Let There Be Water*, 28.

42   Siegel, *Let There Be Water*, 28, 29.

43   Compare, for example, the annual flow of the Nile of 84,000 million cubic metres,
sixty-five times greater than the flow of the Jordan.

44   Eaton in Isaac and Shuval 1994, 104 Note 5.

45   Eaton in Isaac and Shuval 1994, 95.

46   Sosland, *Cooperating Rivals*, 27.

47   Sosland, *Cooperating Rivals*, 27.

48   *Ghor* – literally 'valley' – refers to the part of the Jordan Valley below Lake Tiberias.
The East Ghor refers to the East Bank, the West Ghor to the west bank.

49   Sosland, *Cooperating Rivals*, 27.

50   Source: Mandate Days, 65. Samuel remained in Palestine throughout the Mandate
and earned a reputation for siding with the Zionists. A description in *Palestine
Studies* of Samuel's 'A Year in Ramallah' is revealing: 'In his year as District Officer
of the Ramallah District in the first decade of the mandate (1925–6), Samuel finds a
countryside ravaged by World War I and "four centuries of Ottoman misrule" with
forests decimated, terraces collapsed and the younger and more energetic rural
population emigrated to the United States (he estimates about a third of the income
in the district is remittances). Samuel begins to visit villages and to diligently jot
down possible improvements in his notebooks. He has some sympathy for the
peasants – many of whom are indebted to moneylenders in Nablus, according
to Samuel – and finds his most unpleasant task is collecting taxes, including
"astronomic arrears" from villagers. His method, however, is somewhat peculiar
involving "fearsome threats in broken Arabic but on biblical models". He gives

an example: "If you pay now what I ask, oh my children, I shall be as dew upon your fields, as honey upon your lips. But if you do not, then I shall come as a wolf in your sheep-fold by night ..." Paternalism does not quite explain this eccentric linguistic display. Samuel's view of himself as a "feudal baron" even if slightly ironic, firmly places "his" peasants in the "eleventh century", even while he acknowledges their "immense demand ... for education". This sketch is adapted from an article by Penny Johnston in Palestine Studies Issue 51 (2012). Under the theme of *Witnesses in Jerusalem: Re-Readings*, Dr Johnston reviews Samuel's book Edwin Samuel, *A Lifetime in Jerusalem: The Memoirs of the Second Viscount Samuel* (Jerusalem: Israel Universities Press, 1970).

51 Pappé, *History of Modern Palestine*, 70, 73.
52 Owen, *Economic Development in Mandatory Palestine, 1918–1948*, 20; Pappé, *History of Modern Palestine*, 72/73.
53 Pappé, *History of Modern Palestine*, 77.
54 Pappé, *History of Modern Palestine*, 75.
55 Pappé, *History of Modern Palestine*, 74, 102.
56 On income tax, see Assaf Likhovski, 'Is Tax Law Culturally Specific? Lessons from the History of Income Tax Law in Mandatory Palestine', *Theoretical Inquiries in Law* 11, no. 2 (2010).
57 Sherman, *Mandate Days*, 65.
58 Pappé, *History of Modern Palestine*, 99, 100–2.
59 Pappé records that Jews and Arabs also co-ran the salt plant at Atlit. The plant is still running in Israel today but there is no mention of this past cooperation. See Pappé, *History of Modern Palestine*, 114.
60 Pappé, *History of Modern Palestine*, 114; Jewish Telegraphic Agency, 20 February 1931.
61 Source: Owen, *Economic Development in Mandatory Palestine, 1918–1948*, 22. Compare exports of less than one million cases annually before the First World War – see Chapter 3.
62 Owen, *Economic Development in Mandatory Palestine, 1918–1948*, 18.
63 See Chapter 5.
64 See the Wikipedia article on Nablus.
65 On water consumption in Tel Aviv and other cities, Karlinsky cites David Smilansky, *What is the Water Supply Situation in Tel Aviv?* Yedi.ot .Iriyat Tel Aviv, 5.8.9 (1934) 348.9; TAMA, 4-1031.
66 That the Israelis now call the Yarkon. The remains of the pumping station can be seen today in the Yarkon-Tel Afek National Park.
67 Source is Karlinsky, who cites: Municipal Corporation of Jaffa, John S. Salah, Municipal Engineer, Jaffa Drainage Scheme, 18.6.1935; J. D. and D. M. Watson, Jaffa Sewerage, April 1937, UK National Archives, CO 733/341/3 248609; 2 March 1937, TAMA, 4-2529; Humphreys, Report upon the Water Supply of Tel Aviv.
68 Karlinsky cites: Helman, *Cleanliness and Squalor in Inter-war Tel Aviv.*
69 Source: Karlinsky, based on Rokach, *Tel Aviv's Current Issues*, 35.
70 Source: Karlinsky, *The Limits of Separation*, quoting a report by Shiffman 'First Meeting with Mr. Watson'. *Emphasis added.*
71 In fact, physical constraints required 5 per cent of Tel Aviv's sewage to be dealt with by Jaffa, and vice versa.
72 On hygiene and the Yishuv, see Dafna Hirsch, 'We are here to bring the West, not only to ourselves': Zionist Occidentalism and the discourse of hygiene in Mandate

Palestine, *International Journal of Middle East Studies,* DOI: https://doi.org/10.1017/S 0020743809990079. Published online: 26 October 2009.

73 Pappé, *History of Modern Palestine,* 76.

74 Abu Jilal, interview with Julia Templin (Zababdeh, West Bank, 8 June 2008).

75 Interview with Julia Templin (Zababdeh, West Bank, 15 June 2008).

76 Despite the apparently inevitable clash of two emerging nationalisms, there were forces favourable to cooperation and cohabitation that might conceivably have fostered other solutions. For example, many cases of economic and occupational cooperation existed. In total, during the Mandate, 1,400 Jewish/Arab commercial partnerships were formed. In rural areas, some Jewish settlements cooperated with Palestinian villages, and even joint agricultural cooperatives were set up. In many locations, the two communities shopped in each other's stores. However, as Ilan Pappé writes, 'Overall, these kinds of cooperation were pragmatic and did little to reduce the politicization of relations or the violence of much interaction between the communities. Nor could they stem the move towards nationalist segregation.' See Pappé, *History of Modern Palestine,* 115–16.

Chapter 5

1 Simon Sebag Montefiore, *Jerusalem: The Biography* (London: Weidenfield and Nicolson, 2011), 468.

2 According to LeBor, even if the owners had remained in Jaffa, the orange groves were still considered 'abandoned assets' and were seized by the new state. See Adam LeBor, 'Zion and the Arabs: Jaffa as a metaphor', *World Policy Journal* 24, no. 4 (Winter, 2007/2008): 61–75; and also Ilan Pappé, *The Ethnic Cleansing of Palestine* (Oxford: One World, 2006).

3 Source: Pappé, *History of Modern Palestine,* 146.

4 Eaton in Isaac and Shuval 1994, 97.

5 This notion of 'carrying capacity' had been around a long time. As we saw in Chapter 4, it had been a factor in British concerns about the number of immigrants that Palestine could absorb. Much of Lowdermilk's work had been driven by a desire to disprove gloomy estimates of this carrying capacity. His ideas, he thought, would allow for four million Jewish immigrants.

6 Source: Sosland, *Cooperating Rivals.*

7 Sosland, *Cooperating Rivals,* 30.

8 In the partition plan, the UN had assigned the Negev to the Palestinian Arab state. However, in October 1948 the Haganah bombarded and then captured Beersheba and 30,000 Arabs fled or were driven out of the area. Siegel reports disingenuously: 'With the Negev marginally settled by Jewish farmers and no superior claims by others, the UN awarded the desert wasteland to the Jewish state.' A reading of Salman Abu Sitta's memoir shows that the better watered north of the Negev between Gaza and Beersheba was well populated and farmed by Palestinians. Nor does Siegel mention the 50,000–70,000 Bedouin whose home the Negev was. [Siegel, *Let There Be Water,* 33].

9 Siegel, *Let There Be Water,* 26, 29.

10 Siegel, *Let There Be Water,* 31/2.

11 There was a limited, largely Christian, concern for the Jordan's integrity as a 'holy river' but the voice of these concerns was faint.

12   Eaton in Isaac and Shuval 1994, 96; Caponera in Isaac and Shuval 1994, 166–7.
13   UNRWA was the agency established in 1949 specifically to care for Palestinian refugees.
14   Sosland, *Cooperating Rivals*.
15   Sosland, *Cooperating Rivals*.
16   Citations in Sosland, *Cooperating Rivals*.
17   Sosland, *Cooperating Rivals*.
18   Sosland, *Cooperating Rivals*, 220. Note 35.
19   Munther J. Haddadin, *Diplomacy on the Jordan: International Conflict and Negotiated Resolution* (Boston: Kluwer Academic Publishers, 2002).
20   Sosland, *Cooperating Rivals*, 31.
21   Sosland, *Cooperating Rivals*, 31.
22   Sosland, *Cooperating Rivals*, 34.
23   The *Point Four Program* was a technical assistance programme for developing countries announced by United States president Harry S. Truman in his inaugural address on 20 January 1949. It took its name from the fact that it was the fourth foreign policy objective mentioned in the speech.
24   Sosland, *Cooperating Rivals*, 34.
25   Awartani in Isaac and Shuval, 10; Sosland, *Cooperating Rivals*.
26   Sources: *Taking Sides: America's Secret Relations with a Militant Israel*, by Stephen Green (New York: William Morrow and Co., 1984). "*The 1953 Aid Cut-off: A Parable for Our Times*", 76–93.
27   Sosland, *Cooperating Rivals*, 39, Wikipedia article on Johnston.
28   Sosland, *Cooperating Rivals*, 39.
29   Sosland, *Cooperating Rivals*, 40.
30   Sosland, *Cooperating Rivals*, 42.
31   Arnon Soffer, *The Relevance of the Johnston Plan to the Reality of 1993 and Beyond* in Isaac and Shuval 1994, 110; Sosland, *Cooperating Rivals*, 42.
32   Soffer in Isaac and Shuval 1994, 111: emphasis added.
33   Soffer in Isaac and Shuval 1994, 111; Siegel, *Let There Be Water*, 36, 39.
34   The Israeli version allocates 40 million cubic metres of Yarmouk water to Israel and 100 million cubic metres of Jordan water to Jordan, specifying that 70 million cubic metres should be of average Tiberias salinity and 30 million cubic metres from diversion of saline springs, whereas in the United States version the shares are 85 million cubic metres and 15 million cubic metres, respectively. See Sosland, *Cooperating Rivals*, 53.
35   Sosland, *Cooperating Rivals*, 49 ff.
36   These plans were only realized very much later – almost fifty years on. Jordan's relative weakness meant that its share of Johnston was completed piecemeal and with very long delays. Whereas Israel was able to enforce its own interpretation of Johnston, including by military intervention when it deemed it necessary, and to finance the capital investment from a range of sources, Jordan was unable to compel Syrian compliance, which was erratic and usually not forthcoming. Jordan was also dependent on US finance for its investment programme and so was obligatorily compliant with US policy towards Israel. Only in 2011 did the dam, renamed the al Wehda or Unity dam, finally become operational.
37   Sosland, *Cooperating Rivals*, 54.
38   Sosland, *Cooperating Rivals*, 49 ff.
39   Sosland, *Cooperating Rivals*, 39.

40 Sosland, *Cooperating Rivals*, 44.
41 Sosland, *Cooperating Rivals*, 44.
42 Kelly in Isaac and Shuval, 295.
43 In 1966, a research project interviewed 216 Palestinian refugees who were farming in the East Ghor. Of these, seventy-one were farming on irrigated parcels developed in the first phase of the Jordan Valley scheme. However, although some of the settlers on the scheme were plainly Palestinian refugees, it was Jordanian policy to deny that resettlement was a purpose of the scheme because this could have been interpreted as impairing their 'right of return' to their original homes. See Claud R. Sutcliffe, 'Palestinian refugee resettlement: Lessons from the East Ghor Canal Project', *Journal of Peace Research* 11, no. 1 (1974): 57–62.
44 Sosland, *Cooperating Rivals*, 57; Eaton in Isaac and Shuval 1994, 100.
45 Sosland, *Cooperating Rivals*, 58.
46 Sosland, *Cooperating Rivals*, 225, citing Nasser's speech of 27 February 1956.
47 Sosland, *Cooperating Rivals*, 60.
48 Sosland, *Cooperating Rivals*, 225.
49 Sosland, *Cooperating Rivals*, 61.
50 Based on US sources, Sosland (page 61 and note 196 on page 228) claims that 'the riparians would dump the excess water the Arab states could not use into the Mediterranean or the Yarmouk so Israel could not use it'. There is no evidence from Arab sources that this was either the plan or the intention. Later proposals (see *The Arab water plan* later in this chapter) would have diverted the waters around Lake Tiberias through Syria to the Yarmouk, where they would be regulated by a Jordanian dam at Mukheibah. Although the feasibility of this scheme is unlikely, it is not a scheme for dumping water but simply for keeping it within the basin.
51 Sosland, *Cooperating Rivals*, 61.
52 Eaton in Isaac and Shuval 1994, 100.
53 An example of appropriation by renaming. Yarkon, which means 'greenish' in Hebrew, replaced the old Nahr al Auja, which means 'the meandering'.
54 Sosland, *Cooperating Rivals*, 68.
55 Sosland, *Cooperating Rivals*, 68.
56 Sosland, *Cooperating Rivals*, 68.
57 Sosland, *Cooperating Rivals*, 69–70.
58 Sosland, *Cooperating Rivals*, 69, 230. Stephen C. Lonergan and David B. Brooks, Watershed: *The Role of Fresh Water in the Israeli-Palestinian Conflict* (Ottawa: IDRC, 1994). Lonergan and Brooks (*Watershed*, 69, the source of this figure), say – citing Schwarz 1992 – that by 1992 this proportion had dropped to 12 per cent, not because of reduced cost of pumping but because overall electricity use had risen. They say that pumping in Jordan also used 20 per cent of total national electricity supply.
59 All the quotations in this paragraph are from Sosland, *Cooperating Rivals*, 70.
60 Siegel, *Let There Be Water*, 20. Siegel calculates that 'on a per capita basis, adjusted for inflation, Israel spent six times more building the NWC than the US did building the Panama Canal'.
61 Siegel, *Let There Be Water*, 39.
62 J. Schwarz, *Management of Israel's Water Resources* in Isaac and Shuval 1994, 70; and 307–8.
63 Siegel, *Let There Be Water*, 20, 40.
64 Siegel, *Let There Be Water*, 40, 278.
65 Sosland, *Cooperating Rivals*, 71.

66 Sosland, *Cooperating Rivals*, 71 ff.
67 Sosland, *Cooperating Rivals*, 71 ff.
68 Sosland, *Cooperating Rivals*, 77.
69 Sosland, *Cooperating Rivals*, 71.
70 Sosland, *Cooperating Rivals*, 78, 80.
71 Sosland, *Cooperating Rivals*, 80–1.
72 Sosland, *Cooperating Rivals*, 87–8.
73 Sosland, *Cooperating Rivals*, 83.
74 Sosland, *Cooperating Rivals*, 84–6.
75 Sosland, *Cooperating Rivals*, 88–9; Pappé, *History of Modern Palestine*, 187.
76 Sosland, *Cooperating Rivals*, 89.
77 Source: Tom Segev, *Israel and the War that Transformed the Middle East* (Little, Brown, 1967), ISBN 978-0-316-72478-4, 399.
78 Sosland, *Cooperating Rivals*, 91–2.
79 In 1947, Arabs outnumbered Jews by two to one – 1,320,000 Arabs to 700,000 Jews. By 1967 there were about 2.4 million Jews and about 1.6 million Arabs – 900,000 in the West Bank, 400,000 in Gaza, and 300,000 within Israel.

Chapter 6

1 *The Economic Development of Jordan* (World Bank, 1955), 56.
2 IBRD 1955, 76–8; 102–3.
3 Munther Haddadin, 'Evolution of water administration and legislation', in *Water Resources in Jordan: Evolving Policies for Development, the Environment, and Conflict Resolution: Resources for the Future*, ed. M. Haddadin (2006), 29–42. ISBN 1-933115-32-7.
4 The World Bank provided a loan of $3.5 million to Jordan for a Jerusalem–Ramallah drinking water pipeline project but this had not been completed by 1967. See Sosland, *Cooperating Rivals*, 254.
5 Sosland, *Cooperating Rivals*, 146.
6 More than three-quarters of this in agriculture.
7 Sosland, *Cooperating Rivals*, 142, 146.
8 Zeitoun, *Power and Water in the Middle East*, 68.
9 Source: Soffer 1992 in Isaac and Shuval 1994, 113.
10 Soffer in Isaac and Shuval 1994, 113.
11 See Jeffrey D. Dillman, 'Water rights in the occupied territories', *Journal of Palestine Studies* 19, no. 1 (Autumn 1989): 52. http://www.jstor.org/stable/2537245 (accessed 18 October 2010).
12 Alwyn R. Rouyer, *Turning Water into Politics*, 2000, ISBN 10: 031222611X ISBN 13: 9 780312226114. See n. 19, 46; Israeli Military Order No. 92 Concerning Powers for the Purpose of the Water Provisions, 15 August 1967, in Israel Law Resource Centre. http://www.israellawresourcecenter.org/israelmilitaryorders/fulltext/mo0092.htm (accessed 24 September 2019). The order was backdated to 'the Prescribed Day' – 7 June 1967.
13 Raja Shehadeh, *Occupier's Law: Israel and the West Bank* (Washington, DC: Institute for Palestine Studies, 1985). See also Rouyer, *Turning Water into Politics*, 19, 47; 'Israel Military Order No. 291 Concerning the Settlement of Disputes over Titles in Land and the Regulation of Water', 19 December 1968, in Israel Law Resource Centre.

14 Sosland, *Cooperating Rivals*, 148.
15 Set up to administer the West Bank, the Civil Administration is part of the unit of the Israeli Ministry of Defence known as the Coordinator of Government Activities in the Territories (COGAT).
16 In total, it was said that 140 water pumps were destroyed along the Jordan and in the Gaza Strip. [SH 129].
17 Sosland, *Cooperating Rivals*, 147–8.
18 Sosland, *Cooperating Rivals*, 148.
19 Much of this part of the story is based on World Bank, *Developing the Occupied Territories*.
20 One possible explanation is that the Israeli official data for 1967 refer to the post-war situation when the irrigation area plummeted under war conditions from 100,000 to 57,000 dunums (from 10,000 to 5,700 hectares). There was, however, a clear advantage to the Israelis to show low use in 1967 and a tripling during the Occupation – it would counter Palestinian claims that Israelis had unreasonably limited Palestinian water use during the Occupation.
21 Source: Sosland, *Cooperating Rivals*, 151.
22 See the table *Estimated Recharge and Estimated Potential* in Chapter 2.
23 Sosland, *Cooperating Rivals*, 151 and note 53 at page 257.
24 Sosland, *Cooperating Rivals*, 151 and note 54 at page 257.
25 Source: World Bank, *Developing the Occupied Territories*, 3.34; xii.
26 Source: Sosland, *Cooperating Rivals*, 151 and note 51 on page 257 for reference.
27 Sosland, *Cooperating Rivals*, 151–2 and note 55 at page 257.
28 See note 55 at Sosland, *Cooperating Rivals*, 257.
29 This section is based on World Bank 1993.
30 World Bank, *Developing the Occupied Territories*, 20.
31 The pace of depletion of wells appears to have speeded up over the following decade as by 2005 the PWA was reporting that *half* of the Palestinian wells existing in 1967 were no longer operational – see Chapter 7.
32 Sosland, *Cooperating Rivals*, 153. For the course of the *intifada* and its impacts, see the section *Intifada* in Chapter 7.
33 Source: Sosland, *Cooperating Rivals*, 153.
34 Statement by Brigadier-General F. Zach, Israeli deputy coordinator for the Occupied Territories, in an article in the *Washington Post*, 13 May 1992 – see Sosland, *Cooperating Rivals*, 152 and note 59 on page 257. This statement is roughly consistent with the table *Water use in the West Bank* – see earlier in this chapter – as 43 million cubic metres annually would give per capita settler use of approximately 430 cubic metres, about three times the West Bank Palestinian per capita use of 126 cubic metres – see the table *Water Use in the Occupied Territories*, also earlier in this chapter.
35 Special report of the State Comptroller of Israel, Miriam Ben-Porat, 1990. The report led to the dismissal of the Water Commissioner.
36 Sosland, *Cooperating Rivals*, 154.
37 Sosland, *Cooperating Rivals*, 153–4.
38 On pollution, see Sosland, *Cooperating Rivals*, 154.
39 See Sosland, *Cooperating Rivals*, 154–5 for details.
40 Sosland's phrase, see Sosland, *Cooperating Rivals*, 98.
41 See Sosland, *Cooperating Rivals*, 99. Despite the continuation of a particularly bitter strain of anti-Israeli rhetoric, the Jordanian government pursued practical although

secret cooperation with Israel. The most closely guarded secret of all was Israel's role in helping to keep the Syrian air force from attacking Jordan during King Hussein's struggle with the Palestinians.

42 The Zarqa river is perennial, with a base flow of about 2–3 million cubic metres per month during the summer months. Winter flows are considerably higher, as much as 5–8 million cubic metres per month. This makes it the second-largest tributary of the lower Jordan River after the Yarmouk, and the third largest river in the region by annual discharge. [Wikipedia]

43 'Gold plated' was the term used in conversation with the authors by Harry Walters, who led the World Bank team working on the project. This view is amply supported in the literature – see, for example, *Development as a Gift: Patterns of Assistance and Refugees Strategies in the Jordan Valley* by Mauro van Aken, in *International Symposium on the Palestinian Refugees and UNRWA in Jordan, the West Bank and Gaza, 1949–1999*.

44 Source: van Aken.

45 Source: van Aken.

46 See the table *Allocations in the Johnston Plan* in Chapter 5.

47 Bunger's dam was 140 metres to store 500 million cubic metres; Johnston's version was 126 metres to store 300 million cubic metres.

48 See Sosland, *Cooperating Rivals*, 107 and 241 on this.

49 Sosland, *Cooperating Rivals*, 108.

50 Sosland, *Cooperating Rivals*, 129–32.

51 Israel had considerable capacity to take this extra water. In 1990 it had pumping capacity from the Yarmouk to Lake Tiberias of 21.5 million cubic metres per month and could collect 5 million cubic metres in the Rutenberg pool. See Sosland, *Cooperating Rivals*, 253 Note 256.

52 Sosland, *Cooperating Rivals*, 134–6.

53 Sosland, *Cooperating Rivals*, 135.

54 This section draws on World Bank 1993 Volume 5 *Infrastructure*.

55 And in Gaza, the Gaza Association of Engineers.

56 Al Khatib and Assaf in Isaac & Shuval 1994, 62.

57 Although only about 10 per cent in Tulkarm.

58 It was suggested at the time that some merging of these departments within a region might enable greater management effectiveness and economies from regional projects. This was held to be equally true for wastewater treatment. See World Bank 1993.

59 In 1993, the Civil Administration maintained to the World Bank that it encouraged sewerage projects, and that constraints on municipal water supply projects had been relaxed and allowed adequate supplies, although irrigation water use was strictly controlled. [Source: World Bank 1993].

60 Source: J. Schwarz, *Israel Water Sector Review*. Report Prepared for the World Bank (Tel Aviv, 1990).

61 For the Israeli Comptroller's strictures on settlements polluting the aquifers with sewage, see the section on *Water stewardship* earlier in this chapter.

62 In fact, this recommendation became part of the Palestinian plans for the water sector almost two decades later, and it is still very much work in progress – see Chapter 10.

63 Source: The excellent study by Julia Templin.

64 Israeli data suggest that in 1992, three-quarters (72 per cent) of rural households in the West Bank had water connections, against only one in ten (10 per cent) in

1974, while the Palestinians maintain that *50* per cent of all villages had no piped water systems. In fact, both contentions may be true as it was the villages with larger populations that were likely to get piped networks first.

65 Source: Alon Tal and David Katz, 'Rehabilitating Israel's streams and rivers', *International Journal of River Basin Management* 10, no. 4 (2012): 317–30, 320. The corrective measures are described in Part 1 of our companion volume.

66 Source: Alon Tal, *The Evolution of Israeli Water Management: The Elusive Search for Environmental Security*, 132.

67 Source: Tal and Katz, 'Rehabilitating Israel's streams and rivers', 324. As we shall see in our companion volume, a small reflooding project – on just 1 square kilometre – has been a huge success. The exiguous new ecosystem provides a magnet for migratory birds and attracts 400,000 visitors a year, demonstrating the economic value of environmental restoration.

68 Sources: Nir Becker and Frank A. Ward. 'Adaptive water management in Israel: Structure and policy options', *International Journal of Water Resources Development* (2014): 1, 6–7; and Tal, *The Evolution of Israeli Water Management*, 128–9.

69 In 2021, after exceptional winter rains, there were reports that water might be spilled from Tiberias into the Lower Jordan 'for the first time in 25 years'. Source: *Jerusalem Post,* 24 November 2020.

70 An elderly lady in a Palestinian village, reported by her grandson and quoted in *Zababdeh: A Palestinian Water History* by Julia S. Templin, MSc thesis, Utah State University, 2011 Templin, Julia S. *All Graduate Theses and Dissertations.* 911. https://digitalcommons.usu.edu/etd/911.

71 And as they were never consulted by the United Nations and those who determined their destiny in 1947–8.

72 Pappé, *History of Modern Palestine*, 204.

73 Source: Templin.

Chapter 7

1 Some of the discussion in this chapter, and much of the data, draws on work we did with the World Bank for the World Bank 2009 report *West Bank & Gaza: Assessment of Restrictions on Palestinian Water Sector Development* (Washington, DC: World Bank, 2009).

2 This section draws largely on *The Palestinian Economy under Occupation* by Yusuf A. Sayigh in *The Palestinian Economy*, ed. George T. Abed (London: Routledge, 1988); and on World Bank, *Developing the Occupied Territories*, Volume 3.

3 Sayigh, *The Palestinian Economy under Occupation*, 259, 262.

4 Others went to the Gulf. In this period it is estimated that altogether some 380,000 West Bank Palestinians were migrant workers.

5 Sayigh, *The Palestinian Economy under Occupation*, 259, 261–2.

6 Excluding any spending on security.

7 Sayigh, *The Palestinian Economy under Occupation*, 264. In the article, Sayigh argues that the 'neglect of education and health has forced the Palestinians into a healthy self-reliance'.

8 Sayigh, *The Palestinian Economy under Occupation*, 259, 260.

9 The case of the Occupied Territories in this period has been cited as an illustration of the nature of 'structural dependency'. Throughout the literature on colonial and

comprador economies, there is a Manichean struggle between the view that all rise together (although some less than others) and the view that 'dependency' distorts economic development and skews the benefits towards the masters and the elites. Even in the late twentieth century there are debates over the manifold examples of a semi-voluntary dependency of weak and poor states on a richer, more powerful neighbour. However, the only recent example other than the Occupied Territories of two economies in a dominant/dependent relationship within the same geographical area and in what is – or recently was – the same political entity is South Africa. These two examples share the distinctive characteristics that the dependent territory had no choice. Israeli occupation, like South African apartheid, gave no choice. Another unusual structural feature (highlighted by Sayigh 266/7) is physical fragmentation, another characteristic shared with apartheid South Africa. Through the layout of road and water infrastructure, the appropriation of large tracts of land, the penetration of settlements, and movement and access restrictions, there is a physical fragmentation of the West Bank that is reinforced by economic policies which inhibit aggregation of enterprises to achieve economies of scale or vertical or horizontal integration. On this, see Sayigh's article *The Palestinian Economy under Occupation*, 266/7.

Eyal Weizman, in his classic work on the politics of architecture *Hollow Land: Israel's Architecture of Occupation* (London: Verso, 2017), goes further, and more poetically (pp. xvii–xix): 'Every Palestinian town and village has thus been fully enveloped by Israeli space in three dimensions. If Palestinians want to drive out of their enclaves, they encounter a fence, a wall or an Israeli checkpoint period. If they want to dig a well, they need Israeli permission to pierce into [the] subterranean volumes. Domination from the air is increasingly enforced by overlapping swarms of unmanned drones, hovering continuously over Palestinian towns and villages. The sound of their engines is the continuous backdrop of Palestinian daily lives. This is an aerially enforced colonization based on the drones' ability to maintain a perpetual surveillance and strike capability … [It is] an economically efficient alternative to the otherwise onerous and expensive tasks of colonial policing in the dense urban mazes of the Gaza Strip. Hunter algorithms programmed to follow patterns of behaviour … learn the art of suspicion and violence …'

10   Sayigh, *The Palestinian Economy under Occupation*, 269–70; Note 21 on page 282.
11   Sayigh, *The Palestinian Economy under Occupation*, 283. What happened on the ground reflected policy and attitudes from on high. Sayigh [283] quotes two extreme examples. In 1973, David Hacohen, chair of the Knesset Foreign Affairs Committee, told a UK parliamentary delegation that Palestinian refugees ' … are not human beings, they are not people, they are Arabs'. Rafael Eitan, former IDF chief of staff told *Time* magazine of 25 April 1983 that Palestinians would be made to 'run about like drugged cockroaches inside a bottle'.
12   Pappé, *History of Modern Palestine*, 231.
13   Pappé, *History of Modern Palestine*, 233.
14   Pappé, *History of Modern Palestine*, 233–4.
15   Pappé, *History of Modern Palestine*, 233–4.
16   Pappé, *History of Modern Palestine*, 234–40.
17   Pappé, *History of Modern Palestine*, 231, 239, 241; al Khatib and Assaf in Isaac and Shuval 1994, 56.
18   Pappé, *History of Modern Palestine*, 241.
19   Pappé, *History of Modern Palestine*, 242–3.
20   Pappé, *History of Modern Palestine*, 244.

21   Pappé, *History of Modern Palestine*, 244.

22   The Oslo II Accord divided the Israeli-occupied West Bank into three administrative segments: Areas A, B and C. The distinct areas were given different statuses, according to their governance pending the final status accord: Area A is exclusively administered by the Palestinian Authority; Area B is administered by both the Palestinian Authority and Israel; and Area C, which contains the Israeli settlements, is administered by Israel. Areas A and B were chosen in such a way as to contain only Palestinians, by drawing lines around Palestinian population centres at the time the Agreement was signed; all areas surrounding Areas A and B were defined as Area C.

    Because no final status agreement has ever been concluded, these provisions essentially remain in force today. As of 2015, Area A comprised approximately 18 per cent of the West Bank and Area B about 22 per cent, together home to some 2.8 million Palestinians. Area C comprised just over 60 per cent of the West Bank. It was home to 150,000 Palestinians in 532 residential areas and also contained 389,250 Israelis, in 135 settlements and 100 'outposts' unrecognized by the Israeli government. Area C forms a contiguous territory, called by the Israelis the Judea and Samaria Area. It is technically administered by the Israel Defence Forces Central Command, and military law is applied. In contrast, under the Oslo II Accord, Areas A and B were subdivided into 165 separate units of land that have no territorial contiguity. [*adapted from the excellent article in Wikipedia*].

23   Source: Pappé, *History of Modern Palestine.*

24   Meron Benvenisti, *The West Bank Data Project: A Survey of Israel's Policies* (Washington and London: American Enterprise Institute for Public Policy Research, 1984).

25   Pappé, *History of Modern Palestine*, 245–6.

26   Pappé, *History of Modern Palestine*, 246.

27   Sosland, *Cooperating Rivals*, 169–70.

28   This, as we shall see, was very much the case with the agreements on water.

29   Pappé, *History of Modern Palestine*, 247.

30   Pappé, *History of Modern Palestine*, 254–5.

31   Pappé, *History of Modern Palestine*, 265.

32   Zeitoun, *Power and Water in the Middle East*, 81–2, 185.

33   Sosland, *Cooperating Rivals*, 171.

34   Zeitoun, *Power and Water in the Middle East*, 64.

35   Pappé, *History of Modern Palestine*, 266–7.

36   Some of the points in this section have been adapted from an article by Uri Shamir, *Water Agreements Between Israel and Its Neighbors* in *Transformations of Middle East Natural Environments*, ed. Jeff Albert, Magnus Bernhardsson and Roger Kenna (Yale F&ES Buletin 103, 1998).

37   For a description of these aquifers, see Chapter 2.

38   Shamir points out that Article 40 calls for coordinated (rather than 'joint') operation, management, and development of water and sewage systems. He considers that 'joint' would mean joint ownership and management of a resource, whereas 'coordinated' indicates that each side is sovereign in its domain but that certain defined matters are managed together.

39   The mission and progressive development of this agency are discussed in detail in our companion volume *Water Security for Palestinians and Israelis Today.*

40   Sosland, *Cooperating Rivals*, 169.

41   Sosland, *Cooperating Rivals*, 169.

42   Sosland, *Cooperating Rivals*, 170.
43   See Jan Selby, *Water, Power and Politics in the Middle East* (I.B. Tauris, 2003), 115.
44   Sosland, *Cooperating Rivals*, 171.
45   Sosland, *Cooperating Rivals*, 169.
46   Alwyn Rouyer, *Turning Water Into Politics*, 227 claims that 'by spring of 1998 JSET members developed good personal relations and inspections were going smoothly'. Although this may have been the case in a brief 'honeymoon' period, it was certainly not the case when Palestinian expectations of a final settlement were disappointed. See also Sosland, *Cooperating Rivals*, 169.
47   Source: Fieldwork interviews, Ramallah, 30 November 2008, Tel Aviv, 1 December 2008.
48   *Water Could Dry Up the Peace Process.* The Gazette (Montreal), 20 August 1998, cited in Sosland, *Cooperating Rivals*, 171.
49   Zeitoun, *Power and Water in the Middle East*, 74.
50   Sosland, *Cooperating Rivals*, 172; Z 87.
51   Zeitoun, *Power and Water in the Middle East*, 91.
52   Much of this account of the events in Jenin is taken from Mark Zeitoun's well-written analysis (Zeitoun, *Power and Water in the Middle East*, 88–93).
53   See A. M. MacDonald et al., 'Mapping groundwater development costs for the transboundary Western Aquifer Basin, Palestine/Israel', *Hydrogeology Journal* 17 (2009): 1579–87.
54   Zeitoun, *Power and Water in the Middle East*, 98.
55   Zeitoun, *Power and Water in the Middle East*, 94.
56   Zeitoun, *Power and Water in the Middle East*, 15–18.
57   According to Article 40 (Schedule 8.1a), increases in extraction above the Article 40 allocations 'shall require the prior approval of the JWC'.
58   For a discussion of the causes of the reduced abstractions, see the companion volume *Water Security*, the section on *Reasons for Palestinian under-abstraction*.
59   The source for this statement is our notes on this meeting, which we attended.
60   The information in this section is drawn from the work the authors did for the World Bank's 2009 *Assessment of Restrictions* report and from the work of Anan Jayyousi: *Israeli Water Crimes on Palestinian Water Resources*, Mimeo 2008.
61   The 2007 figures are based on West Bank Palestinians – 105.9 million cubic metres (113 .5 million cubic metres from the table *Palestinian abstractions* less 7.1 million cubic metres brackish water) and population of 2.35 million (PCBS census December 2007); and Israel – 1,408.6 million cubic metres and population of 7.1 million (source: Israeli Water Authority, data provided November 2008 to the Israeli press for a Global Water Intelligence report Water Market Middle East). In addition, Israel had the use of a further 277 million cubic metres of brackish water and storm water, and produced (in 2006) a further 450 million cubic metres of non- conventional water from wastewater treatment and desalination. Taken together, these resources equal a further 280 lcd, making an aggregate of 824 lcd, more than six times the water availability for West Bank Palestinians.
62   The Palestinians resumed their participation in 2018.
63   The other was the Joint Economic Committee.
64   When we wrote about this in 2009, the PWA commented as follows: 'Since the signing of the Oslo Agreement, the parties have not been able to establish formal protocols on process and interaction, making the mechanism susceptible to political events and individual interpretation. Further, the accurate number of meetings of the

Joint Water Committee, the Joint Technical Committee, and the Subcommittees is difficult to determine because of the number of informal meetings or undocumented meetings between the parties. Even if the frequency of these meetings had continued since 2001 at relatively the same pace as prior to the al Aqsa *intifada*, the resulting outcome had little positive impact for Palestinians. Additional meetings have not led to improved development of the Palestinian water sector; in fact, since 2001 there has been a marked decrease in Israel's approval of projects and in the ability to implement projects that received JWC approval as a result of the additional administrative harassment in the form of Civil Administration processing.' See World Bank, *West Bank & Gaza*.

65 Zeitoun, *Power and Water in the Middle East*, 17.
66 See the companion volume *Water Security* for a detailed discussion of these issues related to wastewater treatment.
67 Settlement administration covers about 42 per cent of the West Bank, including four cities, thirteen local councils and six regional councils.
68 For example, the case of the Hebron wastewater treatment plant, on which see the discussion in our companion volume *Winning Water Security*.
69 See the PWA *Water Strategy 2000*.
70 Source: Interviews with PWA, Ramallah, 17 November 2008.
71 World Bank, *Economic Effects of Restricted Access to Land in the West Bank* (2008).
72 Source: Letter of October 2008 from the Head of the Civil Administration to the PWA.
73 Source: Fieldwork interview, Jerusalem, 27 November 2008.
74 All these comments were made to us during our visits to the West Bank in 2008–9.
75 As in the South Hebron hills and at Massafer Yatta in 2006–7.
76 Source: Fieldwork interview, Ramallah, 17 November 2008.
77 Source: Fieldwork interview, Jerusalem, 18 November 2008.
78 On the topic of unlicensed wells, PWA commented in 2009: 'all unlicensed Palestinian wells in the West Bank are drilled into the shallow aquifers (either Eocene in Jenin, or Pleistocene in the Jordan Valley) and therefore are not part of the Mountain Aquifer system regulated under Oslo. These wells only draw on Palestinian resources and do not impact Israeli wells.'
79 Source: Fieldwork interviews and focus groups, Jenin Governorate, 19–20 November 2008.

BIBLIOGRAPHY

Aaronsohn, Aaron. *Agricultural and Botanic Explorations in Palestine*. Washington DC: US Government Printing Office, 1910.

Abed, George T. *The Palestinian Economy: Studies in Development under Prolonged Occupation*. Edited by George T. Abed. London: Routledge, 1988, 358.

Abu Nasar, A. 'Relation of Nitrate Contamination of Groundwater with the Haemoglobin Level Among Infants in Gaza'. *Eastern Mediterranean Health Journal* 13 (September–October 2007). http://www.emro.who.int.

Ahiram, Ephraim and Hanna Siniora. 'The Gaza Strip Water Problem'. In *Water and Peace in the Middle East, Proceedings of the First Israeli-Palestinian International Academic Conference on Water, 10-13 December 1992*, edited by J. Isaac and H. Shuval. Zürich, Switzerland, 1994.

Albright, W. F. *The Archaelogy of Palestine: A Survey of the Ancient Peoples and Cultures of the Holy Land*. London: Penguin Books, 1949, 171.

Al Khatib, Nader and Karen Assaf. *Palestine Water Supplies and Demands*. Zurich: Isaac and Shuval, 1994.

Al Jazeera. 'Israel Reopens Gaza Commercial Crossing'. Article in *al Jazeera*, 15 August 2018. https://www.aljazeera.com/news/2018/08/israel-reopens-gaza-commercial-cross ing-month-long-closure-180815074300410.html.

Aliewi, Amjad. 'Water Resources: The Palestinian Perspective'. In *Water Wisdom*, edited by Alon Tal and Alfred Abed Rabbo. New Jersey: Rutgers University Press, 2010, 231–52.

Aliewi, Amjad, Karen Assaf, and Anan Jayyousi, eds. *Sustainable Development and Management of Water in Palestine*. Ramallah, Palestine: House of Water and Environment, 2008, 567.

Allan, J. A. *Water, Peace and The Middle East: Negotiating Resources in the Jordan Basin*. London: IB Tauris, 1996, 250.

Allen, Tony. *Virtual Water: Tackling the Threat to Our Planet's Most Precious Resource*. London: IB Tauris, 2011.

Attili, Dr Shaddad. *Statement by the Head of the Palestinian Water Authority*, January, 2008, 4.

Al Yaqoubi, Ahmed S. *Country Paper: Water Resources Statistical Records in Palestine*. United Nations EGM on the Production of Statistics on Natural Resources and Environment, June, 2007.

Aqraba. *Town Profile* by ARU. 2013. http:///vprofile.arij.org/nablus/pdfs/vprofile/Aqraba.

ARIJ. *Status of the Environment in the State of Palestine*. Applied Research Institute, Jerusalem, 2016.

Ashly, Jaclynn. 'Drowning in the Waste of Israel Settlers'. *Al Jazeera*, 18 September 2017. https://www.aljazeera.com/indepth/features/2017/09/drowning-waste-israel-settler s170916120027885.htm.

Assaf, Karen. *Replenishment of Palestinian Waters by Artificial Recharge*. Isaac & Shuval, 1994, 302, 307.

Associated Press. *Press Release on World Bank Statements on Easing Israeli Restrictions*. 6 November 2008, 2.

Aviram, Ram, David Katz and Deborah Shmueli. 'Desalination as a Game-changer in Transboundary Hydro-Politics'. *Water Policy* 16 (2014): 609–24.

Avitsur, Shmuel. 'The First Project for the Intensive Exploitation of the Yarkon Waters (The Frangija-Navon Scheme of 1893)'. *Haaretz Museum Bulletin* 6 (1964): 80–8.

Avnieri, Arie L. *The Claim of Dispossession – Jewish Land Settlement and the Arabs 1878–1948.* Efal, Israel: Yad Tabenkin, 1982.

Awartami, Hisham. 'Economic Aspects of the Agricultural Sector in the Occupied Territories'. 3 (1986): 78–89.

Bach, Roberto. *The Population of Israel*. Institute of Contemporary Jewry of the Hebrew University of Jerusalem, 1974, 133, 390–4.

Bard, Mitchell G. *Myths and Facts: A Guide to the Arab-Israeli Conflict*. American-Israeli Cooperative Enterprise (AICE), 2012.

Bargouth, J. M. and R. M. Y. Al-Saed. 'Sustainability of Ancient Water Supply Facilities in Jerusalem'. *Sustainability* 1 (2009): 1106–19.

Becker, Nir and Frank A. Ward. 'Adaptive Water Management in Israel: Structure and Policy Options'. *International Journal of Water Resources Development* (2014): 1–18.

Beltrain, Maria and Giorgos Kallis. 'How does Virtual Water Flow in Palestine? A Political Ecology Analysis.' *Ecological Economics* 143, issue C (2018): 17–26.

Ben-Gurion, David. *Diary*. Sede Boker, Israel: The Ben-Gurion Archive.

Ben-Porat, Miriam. *Special Report of the State Comptroller of Israel*. 1987.

Ben-Reuven, MK Maj Gen. Eyal. Sderot Conference on the Gaza Water and Sanitation Crisis, EcoPeace Conference Summary. 6 March 2018.

Benvenisti, Meron. *The West Bank Data Project: A Survey of Israel's Policies*. Washington and London: American Enterprise Institute for Public Policy Research, 1984, 97.

Benevenisti, Meron. *Sacred Landscape: The Buried History of the Holy Land since 1948.* London and Los Angeles: University of California Press, 2000, 366.

BIMKOM. *Under the Guise of Security: Routing the Separation Barrier to Enable the Expansion of Israeli Settlements in the West Bank.* BIMKOM/B'tselem. 2005. August 2004, 93.

Biswas, Asit K., John Kolars, Masahiro Murakami, John Waterbury and Aaron Wolf. *Core and Periphery: A Comprehensive Approach to Middle Eastern Water*. Oxford India Paperbacks, Water Resources Management Series, New Delhi: OUP 1997, 160.

Black, Ian. *Enemies and Neighbours: Arabs and Jews in Palestine and Israel, 1917–2017.* Penguin, Random House, 2018, 606.

Bouillon, Markus E. *The Peace Business: Money and Power in the Palestine-Israel Conflict.* London, 2004, 247.

Bromberg, Gidon (Israeli Director), Nada Majdalani (Palestinian Director), Yana Abu Taleb (Jordanian Director). *A Green Blue Deal for the Middle East*. December 2020, Tel Aviv, Ramallah and Amman.

Bunton, Martin. *The Palestinian – Israeli Conflict: A Very Short Introduction*. Oxford and London: OUP, 2013, 132.

B'Tselem. *Forbidden Roads: Israel's Discriminatory Road Regime in the West Bank.* B'Tselem. Israeli Information Center for Human Rights in the Occupied Territories. August, 2004, 55

B'Tselem. *Means of Expulsion: Violence and Harassment in the Southern Hebron Hills.* July, 2005, 59.

B'Tselem. *A Wall in Jerusalem: Obstacles to Human Rights in the Holy City*. Tel Aviv: B'Tselem, 2007a.

B'Tselem. *Ghost Town: Israel's Separation Policy in Hebron*. Tel Aviv: B'Tselem, May 2007b, 107.

B'Tselem. *Ground to a Halt: Denial of Palestinian's Freedom of Movement in the West Bank.* August, 2007c, 118.

B'Tselem. *Human Rights in the Occupied Territories: Annual Report 2007.* January, 2008, 57.

Caponera, Dante A. *Principles of Water Law and Administration: National and International.* Rotterdam, Netherlands: A. A. Balkema Publishers, 1992, 71; Z74; IS 97.

Carey, John. *The Unexpected Professor: An Oxford Life in Books.* London: Faber & Faber, 2014, 361.

Centre of Housing Rights and Evictions. *Policies of Denial: Lack of Access to Water in the West Bank.* December 2008, 37.

Centre of Housing Rights and Evictions. *Position Paper. Hostage to Politics: The Impact of Sanctions and the Blockade on the Human Right to Water and Sanitation in Gaza.* 2008.

CIHEAM. *Options Mediterraneennes: Serie A, Seminaires Mediterraneens.* Bari: CIHEAM. No. 65, 2005, 119–122.

Chomsky, Noam. *Occupy.* London, 2012, 121.

Chomsky, Noam and Ilan Pappe. *Gaza in Crisis: Reflections on Israel's War against the Palestinians.* London: Haymarket Books, 2011, 242.

Conder, C. R. *Tent Work in Palestine.* USA: Jefferson Publication, 2015, 133.

Consulate of Spain. *A Review of the Palestinian Agricultural Sector.* Spain, 2007, 76.

Coutinho, Frank. 'How is the Water Industry in Israel Faring?'. *Times of Israel*, 4 August 2018. https://blogs.timesofisrael.com/how-is-the-water-industry-in-Israel-faring/

Dajani, cited in Lane, 1994: 4, Development as a Gift: Patterns of Assistance and Refugees Strategies in the Jordan Valley by Mauro van Aken. *International Symposium on the Palestinian Refugees and UNRWA in Jordan, the West Bank and Gaza, 1949–1999.*

Dershowitz, Alan. *The Case for Israel.* Hoboken, NJ: Published by John Wiley and Sons, 2003, 265.

Dillman, Jeffrey D. 'Water Rights in the Occupied Territories'. *Journal of Palestine Studies* 19, no. 1 (Autumn 1989): 52. http://www.jstor.org/stable/2537245 (accessed 18 October 2010).

Eastern Mediterranean Health Journal. 'Relation of Nitrate Contamination of Groundwater with Methaemoglobin Level among Infants in Gaza'. *Eastern Mediterranean Health Journal* 13, no. 5. http//www.emro.who.int.

Eaton, J. W. and D. J. Eaton. *Water Utilization in the Yarmouk-Jordan.* Zurich: Isaac and Shuval, 1994.

Ecopeace. *Speech of Rotem Caro Weizman.* EcoPeace Conference Summary 6 March 2018. http://ecopeaceme.org/projects/lower-jordan-rotem@foeme.org.

EcoPeace. *Let the Dead Sea Live.* Tel Aviv: B'Tselem, 2000, 31.

El Musa, Sharif S. *Water Conflict: Economics, Politics, Law and the Palestinian-Israeli Water Resources.* Washington, DC: Institute for Palestine Studies, 1997.

Ehrenreich, Ben. *The Way to the Spring: Life and Death in Palestine.* London, 2017, 428.

Environment and Security in the Middle East. The Effects of the Israeli-Palestinian Conflict on the Hydraulic Resources of the Jordan Basin.

ESCWA. *Inventory of Shared Water Resources in Western Asia.* Beirut: ESCWA, 2013. https ://waterinventory.org/surfacewater/jordan-river-basin.

EWASH (Emergency Water and Sanitation-Hygiene Group). *EWASH Concerned by Water Restrictions in the West Bank Resulting from Israeli Discriminatory Policies.* EWASH Press Release, 21 June 2016.

Falkenmark, Malin and Carl Folke. 'Ecohydrosolidarity: A New Ethics for Stewardship of Value-Adding Rainfall'. In *Water Ethics: Foundational Readings for Students and Professionals*, edited by Peter G. Brown and Jeremy J. Schmidt, 247–64. Washington, DC: Island Press, 2010.

Fallon, Michael. 'Stability in the Middle East Now Depends on How Serious We Are about Tackling Climate Change'. *The Independent*, 12 April 2021.

Faruqui, Naser, Asit K. Biswas and Murad J. Bino, eds. *Water Management in Islam*. USA: United Nations University Press, 2001, 147.

Feitelson, Eran and Marwan Haddad, ed. *Management of Shared Groundwater Resources: The Israel-Palestinian Case with an International Perspective*. USA: Kluwer Academic Publishers, 2000, 496.

Fischhendler, Itay, Shlomi Dinar and David Katz. 'The Politics of Unilateral Environmentalism: Cooperation and Conflict over Water Management along the Israeli-Palestinian Border'. *Global Environmental Politics* 11, no. 1 (2011): 36–61.

Fisher, Franklin M. and Annette Huber-Lee, et al. *Liquid Assets. An Economic Approach for Water Management and Conflict Resolution in the Middle East and Beyond*. Washington, DC: Resources for the Future, 2005, 242.

Fischhendler, Itay. *The Politics of Unilateral Environmentalism: Wastewater Treatment along the Israeli-Palestinian Border*. Hebrew University, 20.

Flappan, Simha. *The Birth of Israel: Myths and Realities*. New York, 1987, 277.

Folke, Carl. 'Freshwater for Resilience: A Shift in Thinking'. *Philosophical Traditions of the Royal Society (B)* 358 (2003): 2027.

Friends of the Earth Middle East. *A Seeping Time Bomb*. February 2004a, 24.

Friends of the Earth Middle East. *Conservation and development of the Dead Sea*. March 2004b, 71.

Friends of the Earth Middle East. *Advancing Conservation and Sustainable Development of the Dead Sea Basin – Broadening the Debate on Economic and Management Issues*. March 2004c, 71.

Friends of the Earth Middle East. *Crossing the Jordan: Bringing Peace to the Lower Jordan*. March 2005a, 32.

Friends of the Earth Middle East. *Pollution of the Mountain Aquifer by Sewage: Finding Solutions*. July 2005b, 8.

Friends of the Earth Middle East. 'Good Water Neighbors: A Model for Community Development Programs in Regions of Conflict'. *FoEME*, August 2005c, 40.

Friends of the Earth Middle East. *A Seeping Time Bomb: Pollution of the Mountain Aquifer by Solid Waste*. January 2006a, 30.

Friends of the Earth Middle East. *Health Crises in the Making: Protecting Water Resources requires Cooperation with the PA*. April 2006b, 4.

Friends of the Earth Middle East. 'Good Water Neighbors: Identifying Common Environmental Problems and Shared Solutions'. *FoEME*, February 2007a, 55.

Friends of the Earth Middle East. *Nature, Agriculture and the Price of Water in Israel*. November 2007b, 16.

Friends of the Earth Middle East. *Environmental Peacebuilding Theory and Practice*. January 2008a, 35.

Friends of the Earth Middle East. *Draft Agreement on Water Cooperation*. June 2008b, 34.

Gabbay, Shoshana. *Water in Israel: Rehabilitation of Israel's Rivers*. https://www.jewishvirtuallibrary.org/rehabilitation-of-israel-s-rivers.

German Technical Cooperation Programme for the Water Sector in the Palestinian Territories. *Factsheet* (In cooperation with the German Financial Cooperation). February, 2007.

Ghosheth, Adnan Farouq Saad Aldin. *Disclosable Version of the ISR – Hebron Regional Wastewater Management Project – Phase 1 – P117449 – Sequence No: 09 (English)*. Washington, DC: World Bank Group, 2019. http://documents.worldbank.org/curated

/en/809911561059624782/Disclosable-Version-of-the-ISR-Hebron-Regional-Wastewa
ter-Management-Project-Phase-1-P117449-Sequence-No-09.

Gilbert, Martin. *The Routledge Atlas of the Arab-Israeli Conflict*. 10th ed. Oxon: Routledge,
2012, 227.

Gilbert, Martin. *The Story of Israel from Theodor Herzl to the Dream for Peace*. London,
2018, 160.

Gilmour, David. *Dispossessed: The Ordeal of the Palestinians 1917–1980*. London, 1980,
218.

Gisha. *Mekorot Responds to Gisha's Freedom of Information Application Regarding Water
Supply to the Gaza Strip*. 2 September 2015. https://gisha.org/legal/5016.

GIZ/PWA/CEP (Deutsche Gesellschaft für Internationale Zusammenarbeit, Palestinian
Water Authority, and Centre for Engineering and Planning). *Survey of Private and Public
Brackish Desalination Plants in Gaza Strip*. Final Analysis Report, September
2015.

Government of Israel. *The Issue of Water between Israel and the Palestinians*. 2009. http://
www.water.gov.il/Hebrew/ProfessionalInfoAndData/2012/22-Water-Issues-Between-I
srael-and-the-Palestinians.pdf (accessed 27 May 2019).

The Government of Israel. *Israel's Chronic Water Problems*. Israel Ministry of Foreign
Affairs, n.d. https://mfa.gov.il/MFA/IsraelExperience/AboutIsrael/Spotlight?Pages/Isra
el-s%20Chronicle%20Water%20Problem.aspx.

The Government of the United Kingdom. *Report of the 1937 Palestine Royal Commission*
Cmd. 5479. 1937.

Green, Stephen. *Taking Sides: America's Secret Relations with a Militant Israel. The
1953 Aid Cut-off: A Parable for Our Times*. New York: William Morrow & Co, 1984,
76–83.

Grey, David. *The Development of the Water Resources of the Occupied Palestinian
Territories: Some Key Issues*. Isaac and Shuval, 1994, 220ff.

Gruen, George E. *Contribution of Water Imports to Israeli-Palestinian-Jordanian Peace*.
Isaac and Shuval, 1994.

GTZ. *Training Needs Assessment: Water Supply and Wastewater Service Providers*.
November 2006, 65.

Guyatt, Nicholas. *The Absence of Peace: Understanding the Israeli-Palestinian Conflict*.
London and New York: Zed Books, 1998, 188.

Gvirtzman, H. *Groundwater Allocation in Judea and Samaria*. Isaac and Shuval, 1994,
214ff.

Haddad, Toufic. *Palestine Ltd. Neoliberalism and Nationalism in the Occupied Territory*.
London: IB Tauris, 2016, 338.

Haddadin, M. J. 'Negotiated Resolution of the Jordan-Israel Water Conflict'. *International
Negotiation* 5, no. 2 (2000): 263–88.

Haddadin, M. J. *Diplomacy on the Jordan: International Conflict and Negotiated Resolution*.
Norwell, MA: Springer, 2001.

Haddadin, M. J. *Diplomacy on the Jordan: International Conflict and Negotiated Resolution*.
Boston: Kluwer Academic Publishers, 2002a, 535.

Haddadin, M. J. 'Response to commentary by Uri Shamir'. *Natural Resources Forum* 26,
no. 3 (2002b): 254–55.

Haddadin, Munther. 'Evolution of Water Administration and Legislation'. In *Water
Resources in Jordan. Evolving Policies for Development, the Environment and Conflict
Resolution*, edited by Munther Haddadin, 29–42. Resources for the Future, 2006. ISBN
1-933115-32-7.

Haddadin, M. J. 'Cooperation and lack thereof on management of the Yarmouk River'. *Water International* 34, no. 4 (2009): 420–431.

Haddadin, M. J. and U. Shamir. The Jordan River Basin, Part I: Water Conflict and Negotiated Resolution Jordan River Case Study, Part II: The Negotiations and the Water Agreement Between the Hashemite Kingdom of Jordan and the State of Israel. 2003. PC-CP Series, No. 15 UNESCO / IHP / WWAP, Paris, France.

Hamdy, A. and R. Monti, eds. *West Bank Water Department: Institutional Reform towards National Bulk Supply Utility.*

Hammond, Jeremy R. *Obstacle to Peace. The US Role in the Israel-Palestinian Conflict.* Michigan: World View Publications, 2016, 508.

Harrington, Cameron. *Fluid Identities: Toward a Critical Security of Water.* PhD thesis. The University of Western Ontario. November 2013.

Hass, Amira. 'PA Farmers Hung Out to Dry while Israelis Flourish in Jordan Valley'. *Haaretz*, 2 December 2012.

Hass, Amira. 'A Bedouin Family Got Evicted by Israel'. *Haaretz*, 18 August 2019. http://www.haaretz.com/news/diplomacy-defense/pa-farmers-hung-out-to-dry-while-israel is-flourish-in-jordan-valley.premium-1.481797105.

Helman, J. *Cleanliness and Squalor in Inter-War Tel-Aviv.*

Herzl, Theodore. *The Old New Land.* German: Altneuland. Original edition 1902, republished by CreateSpace Independent Publisher, 2012.

Hirsch, Dafna. '"We are Here to Bring the West, Not Only to Ourselves": Zionisst Occidentlism and the Discourse of Hygiene in Mandate Palestine'. *International Journal of Middle East Studies.* https://doi.org/10.1017/S0020743809990079 (accessed 26 October, 2009).

Hodgkin, Thomas. *Letters from Palestine, 1932 – 36.* Edited by E. C. Hodgkin. London, 1986, 202.

Hourani, Albert. *Arabic Thought in the Liberal Age 1798–1939.* Oxford Paperbacks, 1970, 403.

Hull, Edward. *Mount Seir, Sinai and Western Palestine.* London: Richard Bentley & Son, 1885.

Husseini, Hiba. *The Palestinian Water Authority: Developments and Challenges Involving the Legal Framework and Capacity of the PWA.* 7.

Hydrological Service of Israel (HIS). *Development of Utilization and Status of Water Resources.* 211, 296–8.

IBNET. *Water Supply and Sanitation Blue Book 2014.* World Bank, 2014.

The International Conference on Water and the Environment (ICWE). 'The Dublin Statement on Water and Sustainable Development'. ICWE Secretariat, World Meteorological Organization, 1992. Web. 16 April 2011. http://www.wmo.int/pages/prog/hwrp/documents/english/icwedece.html#p4.

Institute for Palestine Studies. *Supplement to Survey of Palestine. Notes Compiled for the Information of the United Nations Special Committee on Palestine.* June, 1947, reprinted 1991 Washington, DC, 153.

International Desalination Association. *The Current State of Desalination.* Retrieved 24 April 2018.

Isaac, Jad and Hilel Shuval. *Water and Peace in the Middle East. Proceedings of the First Israeli-Palestinian International Academic Conference on Water,* Zurich, Switzerland, *10–13 December 1992* Studies in Environmental Science 58 Published by Elsevier, 1994.

Government of Israel. *Israel Water Sector – Key Issues.* The Knesset Research and Information Centre, February 2018.

Government of Israel. *The Issue of Water between Israel and the Palestinians.* http://www
   .water.gov.il/HebrewProfessionalinfoAndData/2012/22-Water-Issues-between-Israel-
   and-the-Palestinians.pdf (accessed 27 May 2019).
Israel Water Authority (IWA). *Water Supply to the Settlements.* October 2008c, 10.
Israel Water Authority (IWA). *The Natural Water Resources Between the Mediterranean Sea
   and the Jordan River.* Jerusalem – 2012 Authors are Gavriel Weinberger (Head of Israel
   Hydrological Service), Yakov Livshitz and Amir Givati.
Israel Water Justice: Water as a Human Right in Israel By Tamar Keinan, Friends of the
   Earth Middle East, Israel Editor: Gidon Bromberg, Friends of the Earth Middle East
   Series' coordinator: Simone Klawitter, Policy Advisor.
Israeli-Palestinian Interim Agreement. Article 40. 1995.
Jaas, M. *West Bank Water Department. Institutional Reform towards National Bulk Supply
   Utility.* Edited by A. Hamdy and R. Monti.
Jad, Isaac and Atif Kubursi. *Dry Peace in the Middle East.* Applied Research Institute of
   Jerusalem and Dept of Economics McMaster University, Ontario, Canada.
Jayyousi, Anan. *Israeli Water Crimes on Palestinian Water Resources.* Mimeo, 2008, 12.
Jayyousi, Anan and Omar Zimmo. *Good Practice Case Studies on the Palestinian Water
   Sector Donor Coordination.* 9.
Johnston, Penny. 'Witness in Jerusalem: Re-Readings'. In *Palestine Studies* Issue 51 2012.
Kahan, David. *Agriculture and Water Resources in the West Bank and Gaza (1967–1987).*
   1987.
Kally, Elisha, with Gideon Fishelson. *Water and Peace. Water Resources and the Arab-
   Israeli Peace Process.* USA: Praeger Publishers, 1993, 127.
Karlinsky, Nahum. *The Limits of Separation: Jaffa and Tel Aviv before 1948: The
   Underground Story.* In: *Tel-Aviv at 100: Myths, Memories and Realities,* edited by Maoz
   Azaryahu and S. Ilan Troen. Indiana University Press.
Karlinsky, Nahum. *California Dreaming: Ideology, Society, and Technology in the Citrus
   Industry of Palestine, 1890–1939.* Albany, 2005.
Kark, Ruth. *Jaffa: A City in Evolution, 1799–1917.* Jerusalem: Yad Izhak Ben-Svi Press,
   1990.
USAID /EHP. *Save the Children Report – Village Water and Sanitation Program Phase II,*
   June 2003.
Israel Water Justice: Water as a Human Right in Israel By Tamar Keinan, Friends of the
   Earth Middle East, Israel Editor: Gidon Bromberg, Friends of the Earth Middle East
   Series' coordinator: Simone Klawitter, Policy Advisor.
Kerem Navot. *Israeli Settlers' Agriculture As A Means Of Land Takeover In The West Bank.*
   2013.
Khalidi, Rashid. *The Iron Cage. The* Story of the Palestinian Struggle for Statehood Oxford,
   2006, 281.
Khalidi, Rashid. *Palestinian Identity The Construction of Modern National Consciousness.*
   New York: Columbia University Press, 1997, 310.
Khalidi, Rashid. *Resurrecting Empire.* Western Footprints and America's Perilous Path in
   the Middle East Boston, USA, 2004, 223.
Khouri, Rami G. The Jordan Valley. *Life and Society below Sea Level.* London and New
   York: Association with the Jordan Valley Authority, 1981, 238.
Kislev, Yoav. *The Water Economy of Israel.* LAP LAMBERT Academic Publishing 2014, 126.
Kloosterman, Karin. *Desalinated Water Use in Israel,* in Health, posted 28 March 2017.
   www.greenprophet.com/2017/03/desalinated-water-use-in-israel-causing-alarming-io
   dine-deficiency-in-people.

Kubovich, Yaniv. 'Israel Advances Gaza Water Project: Passage of Equipment to Construct Desalination Plant and Water Reservoirs Okayed by Defense Ministry'. *Haaretz*, 2 August 2018.

Kuttab, Jonathan and Isaac, Jad. *Approaches to the Legal Aspects of Conflict on Water Rights in Palestine/Israel.* Isaac and Shuval, 1994, 241.

Lambton, Professor Ann K. S. *The Persian Land Reform 1962–1966.* Oxford: Clarendon Press, 1969, 386.

LeBor, Adam. 'Zion and the Arabs. Jaffa as a Metaphor'. *World Policy Journal*, 24, no. 4 (Winter 2007/2008): 61–75.

LeBor, Adam. *City of Oranges. Arabs and Jews in Jaffa.* London, 2006, 357.

Lemire, Vincent 2000, *Water in Jerusalem at the End of the Ottoman Period (1850–1920)*, Bulletin du Centre de recherche français à Jérusalem [En ligne], 7 | 2000, mis en ligne le 13 mars 2008, Consulted 4 February 2019. http://journals.openedition.org/bcr fj/2572.

LeVine, Mark, 2005. *Overthrowing geography: Jaffa, Tel Aviv and the struggle for Palestine 1880–1948.* University of California Press, 2005.

Levy, Gideon and Levac, Alex. 'Down in the Jordan Valley, the Cruel Wheels of the Israeli Occupation Keep on Turning'. *Haaretz*, 20 September 2019. https://www.haaretz.com/i srael-news/.premium-in-the-jordan-valley-the-cruel-wheels-of-the-israeli-occupation -keep-turning-1.7867122?=&utm_source=Push_Notification&utm_medium=web_pu sh&utm_campaign=General&ts=_1569149378675.

The Local Government Performance Assessment (LPGA) Survey.

Lidman, Melanie, 'In Gaza, Using Agriculture to Grow the Economy'. *Times of Israel*, 17 May 2016. https://www.timesofisrael.com/in-gaza-using-agriculture-to-grow-the-ec onomy/.

Lidman, Melanie. 'Baptism by mire in Jordan River'. *Times of Israel*, 25 May 2019. https:// www.timesofisrael.com/baptism-by-mire-in-jordan-river-sewage-mucks-up-christian -rite/.

Likhovski , Assaf. 'Is Tax Law Culturally Specific? Lessons from the History of Income Tax Law in Mandatory Palestine'. *Theoretical Inquiries in Law* 11, no. 2 (2010): 43–70.

Lonergan, Stephen C. and Brooks, David B. *Watershed: The Role of Fresh Water in the Israeli-Palestinian Conflict.* Ottawa: IDRC, 1994.

Lowdermilk, Walter C. *Palestine, Land of Promise.* London, 1944, 167.

MacDonald et al. 'Mapping groundwater development costs for the transboundary Western Aquifer Basin, Palestine/Israel. A.M. MacDonald, B. É. Ó Dochartaigh, R. C. Calow, Y. Shalabi, K. Selah, and S. Merrett'. *Hydrogeology Journal* 17 (2009): 1579–87.

MacIntyre, Donald. *Gaza: Preparing for Dawn.* London, 2018, 352.

Marie, Amer and Imad Abu-Kishk. 'Review of Water Legislation from the Pre-British Mandate Period through the Israeli Occupation'. *Palestine-Israel Journal* 19, no. 4 & 20, no. 1 (2014) / Natural Resources and the Arab-Israeli Conflict.

MAS. *Effects of Movement and Access Controls on Water for the Palestinian Agriculture Sector.* Preliminary Assessment. 2009 (draft).

MAS-Palestinian Economic Policy Research Institute. *Economic Impacts of Water Restrictions in Palestine.* Preliminary Estimates. March 2009, 74.

Masterman, E. W. G. 'Agricultural Life in Palestine'. *The Biblical World* 15, no. 3 (March 1900): 189. http://www.jstor.org/stable/3137064.

Matthews, Elizabeth, Ed. With Newman, David and Daoudi, Mohammed S. Dajani. *The Israel-Palestine Conflict. Parallel Discourses.* Oxford, 2011, 276.

Mekorot, Israel National Water Co. *Main Facts & Figures.* 31 July 2018.

Messerchmit. 2008.

Minorities at Risk 2008 *Assessment for Arabs in Israel.*

Montefiore, Simon Sebag. *Jerusalem, the Biography.* London: Weidenfeld and Nicolson, 2011, 638.

Morris, Benny. *Righteous Victims: A History of the Zionist-Arab Conflict 1881–1999.* London, 2000, 751

Nablus Municipality 2017. *Wastewater Treatment Plant Nablus West Annual Report for Operations and Reuse 2017* Eng. Suleiman Abu Ghosh Eng. Yousef Abu Jaffal Mr. Sameh Bitar Eng. Mohammad Homeidan Eng.Yazan Odeh. http://wwtp.nablus.org /wp-content/uploads/2018/02/Final-2017-report-20-2-2018.pdf (accessed 4 August 2019).

Netherlands Representative Office (NRO). 'Palestinian Territories: Gaza Exports to Europe with Dutch Support' by Market Insider'. *Wednesday,* 18 December 2013. http: //www.intracen.org/Gaza-exports-to-Europe-with-Dutch-support/#sthash.lS3FO1Dl .dpuf.

New Scientist. 'Desalination: Israel Lays Claim to Palestine's Water'. *New Scientist,* 27 May 2004. https://www.newscientist.com/article/dn5037-israel-lays-claim-to-palestines -water/#ixzz5ySpdLjYM.

Abu Nasar, A et al. 'Relation of Nitrate Contamination of Groundwater with Methaemoglobin Level Among Infants in Gaza'. *Eastern Mediterranean Health Journal* 13, no. 5 (September–October 2007). http://www.emro.who.int.

Niksic, Orhan, and Nur Nasser Eddin. *Public Expenditure Review–Palestinian Territories.* Washington, DC: World Bank Group, 2016. http://documents.worldbank.org/curated/ en/320891473688227759/Public-Expenditure-Review-Palestinian-territories.

Norris, Jacob. 'Toxic Waters: Ibrahim Hazboun and the Struggle for a Dead Sea Concession, 1913–1948'. *Jerusalem Quarterly* 45: 25–42. ISSN 1565-2254. Available from Sussex Research Online https://sro.sussex.ac.uk/id/eprint/43631.

Oren, Michael *Six Days of War June 1967 and the Making of the Modern Middle East* OUP, 2002, 446.

Owen, E. R. J. *Economic Development in Mandatory Palestine 1918–1948 in The Palestinian Economy.* Edited by George T. Abed. London: Routledge, 1988.

Palestinian Central Bureau of Statistics (PCBS). *Agricultural Statistics* 2005/6. December 2007, 39.

Palestinian Central Bureau of Statistics (PCBS). *Survey on the Impact of the Expansion and Annexation Wall on the Socio-Economic Conditions of Palestinian Localities which the Wall Passes Through.* September 2008, 19.

Palestinian Central Bureau of Statistics (PCBS). 'Poverty Profile in Palestine, 2017'. *Palestine,* 2017. http://www.pcbs.gov.ps/Document/pdf/txte_poverty2017.pdf?date =16

Palestinian Central Bureau of Statistics (PCBS) and the World Bank. *Deep Palestinian Poverty in the Midst of Economic Crisis.* October 2004. In English and Arabic. 71.

Palestinian Hydrology Group. *Water for Life. Israeli Assault on Palestinian Water during the Intifida.* 2004 Report, 204.

Palestinian Hydrology Group. *Water for Life. Water, Sanitation and Hygiene Monitoring Program.* 2005 Report, 204.

Palestinian Water Agenda 2008–2010. *Strategy Notes for Short-term Priority. Investments in the Water Supply and Wastewater Sector in Palestine.* May 2008.

PASSIA. *Water and Environment: Water Data.* No date.

Palestine Authority, Ministry of Agriculture. *Strategy for Sustainable Agriculture.* 2004.

Palestine Authority, Ministry of Agriculture. *National Agricultural Sector Strategy 2017–2022*. November 2016.

Pappe, Ilan. *History of Modern Palestine. One Land, Two Peoples* Cambridge: Cambridge University Press, 2004, 333.

Pappe, Ilan. *The Ethnic Cleansing of Palestine*. Oxford: One World, 2006, 313.

Pappe, Ilan. *The Making of the Arab-Israeli Conflict 1947–1951*. London, 2006, 324.

Pappe, Ilan. *The Rise and Fall of a Palestinian Dynasty. The Husaynis 1700–1948*. London: Saqi Books, 2010, 399.

Pappe, Ilan. *The Idea of Israel. A History of Power and Knowledge*. London, 2015.

Pappe, Ilan. *The Biggest Prison on Earth. A History of the Occupied Territories*. London: Oneworld Publications, 2017, 273.

Pappe, Ilan. *Ten Myths about Israel* London, 2017, 171.

Peake, A. S. *Peake' Commentary on the Bible*. Edited by by Matthew Black, Harold Henry Rowley and Arthur Samuel Peake. Thomas Nelson: London, 1962.

PECDAR. *Palestinian Water Strategic Planning Study*. 2001, 140.

Plant, Steven. 'Water Policy in Israel'. *Policy Studies* 47 (July 2000). Jerusalem: Institute for Advanced Strategic and Political Studies.

Pope Francis. http://w2.vatican.va/content/francesco/en/encyclicals/documents/papa-f rancesco. 20150524 enciclica-laudato-si.html (accessed 25 May 2019).

PNA/PWA. *Letter from PWA to B'Tselem*. 14 August 2008, 5.

PWA. *Water Strategy 2000*. Ramallah, 2000.

PWA. *An Audit of the Operations and Projects in the Water Sector in Palestine: The Strategic Refocusing of Water Sector Infrastructure in Palestine*. Final Report, 18 November 2008a. Funded by the Norwegian Representative Office in Palestine, 90.

PWA. *Water Sector Status in West Bank. Summary Report with West Bank Governorates Emergency and Development Plan*. Draft, October 2008b, 50.

PWA. *Water Governance Programme: Building the Capacity for Institutional Reform of the Water Sector*. Ramallah, Report prepared by the PWA with support from the United Nations Development Programme, 15 March 2009.

PWA. *White Paper on Water Sector Reform in Palestine*, April 2012.

PWA. *Status Report of Water Resources in the Occupied State of Palestine*. Ramallah: PWA, 2013. http://www.pwa.ps/.

PWA. *PWA Water Tables 2014*. Palestinian Water Authority Water Information System. 2014.

PWA. *Desalinated Water Chain in the Gaza Strip "From Source to Mouth."* Analysis Report. PWA, GiZ, Norwegian MFA, ECHO, NRC, ACF, GVC, IOCC, Islamic Relief, Oxfam, and Save the Children, 2015a.

PWA. *Gaza Strip: Desalination Facility Project: Necessity, Politics and Energy*. PWA, 2015b. http://www.pwa.ps/userfiles.

PWA. *Water Crisis in Gaza: The Future Depends on Sustainable Solutions* (in Arabic). Ramallah: PWA, 2015c. http://www.pwa.ps.

PWA/Hydroconseil. *National Water Company Draft Action Plan*. 2016.

PWA/Orgut. *Roadmap for the Creation of Regional Water utilities in the Frame of the Water Sector Reform in Palestine. Draft Phase 2*. Completion Report. Palestinian Water Authority/Orgut Consulting AB, February 2017.

PWA/Hydroconseil. *National Water Company Draft Action Plan* (2016). PWA/ Hydroconseil. 2016.

PWA/WASH Partners/GIZ (Palestinian Water Authority, WASH Partners, and Deutsche Gesellschaft für Internationale Zusammenarbeit). *"Surveying Private & Public Brackish*

Water Desalination Plants in the Gaza Strip & Studying the Water Supply Chain."
Dissemination Workshop PowerPoint, September 2015.

PWA/Norway. *Audit of the Operations and Projects of the PWA*. Draft, 5 October 2008, 73.

PWA. *Gaza Central Desalination Plant and Associated Works Program. Donor Information Handbook*. Ramallah, 2018.

Rinat, Zafrir. 'And a Cleaner Yarkon River Runs Through It'. *Haaretz* 18 July 2013. https://www.haaretz.com/israel-news/sports/premium-and-a-cleaner-river-runs-through-it 1.5292956 (accessed 26 May 2019).

Ring, Kenneth PhD. Abdullah Ghassan Letters *from Palestine. Palestinians Speak Out about Their Lives, Their Country, and the Power of Nonviolence*. Tucson, Arizona, 2010.

Rogan, Eugene and Avi Shlaim. *The War for Palestine: Rewriting the History of 1948*. Cambridge: Cambridge University Press, 2001.

Rogan, Eugene. *The Fall of the Ottomans. The Great War in the Middle East 1914–1920*. Allen Lane, Great Britain, 2015, 485.

Rogers, Peter and Lydon, Peter. (Eds) *Water in the Arab World. Perspectives and Prognoses Eleven Essays*. Harvard, 1994, 369.

Romeo, Leonardo G. *Assessment of the Strategic Development and Investment Planning (SDIP) Process: A Rapid Assessment of Policy and Selected Technical Issues*. LDI (Local Development International LLC), 2017.

Rouyer, Alwyn R. *Turning Water into Politics: The Water Issue in the Palestinian-Israeli Conflict*. Palgrave Macmillan, 1999.

Sadoff, C. and Grey D. '(Sink or swim? Water security for growth and development'. *Water Policy* 9, no. 6 (2007): 545–571.

Said, Edward W. *Orientalism*. London, 1978, 368.

Said, Edward *Peace and Its Discontents: Essays on Palestine in the Middle East Peace Process*. With a Preface by Christopher Hitchens. New York, 1995, 188.

Said, Edward W. and Hitchens, Christopher, eds. *Blaming the Victims. Spurious Scholarship and the Palestinian Question*. London, 2001, 296.

Salah, John S. 'Jaffa Drainage Scheme'. *Municipal Corporation of Jaffa* 18, no. 6 (1935).

Samuel, Edwin. *A Lifetime in Jerusalem: The Memoirs of the Second Viscount Samuel*. Jerusalem: Israel Universities Press, 1970.

Sand, Shlomo. *The Invention of the Jewish People*. London and New York: Verso, 2009, 332.

Sayigh, Yusuf A. 'The Palestinian Economy under Occupation'. In *The Palestinian Economy*, edited by George T. Abed. London: Routledge, 1988.

Schama, Simon. *Belonging. The Story of the Jews 1492–1900*. London: Penguin, Random House, 2017, 790.

Schlaim, Avi The Iron Wall. *Israel and the Arab World*. London, 2000, 670.

Schlaim, Avi. *Israel and Palestine. Reappraisals, Revisions, Refutations*. London, 2010, 392.

Schoenfeld, Stuart, Eric Abitbol and Francesca de Chatel. *Retelling the Story of Water in the Middle East: Reflections on and about a Conversation at the Dead Sea*. Ontario, Canada: York University, 2007.

Schwarz, J. *Management of Israel's Water Resources*. Isaac and Shuval, 1994.

Schwartz, J. *Israel Water Sector Review*. Report prepared for the World Bank, Tel Aviv 1990.

Segev, Tom. *Israel and the War that Transformed the Middle East*. Little, Brown, 1967.

Selby, Jan. *Water, Power and Politics in the Middle East*. IB Tauris, 2003, 275

Selby, Jan. '"New Security Thinking" In Israeli-Palestinian Water Relations'. *Facing Global Environmental Change: Environmental, Energy, Food, Health, and Water Security Concepts*. Edited by Hans, 2009.

Günter Brauch, Hans Günter Brauch, Úrsula Oswald Spring, John Grin, Czeslaw
    Mesjasz, Patricia Kameri-Mbote, Navnita Chadha Behera, Béchir Chourou, Heinz
    Krummenacher. Berlin, Heidelberg: Springer, 2009, 623–31.
Selby Jan. *Dependencies, Independence, and Interdependence in the Palestinian Water
    Sector,* 2011.
Selby, Jan. 'Cooperation, Domination and Colonization: The Israeli Palestinian Joint Water
    Committee'. *Water Alternatives* 6, no. 1 (2013): 1–24. ISSN 1965-0175.
Selby, Jan and Messerschmid, Clemens. 'Misrepresenting the Jordan River Basin'. *Water
    Alternatives* 8, no. 2 (2015): 258–79. ISSN 1965-0175.
Shamir, Uri. 'Water Agreements between Israel and its Neighbours'. In *Transformations of
    Middle East Natural Environments,* edited by Jeff Albert, Magnus Bernhardsson and
    Roger Kenna. Yale F & ES Bulletin 103, 1998.
Shapland, Greg. *Rivers of Discord. International Water Disputes in the Middle East.*
    London: C. Hurst & Co., 1997, 183.
Shawa, Issam R. *Water Situation in the Gaza Strip,* Isaac & Shuval, 1994.
Shehadeh, Raja. *Palestinian Walks: Notes on a Vanishing Landscape.* London, 2008.
Shehadeh, Raja. *Occupier's Law: Israel and the West Bank.* Washington, DC: Institute for
    Palestine Studies, 1985.
Sherman, A. J. *Mandate Days: British Lives in Palestine 1918–1948.* London: Thames &
    Hudson, 1997, 264.
Shuval, Hillel. 'Meeting Vital Human Needs: Equitable Resolution of Conflicts Over
    Shared Water Resources of Israelis and Palestinians'. In *Water Resources in the Middle
    East,* edited by Shuval and Dweik, 3–16. Berlin: Springer, 2007.
Shuval, Hillel and Hassan Dweik, eds. *Water Resources in the Middle East .Israel-
    Palestinian Water Issues – From Conflict to Cooperation.* Volume 2, Hexagon series on
    Human and Environmental Security and Peace. Berlin: Springer, 2007, 454.
Shuval, Hillel. *Evaluating the WHO 2006 Health guidelines for wastewater reuse in
    agriculture for Palestinian requirements* Power point presentation. 5 November 2008, 4.
Siegel, Seth M. *Let There Be Water.* New York: St Martin's Press, 2015, 337.
Siegel 2015: 252. Of the Approximately, 318 Million m³ of Water Used in Israeli
    Agriculture in 2016, about 195 Million m³ was from Treated Wastewater (62 Per Cent).
Smilansky, David. *What is the Water Supply Situation in Tel Aviv?* Yedi.ot.Iriyat. Tel
    Aviv.5.8.9. (1934).
Smith, Charles D. *Palestine and the Arab-Israeli Conflict. A History with Documents*
    Bedford/St Martin's, USA 2017, 597.
Society for Austro-Arab Relations. *Development Perspectives for Agriculture in the
    Occupied Palestinian Territories.* 1992.
Soffer, Arnon. *The Relevance of the Johnston Plan to the Reality of 1993 and Beyond.* Isaac
    and Shuval, 1994.
Sokmen, Muge Gursoy and Ertur Basak, eds. *Waiting for the Barbarians.* A Tribute to
    Edward W Said. Verso, 2008.
Sosland, Jeffrey K. *Cooperating Rivals: The Riparian Politics of the Jordan River Basin.*
    Albany: State University of New York, 2007.
Surkes, Sue. 'White Foam Covers Sections of the Yarkon River'. Article in the *Times of
    Israel,* 11 October 2017. https://www.timesofisrael.com/white-foam-covers-sections
    -of-yarkon-river-despite-cleanup-efforts.
*A Survey of Palestine Prepared in December 1945 and January, 1946. For the information of
    the Anglo-American Committee of Inquiry.* Volume I and Volume II Reprinted by The
    Institute for Palestine Studies, Washington, DC, 1991 Volume I, 534 Volume II, 1139.

SUSMAQ. *The Susmaq Project: Sustainable Management of the West Bank and Gaza Aquifers: Summary Report*, 2006, 44.

Sutcliffe, Claud R. 'Palestinian Refugee Resettlement: Lessons from the East Ghor Canal Project'. *Journal of Peace Research* 11, no. 1 (1974): 57–62.

Tal, Alon. *The Evolution of Israeli Water Management: The Elusive Search for Environmental Security*. Chapter 5.

Tal, Professor Alon and Abed-Rabbo, Dr Alfred. *Water Wisdom: Preparing the Groundwork for Cooperative and Sustainable Water Management in the Middle East*. Rutgers University Press, September, 2010, 371.

Tal, Alon. *All the Trees of the Forest. Israel's Woodlands from the Bible to the Present*. Yale University Press, 2013, 348.

Tal, Alon and David Katz. 'Rehabilitating Israel's Streams and Rivers'. *International Journal of River Basin Management* 10, no. 4 (2012): 317–30.

Talmon, J. L. *The Origins of Totalitarian Democracy*. London: Sphere Books, 1970, 355.

Templin, Julia S. *Zababdeh: A Palestinian Water History*. Julia S. Templin, MSc thesis, Utah State University, 2011. *All Graduate Theses and Dissertations*, 911. https://digitalcommons.usu.edu/etd/911.

Thomson, W. M. *The Land and the Book*. Thomas Nelson & Son, 1911.

Trottier, Julie and Perrier, Jeanne. 'Water-Driven Palestinian Agricultural Frontiers: The Global Ramifications of Transforming Local Irrigation'. *Journal of Political Ecology* 25 (2018): 304.

Tuchman, Barbara W. *Bible and Sword. England and Palestine from the Bronze Age to Balfour*. New York, 1984, 412.

Tzuri, Matan. 'Israel to Build Pipeline to Absorb Sewage from Gaza'. *Ynet News*, 7 January 2017. https://www.ynetnews.com/articles/0,7340,L-4983174,00.html.

Udasin, Sharon and Lazaroff, Tovah. 'Gaza Sewage Forces Shutdown of Israeli Beach: Israel May Build a Pipeline to Sderot to Treat Waste'. Article in the *Jerusalem Post*, 6 July 2017.

UNCTAD. *Population and Demographic Developments in the West Bank and Gaza Strip until 1990*. UNCTAD/ECDC/SEU/1 United Nations Conference on Trade and Development, 1990. https://unctaf.org/en/docs/poecdeseudi1.en.pdf.

UNCTAD. *The Besieged Palestinian agricultural sector*. New York: UNCTAD, 2015.

UNDP. *West Bank and Gaza Environment Priorities Note (P169628)*.

UNICEF. *UNICEF Seawater Desalination Plant Helps Head Off Gaza Water Crisis*. 2019. https://www.unicef.org/stories/unicef-seawater-desalination-plant-helps-head-gaza-water-crisis.

UNISPAL *Water Resources of the Occupied Palestinian Territory*. Committee on the Exercise of he Inalienable Rights of the Palestinian People, New York, United Nations, 1992. https://unispal.un.org/UNISPAL.NSF/0/296EE705038AC9FC852561170067E)5F

UNOCHA. Unitedd Nations Office for the Coordination of Humanitarian Assistance. 2019. https://www.ochaopt.org/theme/food-security (accessed 14 June 2019).

UNOCHA. Socio-Economic and Food Security Survey (SefSec). 2018.

UNOCHA. *WBG Closure Maps*. April 2008, 19.

UNOCHA. *Gaza Strip Inter-Agency Humanitarian Fact Sheet*. June 2008, 2.

UNOCHA. *Gaza Humanitarian Situation Reports*, 29 April, 2008, 17 November, 2008.

USAID /EHP. Save the Children Report – *Village Water and Sanitation Program Phase II*, June 2003.

Van Aken, Mauro *Development as a Gift: Patterns of Assistance and Refugees Strategies in the Jordan Valley*. In International Symposium on the Palestinian Refugees and UNRWA in Jordan, the West Bank and Gaza, 1949–1999.

Vishwanath, Tara, Brian Blankespoor, Faythe Calandra, Nandini Krishnan, Meera Mahadevan, and Mobuo Yoshida. *Seeing is Believing: Poverty in the Palestinian Territories*. Washington, DC: World Bank Group, 2014.

von Medeazza, Gregor. *Searching for clean water in Gaza*, 10 January, 2019.

WANA. *Decoupling National Water Needs for National Water Supplies: Insights and Potential for Countries in the Jordan Basin*. West Africa-North Africa Institute, June 2017.

Ward, Christopher and Sandra Ruckstuhl. *Water Scarcity, Climate Change and Conflict in the Middle East*. London: IB Tauris, 2017, 343.

Weinthal, Erika and Sowers, Jeannie. *Targeting Infrastructure and livelihoods in the West Bank and Gaza*. OUP.

Weizman, Rotem Caro. *Speech at EcoPeace Conference* Summary, 6 March 2018.

Weizman, Eyal. *Hollow Land: Israel's Architecture of Occupation*. New Edition. London: Verso, 2017, 318.

World Bank. *The Economic Development of Jordan*. Washington, DC: World Bank, 1955.

World Bank. *Developing the Occupied Territories: An Investment in Peace* Vol 1: Overview and Key Findings Vol II: Strategic Choices at the Macro Level. Vol III: Performance of the Private Sector. Vol IV: The Agricultural Sector Vol V: Infrastructure sectors Vol VI: Human Resource Development, 1993.

World Bank. *Peace and the Jordanian Economy*. 1994, 62.

World Bank. *The Hashemite Kingdom of Jordan: Agricultural Sector Adjustment Operation and Agricultural Sector Technical Support Project*. Working Papers Volume II (Papers 9 –14 Statistical Annex and Bibliography) 30 March 1995.

World Bank. *Poverty in West Bank and Gaza: Summary*. May 2001, 21

World Bank. *Palestinian Economic Crisis*. March 2002a, 141.

World Bank. *Long Term Policy Options for the Palestinian Economy*. July 2002b, 129.

World Bank. *Report on the Impact of the Intifada*. Washington, DC: World Bank, 2003.

World Bank. *West Bank and Gaza Infrastructure Assessment*. December 2004a, 43.

World Bank. *Palestinian Economic Crisis*. October 2004b, 93.

World Bank. *Socio-Political Structures, Development and State-Building in West Bank and Gaza: A Country Social Analysis*. Washington, DC: The World Bank, June 2006a, 46.

World Bank. *Country Economic Memorandum: Growth in WBG: Opportunities and Constraints*. September 2006b. Vol I 80 Vol II 72.

World Bank. *West Bank and Gaza Public Expenditure Review: From Crisis to Greater Fiscal Independence*. March 2007a. Vol I 50.

World Bank. *West Bank and Gaza Water Sector Update*. Draft Final, 1 November 2007b. Text: 37 Tables: 40.

World Bank. *Two Years after London: Restarting Palestinian Economic Recovery*. Report to the Ad Hoc Liaison Committee. 24 September 2007c, 35.

World Bank. *West Bank and Gaza Update*. March 2008a, 24.

World Bank. *West Bank and Gaza Update*. June 2008b, 24.

World Bank. *Political Economy of Policy Reform – Issues and Implications for Policy Dialogue and Development Operations*. Report No. 44288-GLB, Social Development Department (SDV). Washington, DC: The World Bank, 2008c.

World Bank. *WBG Water Sector Institutional Support Study*. February 2008d, 39.

World Bank. *Economic Effects of Restricted Access to Land in the West Bank*. 2008e, 41.

World Bank. *Issues Paper: Interim Technical Assistance Note on Water*, June 2008f, 13.

World Bank. *West Bank and Gaza. Palestinian Trade: West Bank Routes*. December 16, 2008g. Report No. 46807, 22.

World Bank. *West Bank and Gaza: Assessment of Restrictions on Palestinian Water Sector Development*. Washington, DC: World Bank, April 2009, 134.

World Bank. *West Bank and Gaza: Coping with Conflict? Poverty and Inclusion in the West Bank and Gaza*. Report No. 61293-GZ, July. Washington, DC: World Bank, 2011.

World Bank. *Area C and the future of the Palestinian economy*. Report No. AUS2922. Washington, DC: World Bank, 2013.

World Bank. *Water Management in Israel*. Washington, DC: World Bank, 2017.

World Bank. *Towards Water Security for Palestinians. West Bank and Gaza Water Supply, Sanitation, and Hygiene Poverty Diagnostic*. Washington, DC: World Bank, 2018, 131.

World Bank. *The Role of Desalination in an Increasingly Water-Scarce World*. Washington, DC: World Bank, March, 2019a, 97.

World Bank. *Palestinian Territories Recent Development*. Washington, DC: World Bank, April, 2019b.

World Bank/TATF. *Building Palestinian Institutional Capacity*. March 2003, 64.

WSRC (Water Sector Regulatory Council). *Bridge to Sustainability: Water and Wastewater Service Providers in Palestine*. Ramallah: WSRC, 2017.

Zeitoun, Mark. *Power and Water in the Middle East: The Hidden Politics of the Palestinian-Israeli Water Conflict*. London: IB Tauris, 2008, 214.

INDEX

* 9 7 8 0 7 5 5 6 3 7 2 0 1 *